The Complete Guide to

# Buying Property Abroad

# The Complete Guide to
# Buying Property Abroad

7th edition

**LIZ HODGKINSON**

**KOGAN PAGE**

London and Philadelphia

First published in Great Britain in 2002 by Kogan Page Limited
Second edition 2003
Third edition 2004
Fourth edition 2005
Fifth edition 2006
Sixth edition 2007
Seventh edition 2008

120 Pentonville Road
London N1 9JN
United Kingdom
www.koganpage.com

525 South 4th Street, #241
Philadelphia PA 19147
USA

© Liz Hodgkinson, 2002, 2003, 2004, 2005, 2006, 2007, 2008

The right of Liz Hodgkinson to be identified as the author of this work has been asserted by her in accordance with the Copyright, Designs and Patents Act 1988.

ISBN    978 0 7494 5240 7

**British Library Cataloguing in Publication Data**

A CIP record for this book is available from the British Library.

**Library of Congress Cataloging-in-Publication Data**

Hodgkinson, Liz.
  The complete guide to buying property abroad / Liz Hodgkinson. -- 7th ed.
    p. cm.
  Includes index.
  ISBN 978-0-7494-5240-7
  1. Real property--Foreign
  HD1375.H687 2008
  332.63 24--dc22

Typeset by Saxon Graphics
Printed and bound in Great

# WRECKS 2 RENOVATION

Of all the countries in the world which come to mind when considering restoring or renovating an old property, Italy, and Tuscany in particularly, is at the forefront.

Before rushing off to Italy, and parting with your well earned cash, it's worth taking a reality check.

Buying a property for refurbishment is at best in your home country a challenge; completing a similar project in a different country presents a greater one.

There are two main routes to progress. One is to decide to do it yourself; to devote your main holiday periods for a couple of years or so to the project. Fit and able individuals with experience in do-it-yourself may be well capable but do bear in mind that certain installations will have to comply with Italian law.

Planning and building regulation knowledge, in another language, is a major consideration as well as organising local craftsmen.

Alternatively, using a local Geometra or architect, who can help you plan and oversee your project, is usually the best way of progressing a restoration. A good Geometra will know the best craftsmen available, help you put together a budget (and stick to it!), submit the plans to the local Comune (the local council) and importantly talk through your plans with that authority.

Getting to know the locals also lets you find people who will manage your property; keeping an eye on the security, cleaning the swimming pool or opening and airing it before you visit.

Borrowing to buy your property, and borrowing to renovate it, may be major considerations. There are lenders who will do both but bear in mind that lending overseas is quite different from the relaxed lending criteria which is, or was, available in the UK until the advent of the credit crunch in 2007/2008. Self certification does not exist, you will be asked for full details of affordability and for renovation projects, a full breakdown of works and copies of planning consents.

This is just a flavour in the seductive art of Italian property ownership; taking the practicalities into account and letting your head rule your heart will avoid it being broken.

Ciao for now.

Chrissie Ballantyne of The Lemon Tree Company
email: **olihamlet@thelemontreecompany.com**

# A DIFFERENT KIND OF SPICE – THE ISLAND OF GRENADA

The catalyst for changing anything, let alone an economy, is often an unexpected occurrence and there can be a little more unexpected event than a hurricane!

The island of Grenada was devastated by Hurricane Ivan, the first to touch this part of the Caribbean for over 50 years, in September 2004. Once one of the Eastern Caribbean's fastest developing economies producing, amongst other spices, one third of the world's supply of nutmeg, the hurricane wrecked havoc, almost completely wiping out the agricultural industry of Grenada.

Out of every cloud comes a silver lining and the island has since turned it's mind to one of their other natural resources, the island's natural physical beauty – stunning coastline with protected bays and secluded beaches, lush rainforests, cascading waterfalls and breathtaking scenery. Add to this a rich culture and the vibrancy of calypso music and you have a perfect recipe.

With a tax regime of no Capital Gains Tax and no Inheritance Tax, the Government turned their minds to other incentives for investors to the island.

A simple formula, and one to now not only benefit the islanders of Grenada and it's sister islands, but also one which provides the international investor with a property based investment of significant levels.

Leading hotel groups throughout the world, and significantly from the United States, where *Service, Service, Service* is on a par with *Location, Location, Location*, have for a few years now sought to diversify their businesses by providing full management opportunities to all-in resorts. They offer holiday destinations combined with 5★ and even now 6★ facilities, (like a luxury hotel spread over acres of ground rather than confined to four brick walls).

A partnership with a top hotel group, who will manage and market the resort to maximise investment yields, enables property owners and investors to have peace of mind that their investment is secure and safe. Top this with several week's personal usage for the owners every year using the property and resort facilities and the investment takes on a welcome lifestyle element too.

So, back to a different kind of spice, the kind which enables an island's peoples to use their natural resources to rekindle their home economy and welcome visitors. They hope that it will be at least another 50 years before another hurricane strikes their island but if and when it does, the infrastructure will this time be built to stricter building codes and construction standards with better defences able to withstand the harsher pick of the pack which nature occasionally deals.

Chrissie Ballantyne of The Lemon Tree Company
email: **bacolet@thelemontreecompany.com**

# Contents

## WE ONLY WORK WITH THE BEST

Guanacaste, particularly Tamarindo area in Costa rica is not on everyone's lips, but take a look at this HOTSPOT for the best property investment that you could make. Costa Rica is a safe, stable and effective US dollar investment country. One of the world's best environments with beautiful golden beaches and eco system. Whether you are buying land or property or want to build your dream home.

We have a local management company on the ground in Costa Rica, with the full support of solicitors, architects and surveyors to ensure you have 100% title deeds and all real estate is purchased in US dollars.

Close to the town of Tamarindo we have large beach side lots, if you want to build your dream home and new building developments, some with established income AND MORE!

**First Choice have just started direct flights from Gatwick to Liberia Airport with Tamarindo only 45 mins away.**

Oro del Sol, top right - 3 bed/3.5 bathrooms from $395,000.

Large building lots with water and electric from $65,000.

**KSK Villa Rentals & Property Sales**
Tel: +44 (0) 7958 414397 (Uk time please)
Fax: + 44 (0)870 240 80 70
Email: info@kskcostarica.com

www.kskcostarica.com

KSK

---

# Central America, COSTA RICA

At this moment it could not be a better time to invest in Costa Rica. As all capital purchases are in US dollars and is $2 = £1, a high for many years and when the US gets going again, your property will gain in value on currency alone!

1. There is no stamp duty
2. No capital gains
3. No corporation tax
4. No VAT on your purchase
5. No inheritance tax in Costa Rica

With the current exchange rate so favourable across Europe, property in Costa Rica is more affordable than ever. Browse through the developments list and discover what can be achieved when one of the most respected developers in the area partners with a designer whose eye for detail and dedication to the surrounding environment results in some simply stunning developments.

for more information e-mail info@kskcostarica.com
www.kskcostarica.com

# Choice Real Estate in a Choice Location

*Waterfront living in El Gouna, where summer is the only season, has proven to be the best real estate investment option on the Red Sea.*

As global demands for waterfront living are on the rise, several companies are scrambling to get a piece of the market. Some are synonymous with quality, while others are not. One interesting company worth watching is Orascom Hotels and Development (OHD).

OHD specializes in the development of fully integrated and self sufficient leisure towns in some of the most desirable locations worldwide. Current projects include a comprehensive community in the Swiss Alps, four developments throughout Oman, a resort in the United Arab Emirates, and plans for a complete destination on Morocco's Atlantic shores.

Thus far, it is Orascom's home-base projects that have shined the most. Egypt is currently in the midst of a real estate boom, with developers from all over the world striving for a piece of the vast amount of Egyptian countryside. Entire cities are rising up from the desert as new communities sprout up everywhere from the outlying areas of Cairo to the far reaches of the Sinai Peninsula. In Egypt, the company currently boasts two fully grown destinations, with another three under planning or construction. Primarily focused on the virtually untouched Egyptian coasts, OHD has capitalized on providing luxury vacation homes to foreigners and Egyptians alike.

The star of OHD's portfolio is its flagship project, El Gouna. Located just north of Hurghada in a matchless natural environment, the town takes its name from the azure lagoons over which it spreads. Built on a multitude of islands set along 10 km of beachfront, this "Jewel of the Red Sea" has become the most sought-after location for second home ownership. Here, the appeal of year round sunshine, luxury amenities, and an overall relaxed atmosphere has drawn throngs to the El Gouna lifestyle. Starting as simply a collection of homes available only to a select group of Egyptians, the town has drastically evolved over the past 10 years and is now home to over 10,000 international residents forming a vibrant multicultural community.

El Gouna is within easy reach of the rest of the world. Nearby Hurghada is home to an international airport that is served by regular scheduled flights as well as charters departing daily from multiple cities around the European Union, placing El Gouna only 4 hours from the heart of Europe. El Gouna is also home to an international marina with yacht charters available to surrounding destinations including El Gouna's sister resort, Taba Heights. These transportation options allow both guests and residents to arrive and depart from El Gouna easily, providing the seclusion of the resort without the hassle of lengthy transfers.

OHD spares no expense in giving El Gouna every possible luxury amenity in an earnest attempt to exceed the community's expectations. An 18-hole professional golf course, literally dozens of dive and kite centres, world-renowned spas, trendy bars, and upscale boutiques are only some of the town's attractions. The dining options in El Gouna come aplenty, with over 100 restaurants offering delicacies from around the world. Everything residents and guests could imagine is to be had, from traditional local dishes to fine international cuisine and gourmet seafood platters.

El Gouna is internationally recognized as Egypt's most environmentally friendly destination. The town's architecture and phased development respect the unique landscape in an effortless blend of mountains, lagoons, and golfing greens set along the beachfront. El Gouna also makes an excellent base to venture into the amazing natural surroundings. Desert excursions, camel and horseback rides on the beach, quad safaris, biking tours, and visits with the Bedouins are just a beginning. On the sea, diving, kite surfing, and sailing are popular ways to enjoy the bountiful Red Sea.

## El Gouna Properties

Properties, from exclusive private villas to cosy apartments, are split into several real estate neighbourhoods, each with its own look and feel. Every El Gouna neighbourhood affords proximity to different luxury amenities, such as world-class spas and championship golf courses along turquoise lagoons.

The **Nubian Villas** are characterized by lofty vaults and domes and soft pastels in traditional Egyptian style. The colourful **Golf Villas** by renowned American architect Michael Graves blend traditional Arab architecture with modern abstract design.

The classic Mediterranean look of the **White Villas** features clean and simple lines while the Italian-styled **Hill Homes** by architect Alfredo Freda offer breathtaking sea views and utmost privacy.

**Marina Apartments**, complete with Yemeni-style arabesque detail, offer every imaginable convenience in the midst of the town's best restaurants and shopping while the new homes at **Fanadir Lagoons** are designed to epitomize the luxury of waterfront living.

Ever raising the bar, El Gouna has also launched the prestigious **Mansions** project that grants residents a piece of land within a recreated medieval Cairo. Here owners build their dream home the way they see fit, choosing any style and design that they prefer.

## Homeowner Privileges

Homeowners are pillars of the El Gouna community, and as such, enjoy special privileges. Owners share benefits enjoyed by guests, including exclusive access to all hotels' pools and beaches. They also receive a myriad of special discounts on dining, shopping, transportation and accommodation with the use of their Owner's Card.

A friendly and efficient Customer Service Department, centrally located downtown, is on hand to handle homeowner requests and concerns. The department also manages the issuance and renewal of Owner Cards. Countless other services are also available in the areas of housekeeping, interior design, laundry, security, insurance, gardening, and more.

El Gouna continues to grow and thrive due to the centralized management of services and responsible development implemented by OHD. And, as new OHD towns take shape around the globe, we are gladly seeing El Gouna quality developments the world over.

**A Sound Investment**

Owning a property in El Gouna is extremely easy, with an easy buying process making the market accessible and desirable. New properties are now rent managed, meaning that El Gouna management and Rentals office will work to rent out your property for you while you are out of town, ensuring a constant return on your investment. Previously available only to permanent residents of El Gouna, you too can now be a part of this international community when you rent an apartment or villa for your next El Gouna vacation the advantage of all the amenities of staying in a hotel, with the space and seclusion of living in your own home. The wide array of services available to renters will guarantee that you feel welcome and enjoy your vacation. Also, if you choose at any time to sell your home, El Gouna's real estate office work with you to remove all the stress and complications of finding a buyer and speed up the process for you This is where El Gouna Management Services can satisfy all your needs.

The steady growth of this town stands as a strong testament to the reliability of OHD as a developer, making buying a home in El Gouna a sound investment.

# THE
## INTERNATIONAL
# PROPERTY LAW
## CENTRE

International Solicitors, Notaries & Advocates
*Part of The Max Gold Partnership Solicitors*

**Don't** buy a property abroad without our advice!

## *FOR INDEPENDENT EXPERT LEGAL ADVICE IN 50 JURISDICTIONS WORLDWIDE...*

• International Residential and Commercial Conveyancing

• Due Diligence Reports on Foreign Developments for Agents and Buyers

• International, Corporate, Civil and Criminal Litigation

• Advice on Capital Gains Tax and Inheritance/Succession Taxes

• International Family and Matrimonial Advice

| LONDON OFFICE | HULL OFFICE |
|---|---|
| **Tel: +44 (0) 207 189 8391** | **Tel: +44 (0)1482 385 649** |
| **Fax: +44 (0)207 189 8393** | **Fax: +44 (0)1482 385 676** |
| 25 Floral Street | Suffolk House |
| Covent Garden | 21 Silver Street |
| London | Hull, Yorkshire |
| WC2E 9DS | HU1 1JG |

Email: internationalproperty@maxgold.com
Website: www.internationalpropertylaw.com

Listen to our expert advice on: OVERSEAS PROPERTY TV, SKY CHANNEL 287

Regulated by The Solicitors Regulation Authority
Senior Partner: M J Gold, S E M Lucatello LLB (Hons) Italian Consular Agent.
Also qualified in Gibraltar. Partner W D C Boddy.

## THE INTERNATIONAL PROPERTY LAW CENTRE

International Solicitors, Notaries & Advocates
*Part of The Max Gold Partnership Solicitors*

### The International Property Law Centre

The International Property Law Centre is the largest International Property Law firm in the U.K. It is the specialist international legal department of The Max Gold Partnership; a firm of English Solicitors, Notaries & International Advocates.

The International Property Law Centre provides the very best independent legal advice for property transactions and a wide range of other legal matters, in more than 50 jurisdictions worldwide.

Our large team of in-house International Lawyers and administrative staff speak 17 languages between them.

The International Property Law Centre is also regulated by The Solicitors Regulation Authority and the usual P.I. cover as you would expect from a professional body.

### Services we provide

Our independent team of solicitors offers a straightforward alternative to the complexity of sourcing legal services overseas, saving you valuable time and money.

These are some of the areas we cover:
- Sale and Purchase of property overseas
- Wills and Trust translations
- Legislation
- Inheritance matters
- Establishing subsidiaries and branches overseas
- Company/Commercial
- Company Administration
- Business start-ups
- Bonds and stock handling
- Bills of exchange
- Bank account opening
- Power of Attorney
- Emigration
  *Applications for Australia, Canada, New Zealand and U.S.A*

We also have a notary who can provide the following additional notarial services:
- Bills of exchange
- Banking
- Bonds and Stock Handling
- Legalisation of documents

## The reasons for having a specialist lawyer

Your expert should advise you on how to purchase your property and in what capacity, the need to prepare a Will after the purchase has been completed and ensuring that the property is registered at the Land Registry in the correct manner.

You should also take advice on residence and the type of property ownership similar to the English law concept of joint tenancy and tenancy in common.

Your expert will raise general and specific enquiries in relation to the property and should deal with aspects such as how much should be declared in the Deed of Sale and whether you should be proceeding by way of reservation/ option contract, or a full preliminary contract.

Lack of familiarity with the language complicates matters. So your independent expert will translate and interpret all documentation and lead you through the maze of intricacies from the initial contact with the Estate Agents to the placing of the deposit, understanding the contract and amending it, if necessary, to safeguard your interest, drawing up a Power of Attorney if you are unable to be there at the final signing ceremony with the Notary as well as the checking over of searches as well as the final conveyance document transferring ownership of your property to you.

Specialist Lawyers will also give due consideration of the budgetary/financial matters including the most suitable mortgages.

## Why do UK buyers prefer English Solicitors?
- No time difference
- Easily contactable
- Explanations of the foreign system in a manner that is understandable to UK buyers
- Greater security, English Solicitors carry negligence insurance

Finding a reputable law firm abroad can be a minefield, a specialist international property Lawyer, based in England, will take the stress out of the legal aspects of your property purchase. The extra fee incurred on a specialist international property Lawyer, will help you to avoid greater expense and heartache in the future.

# Introduction

Nowadays, you can buy almost any type of property in almost any country. In fact, the choice of homes and locations abroad has become totally bewildering for anybody who has even remotely considered the possibility of having a place to call their own in a foreign country.

Should you go for a brand-new apartment in a modern development, or buy a beautiful abandoned rustic farmhouse that will take a lifetime to renovate? Why are you buying abroad in the first place? To have somewhere to retire to? Somewhere for the family to stay? Or are you more interested in the investment possibilities? Which country should you choose? Is it better to buy inland or right on the coast? And what about tax, insurance, mortgages, bank accounts? Can you make money from renting out your second home when you're not there yourself? Can you make a profit when you sell? What about if you decide you want to settle in your adopted country permanently?

There are very many questions to ask yourself when considering all the vast possibilities of 'abroad' and this book answers all (or at least most) of the vexing questions about the highly complex and often fraught, although increasingly popular, business of buying property in other countries. It also has a section on the important questions to ask yourself before taking the plunge and maybe making a very expensive mistake.

Hard information and advice is interspersed with case histories and stories of those who have been brave enough to purchase a home in another country, and actually managed to get on top of all the bureaucracy and paperwork involved. Buying a home in one's own country is often a traumatic enough transaction, with things to go wrong at every stage. Imagine how much more can go wrong when trying to close a deal in a strange country and using unfamiliar language.

But although buying any property, and particularly one in another country, can be nerve-racking from beginning to end, it is also exciting, and intensely rewarding when you get it right. Although 'pure investors' are becoming ever more common, it is still the case that most people who go through the difficulties of buying a second home abroad do so to improve their quality of life. They agree that there is no sensation quite like driving up to your very own beautiful apartment or villa, opening a bottle of wine and sitting on the terrace watching the setting sun. It's a sensation, they agree, which cannot be matched when staying in even the most wonderful hotel or rented apartment. The fact that it's yours for ever and ever allows love and commitment to be invested in the place, as with an intimate relationship with another person.

Buying a home abroad can be counted as one of the great achievements of life, and nowadays it's not just a luxury for the very rich. Now that foreign mortgages and home loans are increasingly easily available, the dream home in another country is within the reach of ever more people.

If you've ever yearned for that place in the sun, or even in the snow, just read this book to help you make up your mind, and beat an easy path through the legal, financial and bureaucratic minefields that can beset you at every turn.

**Past, present and future**

In the early days of second and holiday home developments, you had to choose between Spain, Portugal and Greece. France and Italy were also possibilities, but buying places there was far more difficult than in Spain or Greece, where it was made easy for you. But now you can have a holiday home more or less anywhere in the world. Nowhere need be too far away to consider as a second home destination.

Thanks to the proliferation of cheap flights and more open political regimes, it is now possible to buy a second home anywhere, from France to Russia, the United States to Australia, South Africa to Thailand. All you have to do is choose your spot and it can be yours. Whilst it is still true to say that most second-homers tend to choose countries relatively near to their main home, this is not always the case. Increasingly, UK nationals are buying homes in Canada and the United States, Singapore and South Africa, and there can be very good reasons for this.

According to a report published in December 2006 by the Institute for Public Policy Research (IPPR), more than 5.5 million Britons (that is, those born in the UK) now live abroad – permanently.

In 2007, a record 250,000 Britons emigrated permanently, with the most popular countries being Australia, New Zealand, France, Spain and the United States. This figure represents a 70 per cent increase on the 140,000 British people who left the country 10 years previously, in 1997.

This means that one Briton every two minutes is now leaving the home country in search of a better quality of life, and this number is set to increase fast. In 2007, Paul Arthur from the Emigration Group, which helps Britons to settle overseas, said: 'During the winter of 2007–08 we have had record numbers of enquiries, with people not just wanting to escape the weather but seek a whole change of lifestyle.'

In many cases, the urge to emigrate or buy a property abroad arises out of intense dissatisfaction with the British way of life.

Writer Leo McKinstry, who has bought a house in Southern France, says, 'What a relief it is to go there, away from the claustrophobia and never-ending construction that is gripping England. In France, where the population density is barely a quarter of England's, there is still room to breathe.'

McKinstry is one of the more than 1 million British people who now own homes abroad. This figure is expected to double within the next five years, as increasing numbers of ordinary people decide to improve their quality of life by buying a wonderful apartment or villa in another country, often for a fraction of the price of a similar property – always supposing you could get a similar property – in the UK.

The most popular places for homes abroad continue to be France, Spain, Florida, Portugal and Italy, although destinations such as Croatia, Turkey, Cyprus, Bulgaria and Morocco are becoming increasingly popular with Britons hoping to pick up a bargain from these rapidly emerging markets.

The IPPR's report also stated that more than 1 million pensioners – or one in 12 Britons over the age of 65 – have now retired abroad. For this sector, the far-flung destinations seem more popular than Europe, with Australia having the largest number of British retirees, followed by Canada and the United States.

The day of the global village has arrived, with holiday properties and second – or even first – homes now being bought almost everywhere in the world by incomers. The internet has helped to make the whole thing even easier. Or, as some might say, more difficult, as we are now totally bewildered by choice.

When you can buy anywhere in the world, what factors affect your choice?

Mainly, the countries that are most popular with foreigners seeking second homes are those that have distinctly better weather than the native land. That's why there are very many Northern Europeans such as Scandinavians, Dutch, Belgians and Germans with second homes in places like Spain and Portugal, but very few

Portuguese dreaming of second homes in Finland or Lapland, for instance, although even this is beginning to change as Finland and Lapland tentatively enter the second-home market.

But weather, although overwhelmingly important for large numbers of people, is not the only decisive factor influencing choice of location for a second home. Some people enjoy skiing, and may buy an apartment in a ski resort to save the time, trouble and expense of booking up hotels or apartments, and lugging ski equipment across several countries. Some people may be golf fanatics and choose a place where they can happily play golf all day long. Very many luxury golf developments in Spain, Portugal and Florida are already in existence and more are being planned all the time. Others might enjoy music festivals, watersports or a place where they can take long walks; it all depends on your preference, and how much you would like the chance to indulge your hobby or passion in ideal climatic conditions.

Ever more people are beginning to feel that life in certain other countries offers more in terms of lifestyle than the UK. Here are two views on the subject.

Keith and Nancy Atkinson, originally from the UK, now divide their time between France and Florida, wintering in the United States and summering in France. Keith says, 'We've always been expats, living in the Middle East, Europe and Africa, and for us, living just in the UK was unthinkable. It is such a badly managed country with a dreadful infrastructure, and "little Englanders" drive us mad.'

Writer Graham Lord and his artist wife Juliet moved out of the UK permanently in 1996, and now live half the year in Nevis, in the Caribbean, and half the year in the South of France. They have no regrets at all about elbowing the UK for good. When asked what he misses about England, Graham snorts, 'Not a thing!' He adds:

> We both got seriously fed up with living in England; not just the dreadful weather, but also the general quality of life and the decline in standards everywhere. I was born in Rhodesia, and lived until I was 17 in Mozambique, and after 35 years in England I came to loathe the grey skies day after day.

> Now, we watch the TV news from England and almost daily we
> bless our good fortune that we no longer live there.

Graham and Juliet sold their London terraced house in order to
finance their life abroad, and now have no UK base at all. When
Graham has to go to the UK to research his books, he stays at the
Chelsea Arts Club for four or five weeks, and then gratefully
decamps to one or other of his exotic homes.

Buying property abroad is a fast-growing market, driven by a
number of factors, such as low and stable interest rates on mortgages; the fact that the buying process is becoming ever easier and
more reliable in every country; the enhanced lifestyle that owning
a place abroad provides; and the ever-increasing media coverage
creating interest among all ages and all income groups.

It seems nowadays that, wherever the travel industry operates,
second-homers follow. Tourism comes first and then, if that is
successful, what are now known as 'emerging markets' follow.
Spain was the first country to be opened up in this way and has
been so successful that it remains the most popular country for
Britons wanting a home abroad, in spite of fierce competition now
from other destinations.

Globalization also has to be a big factor. 'Abroad' seems vastly
less foreign than it used to, with golf and sports developments
being opened up all over the world, and most familiar products
now being obtainable at the furthest reaches of the earth. Thanks
to ever-improving technology, it is becoming ever easier to work
abroad as well. Graphic designer Hilary Sadler finally moved with
his family to Spain in 2006, after several years of trying. He sold his
South Coast home and now, courtesy of the internet, has retained
all his UK clients and added some new Spanish ones. His three
children are installed in local schools – and are even taking GCSEs!

It is also becoming ever easier to borrow money for an overseas
purchase. One important aspect here, according to Nicholas Marr,
of property marketing company Marr International Ltd, is that
borrowers are having to be more international and much more
inventive, as huge and continuing increases in UK house prices

are making it difficult for young Britons to get on the property ladder. Frustrated by not being able to own a property in the UK, younger people are now thinking seriously about buying their first property abroad. And when you can get a fantastic apartment in Turkey for under £40,000 or a seafront property in Bulgaria for £35,000, who can blame them?

There is also the fact that many formerly inaccessible or inhospitable countries are now bending over backwards to make themselves attractive to foreigners and are giving themselves alluring makeovers, such as building new roads and airports, embarking on ambitious building and development programmes and making the buying process ever easier so as to entice property-buying incomers, and all that lovely foreign money, to their shores.

For instance, you can now buy a smart apartment or luxury log cabin in Lapland, and I hear these properties are going, if not exactly like hot cakes in this region of frozen wastes, then at least like Mars Bar ice creams. There has been no talk of freezing prices, though.

New entrants to the EU, such as Bulgaria and Romania, are now also marketing themselves professionally, and making strenuous efforts to improve and ease the buying process for incomers.

The average buyer spends £150,000 on a property abroad, mostly, nowadays, raised by borrowing.

Often known as the Sunset Surfers, increasing numbers of people currently coming up to retirement are healthy and wealthy and are deciding to live the dream, rather than merely drool about it. Many roadside property advertisements in Spain, for instance, are urging the British to spend their 'third age' on the costas instead of in a sheltered home on the South Coast.

Older people are often seen as draining the economy, in that they are no longer economically active. But in Florida, the ever-growing influxes of foreigners are actually boosting the economy. When compared with the most popular second-home destinations such as Florida, Tuscany, Spain, France or Australia, all of which have vastly better weather than the UK, it is unlikely that Britain will ever become a sought-after retirement country. We could even envisage a future where there are simply no older people at all in Britain, as they are all sunning themselves abroad!

But it is not just the elderly who are moving to sunnier countries. Younger people with continuing earning capacity are also increasingly deciding to move to hotter climes, either permanently or for as much of the year as they can afford. Alexander Chancellor, writing in the *Guardian*, commented that France is fast becoming a nation of asylum seekers: not the 'bogus' ones, but Britons for whom life in the home country has become intolerable.

Some people are passionate about a particular country, and long to be there, whatever the weather. Francophiles fall into this category: for them, it's not so much a matter of basking in wonderful weather as being in the country they love above all others.

But for most of us, it's simply more pleasant to potter about in hot weather, so long as it's not too hot, of course. The success of the Center Parcs holiday concept has hinged on the fact that weather doesn't matter. Because these complexes are a vast indoors, they have been able to attract holidaymakers with their inducement that you can have a good time 'whatever the weather'.

However important, or even essential, good weather is for you, it's vital to bear in mind that the country with perfect year-round weather does not exist. The sybaritic south of France can be well below freezing in winter, and sunny, relaxed sub-tropical Florida can be subject to hurricanes, twisters, lightning and torrential downpours and floods. Even the south of Spain is not always warm and, although it is often said that the Canary Islands have eternal spring, sometimes that spring is rather like the British spring in early March.

# Investment or luxury?

Some people may regard buying a property in another country as a hard-headed business investment, but for the great majority of purchasers the second home is seen rather as a yacht or expensive car: in other words, as a luxury. They hope they may claw something back on resale, or cover some of their costs through letting and renting for part of the year, but investment potential is not the prime consideration for most second-home buyers. It is, rather, something they treat themselves to when they believe they can afford it or deserve it. It has been estimated by property developers that over 90 per cent of those buying a home abroad do so to improve the quality of their life rather than to make money.

Here is a considered view from one second-home owner, now retired from work, who has had a house in Miami, Florida, since the early 1990s:

Why have a second home abroad? The answer, in my case, was simply that I had accepted a job with an overseas company in a beautiful location in a sub-tropical climate. But when I gave up that job a choice had to be made. Did I say goodbye to all that sunshine, or keep my second home so that I could return to paradise whenever I liked? Paradise won – at a price!

The price is the time you need to spend over there, not only to look after your new place, but also to get some value for the money you laid out to buy it. If your running costs are high you are going to get less value if you only visit your second home for six or seven weeks a year – unless you let your property, which should not be a problem in most cases. However, some people do not want to do that and I am stubbornly, and perhaps stupidly, one of them.

In the no-letting situation a second home would be more economically justifiable if one spent five months a year there, but if that's not possible I would settle for three months. Much depends on your fixed running costs. If these are very high because you are in a fashionable location, you may sometimes look at the bills and think that you would be better off selling the place and using the proceeds to live up the road at the Ritz Carlton for three months a year.

But there are considerations apart from money. You have now got yourself another responsibility, possibly at a time when you could well do without some of the responsibilities you already have. When absent from your home, you will dread a call from one of your overseas neighbours saying that there is water coming through your front door. To avoid that kind of situation you may have to come to some arrangement with a friend or paid minder to visit your property regularly while you are away.

Spending all your free time in your overseas paradise is fine and dandy for a beginning, but you then begin to realize that, because you want to get best value from your second home, you will have to keep putting off that trip you promised yourself to the Galapagos Islands.

But there is an answer to that: when your second home gets to be a drag, sell it and enjoy the proceeds. You may make a profit, but even if you just get your money back you will probably have made your life more enjoyable than if you had stayed home in the first place just counting your cash.

Expenditure on improving the quality of your life is not wasted. It is a just reward for your labours. A woman who buys an absurdly expensive hat knows it's a luxury, not a necessity, but it makes her feel good. That's what money is for, she might say. And she's right!

However, this attitude is beginning to change, as ever more people are starting to consider buying property abroad as an investment, or pension alternative, as part of their property portfolio.

Buying for pure investment overseas has taken off in the last few years for several important reasons:

1. Mortgage lenders are offering ever better deals on foreign property, demanding lower deposits and offering a greater variety of mortgages.
2. Accession to the EU for many new countries since 2004 has given developers, tourists and industries greater confidence to build, visit and relocate.
3. There is a massive building programme going on all over the world in present or future investment hotspots.
4. Many emerging markets have been experiencing annual property price increases of between 25 and 40 per cent.
5. Ever more countries are becoming accessible to tourism, with better roads and vastly improved air transport.

Remember, there are three main reasons why people buy property abroad: for a holiday home, to retire to or as an investment. It may not be possible for one purchase to fulfil all three requirements.

In fact, people are becoming ever more hard-headed now that property anywhere, whether in the home country or abroad, is increasingly being seen as an investment, as something that will give a good return, rather than just being a luxury or simply a fun thing. Everybody is now becoming a property investor or developer, and hoping to make money from the purchase.

According to the law firm The International Law Partnership (LLP), which specializes in properties abroad, the proportion of clients who buy foreign properties purely for investment rose from less than 5 per cent in 1999 to more than 60 per cent in 2008. The main reason for this appears to be dissatisfaction with conventional stocks, shares and pension schemes – plus, of course, seductive advertisements that give people the idea that they might buy abroad for profit.

The new emphasis on investment, rather than having a holiday home for relaxation and eventual retirement, has encouraged investors to seek properties ever further afield, and in markets much newer and riskier than the most established countries. And these new investments are not just for the rich. A new report by the research group Datamonitor found that average-income earners – those on around £25,000 a year – are also now buying properties abroad mainly for investment purposes.

Instant Access Properties specializes in finding properties for clients purely as an investment. This company began by offering UK properties only, but 30 per cent of its business now consists in locating suitable properties in other countries for investors. Their business analyst James Kitto says:

In the UK, the market is clear cut, as, apart from perhaps their main home, everybody buys property nowadays purely for investment. Overseas, the market is more of a hybrid as most people, even professional investors, will want to visit their properties for holidays. There is also the dream element, which can never be entirely discounted.

The main difference between the dedicated investor and the lifestyle purchaser is that the main aim of the former is to make money from the property abroad.

James Kitto advises:

When buying property abroad purely or mainly for investment purposes as part of a property portfolio, the trick is to minimize the risk and maximize the return. And some countries are more of a known quantity than others. For instance, Spain has a well-developed infrastructure, a massive tourist industry and a stable currency. There is also a thriving rental market, and you can count on 60 per cent holidaymaker occupancy, year-round if you rent out your property.

But Bulgaria, for instance, a new entrant to this market, is a much higher risk. Although the returns may be fantastic, there is as yet hardly any tourism and nobody knows how long it might take for the investment to come into profit – or even whether you could sell it or rent it out at all.

Nowadays, even billionaires want to make yet more money from their homes abroad. Super-rich celebs such as Mick Jagger, Richard Branson and Cliff Richard do not keep their holiday homes in exotic locations just for the hell of it. No, they aim to make money from their tropical paradises by renting them out at huge sums. Mick Jagger's six-bedroom villa on Mustique, for instance, a tiny Caribbean island 1 mile long and 3 miles wide, is available for such as you or I to rent at 'only' £9,000 a week in high season. Apparently, Mick vets all his tenants; one wonders what qualities are needed to pass muster!

Richard Branson's 18-person ski lodge in Verbier is the most expensive chalet in the Alps, where a week's stay in high season costs in excess of £60,000. The Lodge opened in December 2007 after a £3.7 million renovation and conversion from a faded three-star hotel. However, you do get limitless champagne on tap, an indoor pool, mini ice rink and spa for that money – so you may consider it is worth it.

Back to the ordinary investor: most financial experts believe that, realistically, the only type of foreign property worth considering for investment purposes is that bought off-plan at a discount.

It is very difficult to make money from buying a wreck and then doing it up to sell; about a million times more difficult than doing the same in the UK – and that is hard enough. It is not easy, either, to sell an apartment or villa several years old at a profit, as by this time it will probably need at least some renovation.

When buying off-plan, you are putting money into something that doesn't yet exist, and you have to use your imagination to visualize the finished result. Also, you will have to tie money up for perhaps two years before the project is completed.

Nowadays, the prospect of owning a property in another country has come within reach of practically everybody. It's not so much that homes in other countries have got cheaper as that more UK people are wealthy – or at least wealthier – than their parents or grandparents. Also, cheap and easy foreign mortgages are now extremely easy to obtain. Anybody who is solvent, who is earning an income and who can secure a mortgage can, if they like, buy somewhere abroad.

Flights seem to be getting cheaper all the time, and enterprising airline companies such as Buzz, Ryanair and easyJet have made getting to France, Italy or Spain cheaper than taking the train from King's Cross to Newcastle.

And 'abroad' offers a vast array of purchasable properties, from tiny studios and cheap holiday apartments to manoirs, chateaux and luxuriously appointed villas in their own expensively manicured grounds. There's everything on offer from brand-new developments to medieval castles and tumbledown farmhouses. You can be right at the centre of a thriving metropolis, away from it all in a quiet sleepy village, on the beach or right inland, depending on your preference, your pocket and how you like to spend your time.

Truly, the world has never been more everybody's oyster. You can choose to own a holiday apartment by the sea to spend just a few weeks of every year; you can decide to live six months of the year in your chosen country and six months in your native country; or you can pull up all your roots and decamp permanently, as ever more people are deciding to do. Just so long as your pocket or borrowing potential can bear the cost, you can have any kind of home abroad that you want.

Bearing in mind that most places abroad are vastly cheaper than properties in the UK, taken like for like, you can if you so choose sell your UK home and, for about half the selling price, buy something really nice in another country. Then you can live off your capital or pension in your chosen country and watch your new world go by without a financial care in the world.

Although it is of course possible to spend millions on your home abroad – celebrities think nothing of spending £2 or £3 million on a foreign hideaway they hardly ever visit – it is the case that in most countries popular with second-homers the value is vastly better than in the UK.

Visiting a friend who had moved permanently to France, I was struck by the high quality of her life, compared to what she could have in the UK. When she moved to France in 2003, after taking early retirement, she exchanged her small cottage in Hampshire for a vast farmhouse with outbuildings, a cellar, private courtyard and extensive gardens – and still had enough money in the bank to fund her retirement.

Her 18th century home in the Cluny area cost just £140,000 – *and* it was in excellent condition, with modern plumbing and lighting. She has enough spare room to put up two or three guests in the main house, and has completed an ambitious renovation of her large barn, which she has turned into a separate self-contained guest suite. She can rent out the barn to friends and family, or to holidaymakers for income, if she chooses.

She grows a lot of her own produce, there are excellent cheap local wines, and she has enthusiastically joined in village life. The nearest small town has art galleries, bookshops, a wine merchant, vegetable market and supermarket. Several retail outlets are run by British people, although my friend speaks excellent French and makes a point of reading a French newspaper every day, listening to local French stations on the radio, and reading novels in French.

In all, so long as you can be sure you will have no lingering attachment to life in the old country, you can feel that you are permanently on holiday, as well as having a sense of belonging, when you up sticks and move to another country.

The one thing you won't have, of course, is close friends and family easily at hand. For some, this might be a disadvantage; for others, a blessed relief. My friend has lots of visitors in the summer, but it can be a bit lonely in winter. If you love reading, though, this solitude is also enjoyable.

As ever, it depends on what you want – and this must be given very careful thought before any boats are inextricably burned.

The French have never been a nation of dedicated house buyers in the same way as the British, and house prices have not risen to anything like the same extent. It is possible to buy a new four-bedroom house in the Nord–Pas de Calais region of France for £120,000, where a similar house in the UK would be £300,000 at least. You can still get an attractive cottage in Normandy, or a fully furnished studio in Nice for £100,000.

A two-bed beach apartment in Spain would normally be under £150,000, and a three-bedroom, two-bathroom detached house with double garage and swimming pool can be bought for £150,000 in the Orlando area of Florida.

You could decide to try to earn your living in your chosen country. Or you could decide to retire early and just enjoy yourself. Maybe you feel it would be nice to bring up your children in a sunnier, easier climate. Or perhaps you've just had enough of cold, grey, wet Northern European winters and long to be somewhere warmer and drier. There are many, many upsides, many advantages, to widening your property horizons beyond the UK.

So what, if any, are the downsides? The questions in the next chapter are not offered necessarily as downsides, but are aspects to bear carefully in mind before getting carried away at a property exhibition or falling in love with a romantic tumbledown wreck whilst on a magical holiday.

# Buying off-plan

There are now very many property exhibitions that try to persuade you to buy brand-new or not-yet-built villas, apartments and houses. There is clearly much more money for the developers in selling new homes in a block than in selling second-hand, or resale, homes one by one, and this is where all the marketing thrust is aimed. Most large construction companies are now into the vastly profitable second- or holiday-home business, and they use highly seductive, proven marketing techniques to shift these properties.

Some buyers vastly prefer new homes because they take advantage of all the latest building and construction techniques. Also, a brand-new home can look very much more appealing than a 10-year-old villa starting to show signs of wear. On the seafront, all buildings are subject to a lot of wear, a constant buffeting from the elements, which doesn't happen so much inland. So they start to show wear and tear far more quickly than inland developments.

Before you buy off-plan, you are required to have all the necessary paperwork in place, plus a deposit of typically 20 per cent. In some cases, you would have to pay the deposit in the UK before you fly out on an inspection trip. Don't forget that salespeople obtain hefty commissions of several thousand pounds for each sale made, so it is in their interests to use all the high-pressure techniques ever invented to persuade you to buy.

In some cases, your house or villa may not be ready for two or three years; in such instances, you would pay in instalments. These payments are clearly detailed on the brochures. The final instalment would be payable when the house or apartment is completed.

Construction companies building expensive new complexes usually also retain legal, financial and real-estate experts, so that the entire deal can be effected in the one operation. Those selling second homes know, like all other salespeople, that if you walk away saying you'll think about it, the sale is lost. Hence the many inducements to buy whilst you're on site, or even at the property exhibition before you make a visit.

The whole enterprise is designed to make you sign on the dotted line there and then, without having time to think better of it, to cool off or to look at other possibilities before signing an irrevocable contract. Such companies also fly out journalists and reporters to write up these developments in glowing terms, on the grounds that an ounce of editorial is worth a ton of advertising. And they're right. A new development given the imprimatur of a respected property journalist will sell units far more quickly than otherwise.

On an inspection trip, you will very likely be shown round a showhome. These have also been proven to shift property units, and they are carefully designed to appeal to the exact market aimed at. If the properties are very expensive, they will have very expensive furniture, curtains, carpets and so on; if middle-market, the furniture and fittings will be slightly lower down the range, and so on.

Although there is not necessarily anything wrong with buying a second home off-plan, it's important to be aware that these properties are probably the most heavily marketed product there is, currently. Even more than with your principal home, these companies are selling you a highly seductive dream. The finished showhome looks wonderful, of course, but you don't know until you move in what building snags there may be. With a resale home, initial construction problems have usually been ironed out.

If interested in buying off-plan, it's also important to remember that in most European countries property does not rise at the same steady level as in the UK. This is even more the case in places like Florida, where huge housing developments are taking place all the time. Over there, your holiday home has to be regarded in the same way as a car or yacht: it may actually lose value as the years go by, as there are so many new houses being built all the time that are far more desirable to the average UK and US buyer than the slightly dingy, tired-looking resale homes.

When deciding whether to buy off-plan, you have to work out what you want. Those buying into lavish new developments marketed in the UK will usually be British people who are not particularly interested in blending in with the natives. In some luxury developments in Portugal, for example, buyers will be 90 per cent British. Developments marketed in Germany will attract Germans, and so on. So with new developments you are buying into an artificial environment created by the construction company. If all you want is the opportunity to play golf or tennis in nice weather and are prepared to pay for the privilege, then a new-build property in a secure gated environment backing on to a professional-standard golf course may be just the thing.

## Discounts

Almost always, off-plan developments are offered to early buyers at discounted prices. The idea is that the earlier you buy, the greater the potential profit will be when you come to sell. The way it happens is that property investment companies negotiate bulk discount prices from developers and builders, then offer these deals to the general public.

The earlier in the game you buy your particular hole in the ground, the greater will be your capital gain, or profit, when you want to sell. Or, at least, this is the idea, and the carrot held out to potential investors. The reason these huge discounts can be offered is because off-plan property is 'unrealized' at the point of sale. In other words, it is not really worth anything until the apartment or villa is completed.

Clearly, there are serious potential risks to buying in this way – that is, purely to make a profit – and a lot of research and care is needed to be sure a) that the development will be completed at all; b) that it will not be competing with other, similar and cheaper properties when completed; c) that the developer does not go bust and all investments are wiped out; and d) that local currency rates remain favourable.

None of this can be known for certain in advance, so the best advice is: proceed with caution! This includes: visiting the development sites yourself, rather than relying on websites and pictures; confirming that all the planning permissions are in place; and, very importantly, comparing similar developments in similar areas.

Experts always advise: be guided by knowledge rather than emotions when buying abroad. It is all too easy to be swayed by the romanticism and excitement of it – and to forget the practical realities.

Be very careful when buying off-plan property, however attractive the discount sounds. There may be no planning permission for the development, no building licence in existence, there may be debts attaching to the property and no habitation certificate when the building is completed.

## What is a habitation certificate?

Habitation certificates vary from country to country but are an essential piece of the paperwork which confers legality and ownership on you, the buyer. These certificates are usually issued by the Town Hall, or local equivalent, and are necessary to ensure you really own the property, whether this is new-build or resale. Very often, new owners in unfamiliar countries, bewildered by all the paperwork, forget about this last but very important document. Also, as the document may have a slightly different name in another language, it can often be overlooked.

This certificate shows that the building has been inspected and certified as being fit for human habitation. With resale properties, the certificate should already be in the bundle of documentation, but with new-builds, you may have to wait for it after completion. Always make sure you chase it up and never rest until you have it, as the importance of the habitation certificate cannot be overestimated.

Also make sure that any property you buy in this fashion will not be affected by land grab – when the government intervenes forcibly, and legally, to take the land back for itself with no compensation or redress offered. Certain areas in Spain have been affected by land grab, leaving many disaffected people who discover to their horror they are no longer second-home owners, and not only their lovely home, but all their investment is wiped out.

Most people believe that the Andalucian land grab stories are just so much media hype, but it can be the case that your wonderful villa in the sun is quite literally bulldozed to the ground. It actually happened in January 2008 to retired British couple Helen and Len Prior when they were summarily evicted from their gorgeous £350,000 villa in Andalucia, which they had lived in for five years. Then they were forced to watch as their lovely villa slowly crumbled into dust.

What went wrong? It seems that the 63-year-olds had been singled out as examples and a dire warning to over-development along the Costas. The Priors believed they had done everything right, including getting planning permission from the town council in the town of Vera, Almeria, but the regional government later maintained that the house was built illegally on greenbelt land.

Helen said: 'We employed a reputable lawyer and did every-thing, as we thought, by the book.' They obtained a building licence before the property was built and all seemed watertight enough. But, it seems, the Andalucia regional council had already warned the local council that their development should not go ahead as it could encourage unwanted urbanization of so-called rustic land. However, even if this was the case the Priors knew nothing about it.

The Seville-based officials first started demanding that the house should be knocked down in May 2006 and the Priors were presented with a 15-day demolition notice. A local judge ratified the order but the Priors were reassured by their lawyer who started an action to challenge the demolition order, and he convinced the couple that the order would never be carried through.

The Priors believed the lawyer, even when they received a second letter on 16 December 2007, informing them that their house would be knocked down at 11 am on 9 January. Even then, they didn't really believe it would happen, but on that date the house came crashing down to the accompaniment of TV cameras. Local TV stations had been alerted by the Mayor so were naturally in attendance to record this dramatic event.

The Priors' Andalucian dream had quite literally crumbled to nothing, but a spokesman for the area maintained: 'We only demolish houses built illegally.' It is possible that the truth behind this sad saga will never be fully known, but it is a stark warning that land grab can happen – even when you thought you had carried out all checks and obtained necessary permissions.

James Kitto, of the Instant Access Group, which specializes in sourcing discounted off-plan property for investors abroad, says:

In our company, we ensure the property has been through a rigorous vetting process before we offer it to our members.

We meet and analyse the developer, look at what they have built previously, investigate how the properties were sold and ensure the appropriate regulations have been met.

We look at developers from country to country as regulations change. Discounts are offered on off-plan developments because the developer needs to start the project with some cash flow and is prepared to sell at a discounted price because investors are buying something that does not yet exist. Because of this, investors have to know they are dealing with developers who will not go bust or leave the project half finished.

When buying off-plan property, you have to know that it is, or will be, an attractive place for holidaymakers and second-homers. Golf, for instance, is a huge driver for developments in Spain, Florida and Portugal.

As all these countries represent mature markets, where mortgages are easily available in the local currency and there is an established tourist industry, the risks of buying discounted off-plan property are relatively low – so long as you make sure you know exactly what you are getting into, and how long it will be before your villa or apartment is ready.

But if you prefer something old, something authentic, in the country of your choice, then you will have to do your own homework and forget about lavish marketing and yet-to-be-built foreign developments.

The best advice one can offer about off-plan purchases is: before even thinking about going to a property exhibition, do your research, do your homework thoroughly. You should have already made your decision on location, country, type of property, overall budget, *before* attending one of these exhibitions. If you go with your mind made up and have already decided what you want, then you will be attending such an exhibition in a very different frame of mind than if you just wander in and allow yourself to be persuaded without thinking the whole thing through very carefully. The Spanish home exhibition has already become a sitcom cliché, so much so that one company advertises itself as 'not just another Spanish exhibition'.

It is a good idea to have already visited the site, or the area, and be at least three-quarters into making a final decision, before going out on an inspection trip. Of course, the developments all seem attractive, stunning, carefully landscaped. Would the developers tell you anything else?

The same goes for second-hand or centuries-old properties. Whether it's a development company employing sophisticated marketing techniques, a local estate agent, or the vendor doing a private deal, they're all interested in one thing: selling you something for the highest possible price. As such, they will talk up the home you're interested in buying as much as they can.

Make sure you get an absolute, absolute, fixed idea of exactly what you want – then make up your mind very slowly indeed as to the actual purchase. There's virtually nothing that's unique; if you lose one property, there will be others, nearly as nice or vastly better. Always remember that you can walk away, especially with such a very expensive, emotive purchase as a dream home in the sun.

## Avoid the obvious pitfalls

Whether you are buying for investment or to have a home in the sun, you don't want to be out of pocket – or to fall foul of the authorities in your new country. Contentment with your foreign property purchase comes from knowing you have made a wise choice, after doing very detailed research and – most importantly – the most accurate number-crunching possible.

To sum up, here are some of the more obvious pitfalls to watch out for when considering buying abroad:

▌ Never rely on budget airlines, or buy somewhere just because a budget airline has started flying there. Cheap airlines are notoriously subject to sudden closure, withdrawal of services, and unreliability over flights. Also, they are not always as 'budget' as the hype leads you to believe.

▌ Always factor in the ongoing costs. Whatever your reason for buying, there will always be maintenance costs and local taxes to pay. You may not always know in advance what these costs will be, but always assume they will be there. Buying abroad does not begin and end with the purchase price, and every country has its equivalent of council tax to pay.

▌ Never ignore tax liability. You will be liable for many taxes, such as income tax, capital gains tax and inheritance tax. There will be tax to pay – somewhere – on income gained from renting out your property. It is always sensible to take specialist tax advice before taking the plunge.

▌ If you are hoping to rent out your property, do extensive research beforehand on the market, length of the rental season and realistic returns. Most experts believe that 5–6 per cent gross is the most you can hope for – and this is unlikely to be year-round, for most destinations. An increasing number of developers are now offering 'guaranteed rentals' for a period of time, particularly in Turkey, Bulgaria and Dubai – all fast-emerging markets. But Stephen Ludlow, of LudlowThompson estate agents, warns: 'These rentals offered by developers are not necessarily based on what rent would actually be achieved if the property were rented out, or even whether the place would rent out at all. The property may be let by the developer at a fraction of the guaranteed rent, and as they have already added the cost of the guaranteed rent into the price, they are still making money.' Always make sure there is a genuine rental market available in your chosen destination.

▌ Does the place need extensive renovation? Again, most experts advise against DIY. You will almost certainly need professional help and may also need to get planning permission.

▌ Is there an exit strategy? In other words, could you sell if you have to? Although very many people buy properties abroad these days, they don't always keep them forever. I have known many second-homers who have suddenly had to sell because their circumstances changed, through illness, redundancy, death, or other unforeseen catastrophe. If you wanted to sell, would it be easy to find a buyer? It sounds obvious, but if buying for investment purposes, it is the selling, not the buying, which creates the hoped-for profit. A property in an emerging market may be extremely cheap to buy, but can you sell it on? It is particularly important to research the resale market when buying off-plan or at an advertised discount. Many timeshare apartments, for instance, have no resale value at all and cannot even be given away. Instead, the owner has to

keep paying the upkeep on however many years are left on the
timeshare deal.

❚ If you put down a deposit on a property, could you get it back
if you decided not to proceed? Buying systems in other countries differ from those in the UK, and in many places putting
down a deposit commits you to buying. So, never hand over
*any* money 'to secure the property' until you are 100 per cent
sure you want to buy.

❚ Be careful about buying a property you have never seen in
reality, but only viewed on a website, or at a property show.
Always visit the property and the site before making a
decision to purchase. Never be swayed by high-pressure sales
talk at shows.

❚ If buying for investment, do not make the mistake of believing
that property values in other countries only ever go up. It is
also dangerous to believe the hype of sales agents when they
are trying to sell you properties for investment and quote
annual rises of 20 per cent or whatever. No investment is ever
100 per cent guaranteed and there is always an element of risk,
*particularly* when buying abroad. Never forget that foreign
properties are very heavily marketed these days, with slick,
seductive campaigns. This does not necessarily mean you will
be sold a pup, but it is essential, when handing over very large
sums of money, to carry out your own independent research
on the area into such aspects as transport links, stability of
currency, popularity with holidaymakers, future planned
developments and political regimes.

# 2 The important questions

Although, as we have seen, any place, anywhere in the world can now be yours in exchange for a simple down payment, because the choice is now so vast it has also become totally mind-blowing. What's better overall: that 15th-century tumbledown farmhouse in need of total renovation, or a spanking new, modern, easy-to-run apartment right on the beach? And which of all the countries in the world would you choose?

Here are the important questions to ask yourself, and remember: don't buy anything until you have satisfied yourself as to the answers.

## For what purpose do I want a foreign home?

The answers to this question will probably influence your choice more than any other consideration:

■ Do you want the second home purely for holidays, to live in permanently or to provide some income from renting? Or are you looking purely for an alternative to stocks, shares and pension schemes?

■ Would you want a place you could divide up so that you could have part of it to yourself and rent out the other part?

■ Are you looking for a family home for family holidays, or a place just for yourself and maybe a partner?

■ Do you have pets you would hate to keep putting in kennels?

■ Would you be looking for a place to which you could eventually retire?

■ Are you fanatical about a particular sport, interest or hobby?

■ Is good weather overwhelmingly important?

■ Are you looking for a place beneficial to health?

■ Are you looking for relaxation, or stimulation?

■ Are you passionately in love with a particular country?

■ What would you do with yourself once you were there?

■ Might you become bored after a very short time?

If relocating permanently, would you need to earn a living in the host country? If so, you should check in advance whether you are allowed to earn a living as a foreign national, before finding out whether your skills are in fact marketable in the foreign country.

Most countries prefer to offer work to their own people and unless you can offer some specific skill that is not readily available in the host country, you could find it difficult to get permission to work. Some countries, also, do not allow foreigners to work unless they have a work permit or visa. These, such as the notorious Green Card, can be extremely difficult to obtain and, in some cases, take years.

You may need permission to rent out your property, or to set up a small hotel or B&B. Most people, also, find it extremely difficult to make a living from setting up a vineyard, or olive grove, or selling other produce.

In some countries, it may be difficult to persuade the authorities that you are working quietly as an author or artist. Writers Derek and Julia Parker emigrated to Australia a few years ago, only to discover they were not allowed to write for Australian publishers, in case they 'took work away' from an Australian author!

All this is to say: you can't be too careful, and if intending to earn a living abroad, every aspect needs to be checked out first – not only that you are allowed to earn money, but that there is a market for your line of work. Some people relocating abroad have discovered it is hard even to earn money doing internet work, which can theoretically be done anywhere, as they can find they lose touch with their contacts.

Some examples: Mike Walker, who with his wife Mary owns an 18th-century house in Gascony, France, loves golf, rugby and

French culture; he also wanted somewhere to retire to that was not too far away from the UK. Because of his sporting interests, he never gets bored in his French home.

Irene Goodman, who has a beautiful studio near Cannes, loves going there, but says her husband gets bored after a few days. The result is that they go very infrequently indeed.

Trevor Roberts, who lives in Italy permanently after retiring, says that many people retire to a beautiful spot or a beautiful country and then discover that life has no purpose, or at least not enough purpose.

It's essential to ask: what would I do with myself there, not just for a week or two, but for three or six months?

## Would I actually want to go to the same place every year?

To make the purchase of a second home make sense, you have to want to keep going back and back to the same place. Some people go to their holiday home abroad every other weekend, or every six weeks or so. Others spend three months there in the summer, and simply wouldn't want to be anywhere else.

For those who have taken the plunge and bought holiday homes, the location is that of their dreams. It has to be. They have fallen totally in love with the place and, although they may want to explore other countries, this place, this hallowed spot, tugs at their heartstrings like nowhere else. Unless you feel a pull as strong as this, don't buy. The thing has to become irresistible to you, otherwise it can all too easily become a burden and something with which to reproach yourself.

Bear in mind that the purchase of your holiday home is the biggest financial commitment you will ever make, after buying your main home. Nowadays, you will almost always be talking about a six-figure sum, especially after you have added on running and maintenance costs, local taxes and utility bills.

And in any case, never buy when your consciousness has been altered by copious amounts of sun, sea and sangria. The best, and indeed the only, way to buy somewhere abroad is to go and stay in the vicinity for the sole purpose of looking for somewhere, rather than trying to combine it with a holiday.

Visit possible places, with estate agents, every single day and don't make an offer until you are 10 million per cent certain that nothing else will do. Don't buy until the home pleads: buy me.

If tempted to go out on an inspection trip offered by a property developer, you should already be 100 per cent certain of the location and type of home required. Otherwise you could be seduced by smooth-talking salespeople into a purchase you will later regret. Don't forget that sales teams on inspection trips and at exhibitions are highly trained high-pressure salespeople. They have to be; their commissions of several thousand pounds per sale closed make them very mean and hungry indeed, even if they seem to be all smiles and charm.

The advantages of a permanent place abroad are: once you've got over the initial outlay, you can spend longer and cheaper holidays than would be possible in hotels or rented apartments; you can go out there on the spur of the moment or when the fancy takes you; you have the opportunity of getting to know another country really well and becoming part of it.

There is also a dramatic pleasure, hard to beat, in actually owning a little part of another country. It's romantic, exotic, satisfying to the soul and delivers the most overwhelming sense of achievement.

## How much time, realistically, would I be able to/want to spend in my second home each year?

Bear in mind that as a holiday home is an expensive purchase with permanent ongoing running costs, you have to be certain that it is worth it, in terms of the amount of time you intend to spend there. If the maximum time you could spare is two weeks in a year, then it is most probably better to rent somewhere, or consider a timeshare option, rather than buy an entire property.

Most people who take the plunge intend to spend at least two months in every year at their second home, although not necessarily all at once. In most countries, you are allowed to spend up to six months in the year at your second home without having to satisfy residency qualifications or paying income tax or social security.

It has to be said that, when first buying a holiday home abroad, not everybody knows just how much time they might spend there. Very often, owners get to like their second home so much they spend far more time than they originally intended, and in many cases have a plan eventually to retire there.

## How important are sunshine and hot weather?

Few, if any, places have hot sun all year round with no climatic disadvantages. Italy is cold in winter – hence all those fur coats – and places like Cyprus, which are becoming popular with British second-homers, have a couple of cold months a year, at least. The Canaries can be cold in winter and are almost always windy. Few parts of Spain are hot all year round. Portugal can be cold, windy and rainy in February.

All parts of France, even the southernmost areas, are cold in winter. If warm weather is of paramount importance, don't choose somewhere that is liable to have long cold stretches. Normandy can be as bitingly cold as the north of Scotland in winter, and Florida is subject to tropical downpours and extreme heat and humidity.

Don't forget that it is always more difficult to occupy your time in a holiday home when the weather is bad. So many activities that people enjoy in a second home are weather dependent: walking, golf, tennis, sailing, sunbathing, sitting outside drinking cold beer. Also, just coping with everyday activities becomes more difficult in rainy or cold weather.

Again, as with all other considerations, it is vital to do your research thoroughly. Spend a February in the location of your choice (if it's in Europe) and see if you still like it. If the weather in the place you like is not much better, or actually worse (if that's possible) than that of the British Isles, then there have to be strong other pulls to that particular place.

Mike Walker, with a house in Gascony, says he is not a sun seeker, and admits that the winters in Gascony can be worse than those in the UK. Hilary Sadler, on the other hand, with a place in Spain, is a 'total sun worshipper', and so had to choose a second home somewhere with plenty of heat for most of the year.

If you are seeking a home abroad primarily for health reasons, it's important to pick your location very carefully indeed. First of all, check out what the health care and medical provisions are like in your favoured country; then research the implications of private health care.

If you already have a chronic health condition, you will most probably want to choose your home with this in mind. As a rough guide, if you suffer from asthma, sinusitis or bronchitis, you'd want a place with little or no air pollution, such as the Caribbean. Sufferers from arthritis or rheumatism should pick somewhere with a bone-dry climate such as Lanzarote, Costa Blanca, La Gomera or Malta.

Heart problems often respond well to the Mediterranean diet and, for poor circulation or hypertension, a flat country should be chosen. The Bahamas and Florida are examples. The Champagne region of France is said to be excellent for depression, and if you suffer from seasonal affective disorder (SAD) don't choose somewhere like Thailand, where there is no evening, and it's pitch-black, summer and winter, by 6 in the evening.

The World Health Organization has designated the Costa Blanca as the world's number one health spot.

# How important is distance from my main home?

Most places take six hours, at least, to get to, door to door, from the UK. There is simply no 'abroad' place that takes much less. Even the north of France can take several hours from your own front door.

Don't be misled either by stated flight times. Although Spain may be only two and a half hours away when in the air, you have to add on two hours or so waiting time at the airport, the time it takes to get to the airport and the time the transfer takes at the other end. Most places are an hour away from major airports, at least. With added airport security since 11 September 2001, checking in and out at most airports takes far longer than it used to.

If there is no convenient airport near your chosen location, would you be happy to drive? It takes around 13 hours to get from London to the French Alps, driving solidly. For some, these very long journeys are daunting. If you have pets that you want to take with you, it may not be possible to fly and you would have to drive to your destination.

Florida, rapidly becoming a popular second home choice, is an eight-hour flight away, and Greece and Cyprus are four hours, at least. The further the distance, the less possible it is to go on a whim, at a moment's notice. Handy flights are not always available, and although very cheap flights are frequently advertised there may be only six seats on the aircraft on offer at a ridiculously low price at any one time. Many people have discovered, for instance, that since 11 September 2001 cheap flights to and from the United States are far more difficult to come by than previously.

Keith Atkinson, with homes in France and Florida, warns that Ryanair (or any other cheap carrier) may well cut your airport off its schedules, so it may not do to rely too much on cheap airlines transporting you or your family at low or no cost. Budget airlines are notoriously fragile and liable to go bust at a minute's notice, so although cheap airfares have revolutionized the second-home industry, they are by no means as reliable as you might like.

If you hate flying or are flying-phobic, then it would not be a good idea to choose a holiday home that involves a long flight. Also remember that for each member of your family flying with you, that's the price of another air ticket. Packing everybody into a car only involves the price of the petrol and ferry, however many people travel.

# How important is it to be able to speak the language?

That depends on how much you want to integrate with the natives. Obviously you get far more out of being in a foreign

# ROUTLEDGE
# COLLOQUIALS

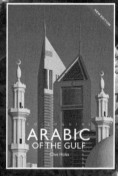

'Undoubtedly the best series of in-depth language courses on the market.'
– *Waterstone's Booksellers*

What makes our *Colloquials* the best choice in language learning? They are:

- interactive – lots of exercises for regular practice

- clear – concise grammar notes

- practical – useful vocabulary and pronunciation guide

- complete – including answer key and special reference section.

Packs contain a book, plus accompanying audio material recorded by native speakers which will help you with listening and pronunciation skills.

'They are always up to date, clear and accessible and enable the reader to communicate effectively in the chosen language.'
– *Blackwell's University Bookshop*

# COLLOQUIAL 2s

*Colloquial 2s* are perfect for those who already have some knowledge of the language and want to progress a stage further. They are also available in packs with a book and audio material, and each is accompanied by a FREE website providing extra information and exercises.

Key features include:

- texts, scripted dialogues and interactive exercises, all recorded by native speakers

- revision material to help build on your basic skills

- a wide range of contemporary authentic documents, both written and audio

- plenty of spoken and written exercises, a grammar reference and a detailed answer key.

*Colloquial 2s* are the only language courses of this type to provide further exercises and resources via the web, and the *Colloquials 2* websites are ABSOLUTELY FREE!

Visit **www.routledge.com/colloquials** to order your copy or for more information on the full range of titles available please email us at colloquials@routledge.com, or telephone 0207 017 6243.

**Routledge**
Taylor & Francis Group

country if you speak the language; this allows you to become friendly with the locals and to be alive to nuances and subtleties that would be lost otherwise.

It is possibly not absolutely essential, but a huge advantage, if you can already speak the language of the country of your choice. It becomes essential if, for instance, you are buying a place that needs renovation or serious work, or if you are having to handle legal documents or deal with officialdom. The better you speak the language, the easier all the practicalities will become.

Mike Walker found himself totally flummoxed by French legal jargon and bureaucracy, by not speaking the language, when he tried to close the deal on his French home.

How would you feel if pages of small print had to be explained to you by somebody else? Another buyer, who does speak fluent French, made the point that technical and legal French is different from the everyday language and that, even if you are fluent, you may still not fully comprehend a legal document.

Again, ability to speak the language depends on your main reason for wanting to be in the country. If you want to spend most of your time with other British expats in a secure gated development, playing golf all day, then speaking the language may not be of prime importance. It all depends on how much you want to integrate. There are whole communities in Spain that speak only English, for instance, and for the type of people who go there that is what they prefer.

But never forget that you are at a distinct disadvantage if you don't speak the language. One of the reasons for the great popularity of Florida as a second-home destination for English-speaking people is that they don't have to learn a new language.

On the other hand, if you are already fluent, or bilingual, then this will most likely influence your choice of destination.

Vicky Harrison, who has bought a house in France, says: 'I don't know how people can imagine they can settle somewhere without the language – buying is the easy bit.' She adds: 'I am being very disciplined and only reading French papers and watching French telly. I very much like inhabiting another language and culture.' Graham and Juliet Lord say they had only O-level French when they first moved there in 1996, but are now reasonably fluent. So long as you have a smattering, it is possible to improve language skills once in the country permanently.

## What about lifestyle, crime rate, the arts?

A tiny village in Spain is hardly likely to have avant-garde art or music shows, although local festivals may appeal. Some places may have a very high crime rate, or a reputation for corruption. Places where crime is rife could pose a security problem when you're not there. Again, it's a matter of doing research thoroughly, and satisfying yourself, rather than being influenced by others. Many places are specifically advertised as having a 'low crime rate', in order to tempt foreign buyers.

So far as lifestyle is concerned, this also has to appeal. Some people like the hustle and bustle of a busy city such as Paris or New York, whilst others prefer the peace and quiet of a lazy village. You have to ask yourself what you are likely to be doing most of in your holiday home, and take it from there. Peace and quiet is wonderful for a few days, but would you enjoy total peace and quiet and isolation for three months?

Some countries, such as Portugal, have become famous for their sports complexes, hence the name 'Sportugal'. If you hate all sport, you are hardly likely to be happy in a place catering for tennis, golf, watersport or sailing fanatics. In fact, you would be extremely miserable.

Do you want to go and read? Sunbathe? Have a hectic nightlife? Visit museums and art galleries? Go to operas? Find some income-producing work to do? Ask yourself what you would do, or most like to do, in your holiday home. The answer will depend on your personality, inclinations, skills, interests and hobbies.

## Who is likely to use the place?

It's essential to be very specific in your requirements. You may want somewhere that can accommodate all your family plus extended family. Are you looking for somewhere for your children or grandchildren to enjoy? If so, the considerations may be different than if you just want a bolthole as an escape. For instance, most of the properties on offer in Florida are three- or four-bedroom detached houses with their own swimming pool.

This is ideal if you are looking for a family home. But if you are a couple, or single, you would be better off with a one-bedroom apartment that needs less maintenance and costs less to run.

## Would I miss my friends, family and neighbours?

If you have thrown down very deep roots in your own country or neighbourhood, it may be difficult to contemplate being in a foreign environment for maybe months at a time. Some people simply do not enjoy being away from their main home for long stretches, and unless you intend to spend several months of the year in your second home its existence will probably not justify itself.

## Would I need to rent out the place to make it pay?

Renting out your second home for part of the year can be a way of making the otherwise unaffordable affordable. But there are many potential problems to this. The main drawback is that the times of highest letting potential are most probably the times when you want to be there yourself.

Also, a lot of work and effort is involved in renting out a place that is also your own home. For one thing, the place has to be kept immaculate, and if you are occupying it yourself for some of the time this might be difficult. Your home has to be cleaned and maintained to a higher standard than you would probably bother with if only using it yourself.

If you intend to rent out your place, you first of all have to pick somewhere with high renting potential. Not everywhere attracts foreign visitors. Places popular with holidaymakers are likely to be busy and the beaches may be packed in summer. The home has to be relatively near airports or main transport links, easy and cheap to get to.

Then it has to be professionally managed in your absence, as linen has to be changed each week, the place has to be thoroughly cleaned after each holidaymaker, and all appliances must be working. Letting agencies insist on certain standards, and also take a hefty fee for their services. Rental companies calculate that you have to forgo at least half of your total rental income if you have the place managed by a local agency.

Then there will be tax to pay on your rental income, either in your own country or the country of your holiday home, and for this you will need to keep all bills and employ an accountant.

It is obviously easier not to rent out your holiday home, but sometimes it is essential. If you are buying on a mortgage, you will most probably have to rent it out at least for part of the year to cover your costs.

It is a sad fact of life that very many people who buy second homes with the intention of renting them out for at least part of the year discover that, once they have made the place their own, they cannot bear to rent it out to strangers.

It's also common for such people to realize that they can't bear, either, to charge members of their family, or even their friends, rent to stay in the place. If you fear this may be you, think very carefully about whether you would actually want to rent the place out to others, or to keep it solely for yourself or members of your family.

When it comes to second or holiday homes, strong emotions come to the fore, as you have to fall in love with the home, the location, the climate, the country, in its entirety, before ever considering the financial side. Big construction companies who sell off-plan are as hard-headed as the hats they wear, of course – but buyers, usually, are not. They just love the place and they have to have it. So much emotion is bound up in the purchase of a holiday home that it can be difficult to separate longing from logic.

If you are buying the place with rental income for all or part of the year in mind, you must first check that you are allowed to let it out. In some areas of France, for instance, you are not allowed to rent out certain properties. It may be considered that you would take trade away from other holiday developments or from hotels, for instance. Some apartment blocks may forbid subletting. Some authorities may allow holiday, but not long-term, lets. Some parts of Florida are not 'zoned' for holiday letting – so don't buy a home in one of these areas and then discover you are not allowed to rent it out.

You also have to be certain that it would rent out successfully. A lovely remote farmhouse in the middle of France may be too far away from airports, towns or good roads to tempt anybody in the summer, and too cold in winter to be a viable rental proposition.

Most countries have very strict rules indeed about rental arrangements, and you would have to check carefully first what is and is not allowed under local or national laws.

Thousands and thousands of second-homers do rent out their homes very successfully, of course, and it may be an idea to check out the rental situation by posing as a possible tenant when on holiday in the area, before deciding to buy. You would also need to know what a particular property would command in rents, in both high and low seasons, and how many, comfortably, it would sleep. A one-bedroom Miami apartment I saw on the internet was advertised as 'sleeping six'. The mind boggles as to where all those six would go!

A two-bedroom flat with a double sofabed could sleep six; most people seem content to crush up together on holiday in a way they would not tolerate in their own home. When calculating rental income, it's also necessary to be able to pack in the highest number of holidaymakers, so as to maximize this income.

You could, of course, decide to rent rather than buy. Most people who have moved abroad permanently advise renting first, before you take what might turn out to be an irrevocable plunge, but Graham and Juliet Lord have taken the decision to rent as a way of life, in both Nevis and the South of France.

Sounds risky, maybe, but Graham reckons their no-going-back decision has definite advantages, in that by renting, they are able to live in far grander style than if they bought, at the same time as having money in the bank. Graham says:

> We decided to sell up and move out permanently, which meant we missed out on the huge boom in property prices, which would have meant I could now have afforded to retire. The house we sold in Fulham in 1996 for £300,000 is now worth about £1.3 million. But we have had 12 glorious years living out of the UK and you can't put a price on that.

> In France, we have a huge house with four bedrooms, two bath-rooms, three loos, a vast salon with a big fireplace, swimming pool, sweeping driveway and separate two-bedroom guest cottage, all for £450 a week. What could you rent in London for that?

On the financial side, Graham adds:

> By not owning a property we are skating financially on thin ice. But I spent 30 years paying off mortgages in England and it's bliss no longer to be responsible for house repairs and maintenance and to have some money in the bank for the first time in my life. Unless you're rich you have to be prepared to take a huge risk, but as a writer and painter, we can work anywhere in the world.

The advantages of renting over buying are that you can more easily calculate your outgoings, and that you are less likely to face an unexpected repair or renovation bill. The disadvantage of no longer having a home to call your own is probably more an attitude of mind than a reality. After all, if Graham and Juliet's finances suddenly took a serious downturn they could easily downsize, whereas it might take many months, or even years, to sell a property. Also, there is no absolute guarantee that your foreign property will increase in value. French property increases by about 3 per cent a year, but in Florida and parts of Spain, property can actually go down in value as new places are built. Where there is no shortage of land, it cannot be taken as automatic that property prices will rise.

Graham and Juliet are the only people I know who have taken a decision to rent as a conscious lifestyle option, but it is worth considering, especially if renting would mean you have a nice lump of money in the bank to go at.

These days, there may be more security in having money in the bank than owning a property. But it all depends on what sort of person you are, and what considerations have to be taken into account.

# Am I looking for a seasonal holiday home or a year-round place?

This question is very important, as it will make a profound difference to the place you choose. Many developments designated as holiday homes are simply not suitable for year-round occupation. For instance, a holiday apartment intended for summer use may not have central heating, which could make it unacceptably cold in winter.

Many holiday resorts are extremely bleak in winter, with restaurants, bars and facilities all closed down. If you are attracted to an apartment right on the beach, this question becomes even more crucial.

An important question to ask is: is the apartment/villa 'winterized'? Non-winterized apartments come cheaper, but are strictly for seasonal occupation. Also, local laws may not allow you to occupy some holiday homes year-round.

# Would I need to earn a living abroad?

It is not, it must be said, easy to earn a living in another country, particularly if you are not absolutely fluent in the language. Also, in some countries there are severe restrictions on incomers taking potential jobs away from nationals.

By far the great majority of second-home owners do not think about earning a living in their adopted country, as in any case, even when allowed, they become involved in huge amounts of bureaucracy and taxation.

Obviously if you are a writer or artist like Graham and Juliet Lord, then nobody can prevent you from working in your second home. But, at least in the first instance, life will be far more enjoyable and less worrying if you do not absolutely have to earn money whilst at your second home. Some people who start off buying seasonal holiday homes discover they like their host country so much they decide to stay there permanently.

In such cases, home owners have become managing agents for other owners, or swimming-pool attendants, or have set up language schools or bed-and-breakfasts, to enable them to remain permanently in their chosen country. Most people in this position admit that they do not earn what they consider a good living, but they tick over, especially if they have capital left over from selling their main UK homes, which many have to do in order to survive abroad.

If, however, you intend to get a 'proper' job abroad, you need to know all about local income tax rules. For instance, if you have a permanent job in the United States, you would only be allowed to enter the UK for 90 days a year – unless you wanted to pay income tax in both countries.

## A few tips about setting up a business abroad

Ever more people buying abroad are interested in setting up a business and making money while they are there. Most popular are running a boutique hotel or B&B, a restaurant or bar, or setting up as a sports instructor. However, you need to know that you would enjoy doing this kind of thing, so the first question to ask is: would I like to do this in the home country, never mind abroad? Running a business abroad is similar, but more difficult as you are coping with an unfamiliar language, and unfamiliar employment and commercial laws. So here are a few tips to bear in mind when considering running a business in another country.

If you want to set up a business in Spain, you will need to apply for residency. The residency document takes you into the tax and benefits system and entitles you to its services. An EU citizen is allowed to work in Spain free of restrictions – but not free of tax. If you buy an existing business, or set up a new one, you will need to get a fiscal number to register your company. The coastal areas of Spain have many English-speaking firms that can organize this for you.

In France, it is not quite so easy to set up a business thanks to bureaucracy, but it is not impossible. France is a country known for high taxes and an expensive welfare system, and the 'enterprise spirit' is not so much encouraged as in Spain. Again, you would need to take tax and residency advice before embarking on any kind of business.

You can set up a business in Turkey if you like, but would have to apply for a work permit and permission to set up a company. You have to prove that you would not be taking away a job from a Turkish native, so you have to be able to offer something unique. In most instances, you would have to set up a limited company and pay in to the social insurance system.

Most countries have many rules and regulations regarding foreigners setting up companies, and it is vital to be au fait with these before embarking on your chosen way of trying to make money in another country.

It is not always easy to be a self-employed writer in another country, as authors Derek and Julia Parker discovered when they emigrated to Australia: the authorities feared they may be taking away a writing job from an Australian author. Not all foreign employment or working laws in other countries are sensible – many countries have rules and laws that are as daft as our own.

## Does my partner like the same things as me?

When contemplating the purchase of a second home, it is vital to be in harmony with your partner, and discuss very thoroughly the kind of place you both want. Very many relationships come to grief over non-shared interests: the husband who wants to go to Spain for the golf, which the wife hates; couples choosing somewhere remote where one partner would prefer a busy social and night life; a tennis village where one plays and the other doesn't.

Unless you have genuine shared interests, the relationship is bound to suffer if one of you enthusiastically looks forward to going to the place and the other starts to hate it. Very often, couples and families are thrown together far more in the foreign home than they ever would be in their principal home.

# Can I actually afford the place abroad?

The expert advice here is: never buy a home abroad unless you can do so without jeopardizing your principal home and way of life. The other big piece of advice is: never buy if rental income absolutely *has* to cover all of your costs. It might – but this can never be guaranteed.

Some second-home owners, it is true, do make money from renting out the place. But if stretching yourself to buy on a mortgage, you have to remember that nobody knows what is going to happen to the economy in five years' time. Nor does anybody know what interest rates or currency fluctuations might be.

Although many properties abroad seem ridiculously cheap compared to those in the UK, the purchase price is of course only one aspect of the expense. In most other countries, the actual purchasing costs are far higher than in the UK; then there will inevitably be ongoing running costs.

You will have to pay local taxes – the equivalent of council tax – and all your utility bills, whether you are there or not. In some countries with severe water shortages, water bills can be extremely high. In the Canaries, for instance, where it hardly ever rains, household water is provided by desalination plants, which are very expensive to run.

You will have to have a bank account in the country of your second home, and this must always be in funds. Otherwise, you will be heavily fined, on top of not being able to pay local bills.

If you do not intend to rent out the property, costs mount up all the time you are not there. One owner of a home in Florida reckoned he could stay in a hotel such as the Ritz or the Raffles for three months for the same price as it costs him to keep his Florida home going each year. This particular owner does not rent out his house when he is not in occupation. It just stands empty.

If you are not there all the time, the property will still have to be maintained. You may have to employ a gardener, somebody to clean the swimming pool, and a maintenance person to make sure pipes do not freeze up and the electricity is still working. A place left empty for nine months of the year will inevitably deteriorate, and need work when you return.

If buying into an apartment block, there will be ongoing costs apart from local bills and taxes. Service and maintenance, or community charges, will have to be paid whether you are there or not. Beware of buying into an apartment block that has communal heating and hot water, as many US condos do, as you will be paying for these in your absence. Many older blocks in the United States, for instance, have these communal systems, which cannot be individually turned on or off, but still have to be paid for. You can find yourself sitting in a US apartment with all the windows wide open, whilst the radiators are belting out heat you cannot turn down.

If you buy a place backing on to a golf course, there will probably be membership and green fees to find on top of everything else. All sports activities cost something, and these will have to be added on to the running costs.

Then there will be the costs of actually getting there. Florida homes are cheap, but the cost of flying out four people two or three times a year will add up significantly. Cheap flights may not always be available, especially if you have to fly out at short notice.

A remote tumbledown farmhouse in France or Italy may be extremely cheap to buy, but how much will it cost to do up? The received wisdom is that it costs far more to buy and renovate a wreck than to buy a much more expensive new or renovated home that does not immediately need major work. Also, if buying something run-down, the business of obtaining planning permission, and employing local architects, surveyors, builders and other workers can soon run away with any budget you may have.

The bottom line is: don't be misled by a suspiciously cheap asking price for the property. It's no good making an offer until you have added up all the nastiest figures – and then added some for unexpected repairs, maintenance, building work or times when you may simply not be able to rent out the place. It's probably safe to assume that there's no such thing as a bargain: if it sounds suspiciously cheap, then there will be something seriously wrong with it.

It's common to consider buying a property abroad if you come into an unexpected legacy or windfall. But although the windfall may cover the price and cost of purchase, would there be enough left over actually to run the place?

Another piece of hard-earned wisdom is: when buying, never ever go more than 10 per cent over your total budget. Don't fall in love with something so much that you allow your heart to rule your head. Mortgage repayments and running costs are relentless; they never go away, and if you can't keep up the payments you will lose your lovely home. Lenders show far less leeway with second or holiday homes than they do when it comes to the main roof over your head.

Karen Robinson, supplements editor of the *Sunday Times*, spent a summer week looking at possible second homes on an unidentified Mediterranean island, and was almost seduced into buying somewhere. She says, 'I came away from the experience with nothing but a keen sense of how easy it would be to have a few glasses too many of the local firewater and end up making a huge mistake.'

Writing in the *Spectator* (25 October 2002), she continues:

We stayed in a villa – the showhome, in fact – on a brand-new development of houses and apartments with its own 'private beach'. But there is no such thing as a private beach in the Mediterranean. So while the pebbly strand was pretty deserted on weekdays, at the weekend the indigenous equivalent of white-van man and his extended family descended, hauling barbecues, beatboxes, beach umbrellas and ancient, black-clad female relatives out of their trucks and disporting themselves in noisy enjoyment.

Karen, who went on a fly'n'buy trip, also makes the point that a quick half-hour spent looking at the property does not show up such potential problems as faulty wiring or the fact that the 'mosaic tiles' in the swimming pool may actually be sticky-backed plastic. Then there are the neighbours to consider. Are they going to be an ever-changing roster of holiday tenants? Or – even worse, to her – golfers from Hertfordshire? She also makes the point that in many holiday home areas, there are far more places to rent than potential tenants.

Addressing the question of affordability, Karen cited two case histories as cautionary tales. One was of a family who were pouring so much money into their Spanish home, where they spent at most six weeks a year, that they were having to downsize on their main home. Another couple, having paid off their UK mortgage, locked themselves into long-term debt to buy an Italian ruin.

She ends on a positive note, however: 'More people piling onto the foreign property bandwagon means an ever greater choice of places to stay when we want to get away.'

## Am I looking for an investment?

Although it is true that some people make money from properties in other countries, these are mainly big construction companies, holiday companies, tour operators and people primarily running holiday rentals businesses.

If the main purpose of the purchase is for holidays for yourself and maybe your family, it is unlikely to prove a worthwhile investment from a financial point of view. It may be a wonderful investment so far as improving your lifestyle goes, of course – the considerations cannot only ever be simply financial ones with this type of transaction.

Although properties are often cheaper in other countries, the actual purchase costs tend to be far higher. Because of this, and because people do not move so much in certain countries as in the UK, property prices do not rise at the same level. Also, it may take a long time to recoup the purchase costs; if you sell within two or three years, you are likely to make an overall loss on the sale. Few people find they make much of a profit on resale. In Florida, for instance, it is almost impossible to make money on resale; and the likelihood is that you will make a loss. It's best to regard your second home as a luxury, rather than a money-making venture.

Rachael Heyhoe-Flint, the former England women's cricket captain, believes that the golf bungalow she and her husband Derrick Flint bought in La Manga club in Spain has been her best investment ever, not perhaps in terms of money but because 'it's a wonderful bolthole, always there for the family. We do not need to plan holidays months in advance. We can whizz down there whenever a few free days emerge.'

Property sales to foreign investors have become big business and, indeed, Spain's economy now depends heavily on sales of homes to foreign buyers. Spain has become the number one destination for Britons, and many other Northern Europeans, to settle permanently. Because of this, high-pressure sales techniques are extremely common and if you are not very careful, you could end up losing all your investment.

Although Spanish developers probably employ the highest-pressure sales techniques, developers in other countries are following suit, so it is as well to bear in mind that, in general, the more heavily marketed the dream villa or apartment, the less likely it is to prove a good financial investment. Developers, architects, lawyers, estate agents and mortgage lenders will all make money from the sale of a home in the sun, but you, the purchaser, may not.

## A cautionary tale

The Watchdog column in the magazine *Homes Worldwide* featured the following cautionary tale. And beware – it could happen to you.

Reader Luis Gladstone had been thinking for some time about investing some of his savings in a property abroad, and decided to go on an inspection trip to Malaga, Spain. His intention at this time was just to look, not to buy. He was then going to go home, crunch the numbers, think about it in the cool light of English weather, and see if it all added up for him without salespeople breathing down his neck.

It didn't turn out that way.

When he was on the trip, the sales agents were so pushy that, against his better judgement, he ended up signing away all his life savings on a new apartment in Malaga. Once back home, he realized he had made a dreadful mistake and asked Spanish lawyer Antonio Guillen of the International Property Law Centre in Hull whether he stood any remote chance of getting his money back.

Guillen replied that, if Mr Gladstone had only signed a *reservation* agreement and paid typically around £4,000, he would have a statutory cooling-off period of 30 days, even though the £4,000 or so would itself normally be non-refundable. It is questionable, though, whether Mr Gladstone would have a defence of duress and harassment, as this would have to be fought in a Spanish court and would in any case be very difficult to prove.

But if he had signed a *purchase* agreement, where he would have put down between 10 and 30 per cent of the purchase price, it is unlikely he would get his money back and he would have to decide between completing the purchase and pursuing it through the Spanish courts. Where sales agents are extremely pushy and you are trying to deal with legal documents in an unfamiliar language, it can be difficult to know exactly what you have signed or to understand the legal differences between the various documents that constitute a binding contract.

Antonio Guillen added that, in order to issue legal proceedings once a purchase agreement has been signed, the buyer would have to have some legal grounds against the vendor, such as defects in the title.

To me, this all sounds very grim indeed, and if you doubt your ability to resist sales talk don't go on inspection trips in the first place. Salespeople are often *very* good at their job, as I realized when I bought a new car recently. Although I recognized the sales talk for what it was, I still fell for it and bought the car – and all the accessories! Never underestimate the persuasive techniques of salespeople, who after all depend on sales for their income, or overestimate your ability to resist sales patter.

# What about 'mouseholing'?

'Mouseholing' is rapidly becoming popular as an alternative to stretching yourself to buying a second home you can barely afford in addition to keeping on your main UK home. The 'mousehole' concept means that you sell your main home in the UK and use the money to buy two, or even three, smaller homes dotted around the globe, which you can either rent out when not in residence yourself or lock up and leave.

Writer Irma Kurtz pioneered the mousehole concept when she sold her three-bed London house to buy a tiny flat in Soho and another in France. Another friend, now in her 60s, sold the big family house following her divorce, and used the money to buy a studio flat in central London, a two-bed apartment in Miami and a one-bed apartment in the south of France. Although she has nowhere to call absolute home, her life is made exciting by flitting around her three mouseholes at will. When she feels like travelling, she contacts local agents to see whether they can let out her non-occupied residence for the time she is away.

Note: in London, a number of agencies now operate 'short lets' whereby immaculate homes can be rented out at premium rents for anything from a week to five months. There are also 'home from home' agencies, which rent out your home to holiday-makers. This can be a way of affording several homes and also ensuring that they are occupied, rather than being attractive to burglars, in your absence.

The 'mousehole' concept is ideal for couples whose children have grown up and left home, for retired people who have the time and leisure to spend several months in another country, for single people with few ties, for self-employed people who can work anywhere they choose or, indeed, for anybody who no longer has need of a family home.

James Barnes, European Manager for Hamptons International, says:

> In the past, the main problem was actually getting to the homes abroad, rather than affording them. But now that air fares are so cheap, and transport generally has improved out of all recognition, ever more people are deciding to sell the family home and buy two or three little homes for the same money. In the same way that rail links enabled people to buy places at the coast in Victorian times, so budget airlines are enabling today's buyers to purchase their little homes in the sun, while keeping a toehold in the UK.

# 3 Money

Whilst it is generally cheaper to buy a property abroad than in the UK, it's no longer as cheap as it once was. A number of factors have driven up prices in recent years.

The first and most important of these was the introduction of the euro, initially in 12 European countries, in early 2002. Many Europeans who had hidden their stash of francs, pesetas or lire under the mattress knew they had to get rid of this cash before it became worthless, or difficult to explain to the tax authorities. What better than to put it into property? Since the late 1990s, many French, Italian and Spanish nationals have been buying up plots of land or second homes in their own countries to get rid of this 'mattress money' before too many awkward questions were asked.

Also, since countries such as Spain and Portugal have become more affluent, many more nationals than ever before have been able to afford second homes in their own countries. If their country is already perfect, why go anywhere else?

Introduction of the euro has also given many Northern Europeans the confidence to buy second homes abroad, as it has become so much easier to compare and calculate prices, now that there is a single currency. This has meant that, in some areas, demand is outstripping supply. There is a limit, for instance, to the number of 17th-century Tuscan farmhouses available, and no more are likely to be built.

Another very important factor, and one that should not be underestimated, although at first it may seem trivial, is the introduction of pet passports in many countries across the world. This development has persuaded many people, who previously would not have wanted to leave their pets behind or put them in quarantine, to take the plunge and purchase second homes in countries that now welcome their cats or dogs.

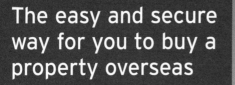

**The easy and secure way for you to buy a property overseas**

Hundreds of overseas buyers are already seeing the benefits of using an Exchange Bond.®

**EXCHANGE BOND**®

An Exchange Bond® is a financial guarantee which allows you to buy property overseas without putting down a cash deposit. It's a stress-free and trusted way to protect your property investment, providing a simpler and often cheaper alternative.

Winners of the Your Mortgage Award 2007 - 2008.

Sponsors of
**newhome** AWARDS:2007
The Daily Telegraph

To find out more or sign-up, visit www.exchangebond.com

EXCHANGE
BOND®

### Realising a dream

Many Britons dream of buying a second home overseas for those long, relaxing holidays in the sun; for others, retirement provides the impetus to live outside the UK more or less permanently.

By 2050, according to a recent survey*, some 3.3 million Britons will be retiring abroad. The number of British and Irish residents owning a foreign property is already substantial amounting to 3.81 million (excluding time share and fractional ownership).**

Buying a property abroad, however, is not entered into lightly. Aside from language difficulties buyers have to cope with the intricacies of property laws which are completely alien to those in the UK. Add to these, well documented cases of poor quality building, fly by night developers and developments which never get beyond an outline drawing and the dream can quickly turn into a nightmare.

### Introducing the Overseas Exchange Bond®

Now there is a product which is helping to remove the barriers to buying property overseas and making the process transparent, simple, secure and stress-free.

The Overseas Exchange Bond® (OEB) is being taken up by a growing number of developers worldwide as a direct replacement for the traditional cash deposit usually required at exchange of contracts in order to secure a property.

Pioneered in the UK by the Exchange Insurance Company (ExCo), the Exchange Bond® is a form of financial guarantee. It has quickly established itself as the industry standard with buyers and developers recognising the benefits of using an Exchange Bond®.

A key attraction of using the OEB is that it removes the need to put down the often substantial cash deposit – which may be as much as 30% of the asking price for an overseas property purchase. Instead the buyer can choose to pay the full agreed deposit amount at completion, which may be several months – and possibly years – ahead. Where stage payments are involved, the OEB still allows the buyer to retain a substantive part of his cash until completion.

## Benefits of using the Overseas Exchange Bond®

Using an Exchange Bond®, issued and underwritten by the ExCo, provides a "win- win" scenario for all parties involved in the property transaction.

- The buyer avoids putting down an often substantial cash sum as a deposit with an overseas developer before completion, as part of a transaction which is subject to local laws.
- It ensures that the bonded amount is not at risk in the event that the developer fails to perform.
- An overseas property can be secured without the need to deploy savings – or expensive bridging finance – so that the buyer's assets can continue to generate a return.
- An Overseas Exchange Bond® is unsecured and inexpensive to buy.
- In many cases, the developer will credit the premium paid to purchase the OEB® at completion so that the buyer is better off financially using the Overseas Exchange Bond®.
- Purchasing an Overseas Exchange Bond® is simple, swift and convenient.
- An Overseas Exchange Bond® can be provided for between three months and five years for new properties.

## Not forgetting the attractive cost

The premium payable to purchase(x) an OEB® is calculated on the basis of the amount of the deposit and the period for which the Overseas Exchange Bond® is required (the period between signing the sale and purchase agreement to completion).

The attraction of using an Exchange Bond® is clear from this typical example of a new property with a purchase price of Euro 200,000 (£157,961). If the buyer ties up Euro 40,000 (£31,592) to cover the 20% deposit required to secure the property for 24 months, this money can be invested at (say) 5% which will largely cover the premium cost for the Overseas Exchange Bond®.

A cheaper property, costing say Euro 100,000 (£78,980), might involve a 20% deposit amounting to Euro 20,000 (£15,796) for a 24 month period. The premium required to purchase an Exchange Bond® to cover the deposit would be Euro 2,240 (£1,769).

ExCo charges a non-refundable Euro 125 application fee for each Bond with the total premium being payable when issued.

## Providing financial flexibility

Among those who have recognised the benefits and the attractions of the Exchange Bond® is Brent Backhouse, commercial director of Evolve Investment Property, a specialist property advice company.

Australian- born Brent explains:
"Our role at Evolve is to identify opportunities and help private investors negotiate as well as secure investments in both niche and growth markets. My familiarity with the deposit bond in Australia – a product similar to the Exchange Bond® that has been established for over 10 years – meant that I had firsthand experience of the benefits of the Exchange Bond®. I knew it would facilitate financial flexibility and increase investment opportunities for my clients.

"Buyers keen to maintain control of their capital for as long as possible – largely with the intention of generating additional funds through further investments – can see immediately that the Exchange Bond® is for them.

"Buying abroad is an increasingly visited option for investors. Anything that makes that choice easier, less costly and more secure is guaranteed to generate interest. A number of my clients have now used an Overseas Exchange Bond® and they are delighted with the experience. With the completion date a year away in most cases, they can continue to invest capital that would otherwise have been tied up in a deposit."

Oceanico Developments is among the steadily expanding number of overseas property development companies which accept the Overseas Exchange Bond® instead of the typical 20-30% deposit and staged payments traditionally required.

The company is one of Portugal's most prestigious property developers and has pioneered the use of the OEB® at two of its five star resorts. Says Oceanic director, Simon Burgess:

"While 'staged payments' are the norm for many overseas developers we feel as an established, well funded company it is good business practice for us to carry the weight of our own development.

"Through the introduction of the Overseas Exchange Bond® we are simplifying the purchasing process and making it financially more attractive. Clients now make just one initial payment, which is significantly less than the traditional deposit or staged payments, with the majority of purchasing funds transferred when the property is completed."

## Growing steadily worldwide

The Overseas Exchange Bond® is being accepted by a rapidly growing number of property development companies worldwide. Presently it is available at selected developments in Cyprus, Greece, Italy, Portugal, Dubai, Canada, Turkey, Hungary and the Caribbean.

Check if the company building your dream home overseas accepts the Exchange Bond® and if they don't, contact Exchange Insurance and they will explain how they can benefit from doing so.

*More information at:*
Website: **www.exchangebond.com**
E-mail: **info@exchangebond.com**
T: **+44 (0)20 7256 3973**

*Source: Survey on behalf of NatWest International, April 2008
**Source: Datamonitor
Currency conversions @ April 2008
(x) Subject to status and certain other criteria

*The Exchange Insurance Company Limited is authorised and regulated by the UK Financial Services Authority.*

The proliferation of property fairs all over Northern Europe plus popular television programmes on the subject are also drawing the attention of ever more people to the possibility of a second-home purchase, something they may previously not have considered.

And the more desirable it seems, the more it becomes a must-have, in much the same way that ownership of a car was once optional but has now become a necessity. Wherever there is high demand, prices inevitably rise.

But in spite of many factors driving up the price of homes abroad, it is still unlikely that the value of the average foreign second home will rise in line with UK properties. UK nationals have got used to their house prices rising far above inflation, but this is not the case in most other countries, whether in Europe or further afield in places like North America or Australia.

In fact, in countries with massive new-build and urbanization programmes the price of your holiday home could actually go down as new and more desirable homes are built in future. In Florida, for instance, a 'used' or resale home is regarded rather as a used car – not so good as the brand-new version.

In areas where there is plenty of land, and hence plenty of room for new housing developments, homes are unlikely to increase much in value. Of course, in areas where no more properties can be built, such as South Beach, Miami, homes are already extremely expensive, and likely to rise.

But the average holiday home, of the type within the reach of the average person, cannot be considered a safe financial investment in the same way as a UK home. Although it may be possible to make it pay for itself through rentals, the capital value of the property is unlikely to rise in line with UK values, especially if any number of similar properties in the same location can be constructed without too much trouble.

Therefore, for most people, the purchase of a second home must be considered a financial luxury rather than a ring-fenced, blue-chip investment. The French, for example, have not traditionally considered their homes as investments: rather, as places to live and maybe pass on to their children or grandchildren. This attitude is slowly changing, but has not yet caught up with the UK's approach to property purchase.

Another point to consider is that, in most European countries, it actually costs more to purchase a home, even though the actual price of the home may be cheaper. Purchase costs and taxes can add as much as 20 per cent on to the purchase price.

Don't forget that, as soon as you buy any property abroad, you should make a will in that country. You should in fact make a will in every country in which you have bought property, and never assume that your British will is able to cover foreign acquisitions. Failure to do this could result in horrendous legal tangles that may take years to sort out. Most countries have inheritance laws that are very different from those in the UK, and expert advice should be taken as soon as you enter into negotiations for your place abroad.

# Ways of buying

There are two main ways of buying your dream home abroad: you can either pay cash and have done with it, or you can buy on a mortgage. Very many UK buyers are selling their UK homes to release enough equity to buy a foreign home outright, and leaving themselves just enough for a bolthole or pied-à-terre in the native country.

But it is also possible to buy on a special foreign mortgage, and make repayments for the next 10, 20 or 30 years. In order to qualify for a foreign mortgage, you must satisfy the lenders that you have sufficient income to make the repayments. For this, a large amount of documentation is needed, and loans will be refused unless this is forthcoming.

Whether paying cash or buying on a mortgage, you will need a bank account in the country of your second home, which must always be kept in credit. You will be fined heavily for any account that goes into the red.

There are advantages and disadvantages both to paying cash and to borrowing. If you pay cash, you do not have to worry about debt, making repayments or having to cover mortgage costs through rental income. But by paying cash, a huge slice of money will instantly become non-liquid and may be difficult to liquidize quickly, should you suddenly need the money.

Also, by paying cash you do not have the safety net that comes when mortgage lenders are involved. A lender will insist on a survey, on a valuation, and will only lend if the home is considered worth the asking price. With a cash deal, it's easy to pay through the nose – especially if you have set your heart on a particular dream home.

Wily vendors can often see the naïve foreigner with loads of cash coming – and up the asking price accordingly. As ever more foreign buyers come on to the market, the prices of homes in many European countries are rising steeply and no longer represent a bargain.

With a mortgage, though, you will eventually be paying maybe two or three times the actual price of the property, by the time several years' interest charges are added on to the actual cost.

These days, highly competitive mortgage packages are easily available, usually in a choice of currencies: you can have either a sterling or a euro mortgage, or, in the United States, a dollar mortgage. As a general rule, you are asked to put down a deposit of around 20 per cent of the asking price out of your own money. You then make repayments over a prearranged number of years, and there are severe penalties both for not making repayments on time and for early redemption. Although it may seem a good idea to redeem your mortgage early, especially if you have come into a legacy, for instance, from the lender's point of view you have reneged on your contract and the lender will penalize you for it.

Most, if not all, mortgage lenders insist that the property is properly insured, and life insurance is also required. Neither of these requirements apply when paying cash, although contents and property insurance make sense, especially if you are not always there.

A second or holiday home is not regarded as a necessity in the same way as the principal roof over your head, but as an optional luxury that you have to be able to afford. Don't expect any mercy from the lenders should you default on repayments. Also keep in mind the possibility of currency fluctuations, which could adversely affect your mortgage repayments. Nobody knows what might happen to currencies or exchange rates in the years to come, so a foreign mortgage is always considered slightly more of a risk than a mortgage for your own home in your own country.

Unlike many UK mortgages, foreign mortgage repayments are often 'fixed'. Do not imagine, though, that this necessarily means fixed for the whole term of the loan; it usually refers to three or five years, after which time interest rates may go up or down.

All mortgages, in whichever currency and however attractively presented, come down to a single basic fact: you are borrowing money on which you will be paying a large amount of interest, just as with your principal mortgage. So it is imperative to sit down and work out, with your accountant if you have one, how and whether you can actually afford this extra financial burden.

When buying a foreign property on a mortgage, you will have to have a mortgage inspection report, and pay for this. A qualified surveyor will prepare a report, which will be sent to the mortgage company. Fees for this report, which are not refundable, vary between around £250 and £450 or more, and paying it does not mean that the lender must offer you a loan. It may be that the valuer decides there is not enough security in the property to lend the necessary amount.

Once satisfactory references have been received, you will receive a written loan proposal, and an offshore company may be set up for the sole purpose of owning the property. It is not necessary for the purchaser to understand all the ins and outs of having an account in a tiny offshore island. It all sounds rather grand, but it is just a convenient way for the banks to lend you money to buy property in another country.

Here are some typical mortgage arrangements for buying abroad: Abbey National France will loan up to 85 per cent of the purchase price, excluding legal and transaction fees. The minimum loan amount is 30,000 euros, and the term between 7 and 20 years. Loans can be arranged for purchase of a main residence, second home, property to be let, new-build, remortgage and home improvement. Loans are available for residential use only, and would not be applicable for any property intended for commercial use such as a holiday development, hotel, language school and so on. There are very many forms to fill in, and an administration fee of 1 per cent of the purchase price is required.

For mortgages on Spanish, Portuguese and Italian properties, the process is pretty similar. In order to qualify for an Iberian (Spanish or Portuguese) mortgage, the property has to be structurally sound, freehold, or have at least 50 years unexpired on the lease, and free from any charges, occupation or arrears. Under Spanish law, the buyer becomes responsible for any unpaid debts on the property at the time of sale.

When looking at a potential property, particularly in Spain or Portugal, where massive development programmes have been instigated in recent years, you need to satisfy yourself as to the following points:

■ Is any major work required on the property, and how much is it likely to cost? Are all the basic services connected? In Spain and Portugal, they may well not be, although things are improving in this area, especially on heavily advertised 'luxury' developments.

■ Could future developments interrupt your view of the sea or countryside? This is very important, as a high-rise block right in front of your lovely villa will greatly reduce its value should you want to resell – and in the meantime ruin your own pleasure in your holiday home.

■ Is your property within a community development or urbanization scheme, which would make community fees payable?

If you are borrowing in euros, your monthly repayments must also be in euros. These funds must be cleared so that they are available on each monthly repayment date. Whether making payments in euros or sterling, your bank account must always be in credit to at least two months' repayments. Cheques from foreign accounts can take up to eight weeks to clear, and are not recommended. Instead, you will have to set up a standing order once the purchase is completed. Euro accounts can be earning interest until the repayments are made.

Mortgages on properties in Spain and Portugal are typically available for 75 per cent of the purchase price. You will have to pay an administration fee to the lender of around £250, refundable only if the application is turned down. The valuer's fee is not refundable in any case, and has to be paid directly to the valuer. There are higher valuation fees to pay if the property is situated in the Canary or Balearic Islands, as you have to pay for the additional travel costs involved: typically an extra £150.

You as the buyer are responsible for the legal fees, taxes, land registry charges and the notary's fees. Notaries, who operate in most European countries, are independent legally qualified people who must inspect and assess all relevant paperwork. They usually act for both buyer and seller, and their fees are paid by the buyer.

If buying on a mortgage, you are responsible for the lender's legal fees as well as your own. When purchasing a Spanish or Portuguese property, legal fees are typically 1 per cent of the purchase price, with a minimum fee of around £1,000.

Obtaining an Italian mortgage or, indeed, a mortgage anywhere in a euro country follows broadly this same pattern.

Comprehensive financial information packs for buying abroad are now provided by most of the major UK banks, such as Barclays, and give up-to-date information on securing mortgages on foreign properties. It is worth remembering that mortgages secured on properties in other countries are not covered by the Financial Services Authority, but are regulated, if at all, by officials in each specific country.

Many mortgage lenders advise potential buyers to study the mortgage situation very carefully, and obtain information packs *before* even deciding on the country, never mind the location or the actual property. It is important to know in advance whether you can actually afford the property, or make the repayments without jeopardizing your main UK home, if you intend to keep this on when buying a property abroad.

Before making a decision to lend you the money, all lenders need to know your exact financial position. As with a UK mortgage, loans are available for up to three times the salary of the main earner. If you intend to make the foreign property pay for itself with rental income, the lender would need proof that this particular property can rent out at a certain amount for so many weeks of the year, and that you are actually allowed to let the place. The lender will not go on guesswork or optimistic forecasts alone, but will take into account rental income, rentability and running costs of similar properties in the area.

Mortgages to buy homes in the United States are available for up to 85 per cent of the property's value. It is possible to obtain either a dollar or sterling mortgage. Many UK residents feel more confident with a sterling mortgage, although interest rates can vary. Dollar mortgages are often offered at a fixed rate of interest for the whole term, but the average rate will be higher.

Fixed-rate mortgages may be a better bet because, as time goes on, the amount means less and the rental income (if applicable) is likely to go up. Financing costs amount to between 2 and 3 per cent of the purchase price, with legal costs averaging $500. Interest rates are between 7 and 9.5 per cent, depending on the type of mortgage, and these rates can vary according to currency fluctuations.

Most people buying property in the United States do buy on a mortgage, and they rely heavily on rental income to make the transaction pay for itself. In fact, the majority of buyers into the US market are looking for rental income as well as a holiday home, which is much less likely to be the case when buying in Europe.

Wherever you are buying, you would need to provide the following information to mortgage companies:

- three years' tax returns;
- P60s for three years;
- payslips for recent months;
- if self-employed, a letter from your accountant showing you are in good standing;
- three items of credit, such as Visa, MasterCard, Amex;
- evidence of mortgage history;
- two reference letters, one from your bank;
- three months' bank statements;
- copy of passport.

You would also need to open a bank account in the country where you wish to buy, and have six months' mortgage payments in this account when the deal is closed. Most lenders recommend that you should make sure you qualify for a foreign mortgage before making an offer on a place.

As to whether it is better overall to pay cash than buy on a mortgage, there are so many pros and cons that it really comes down to a matter of personality, anxiety levels and lifestyle. The advantage of paying cash, if you can, is that you don't have to worry about making the place pay for itself, although of course there will still be running, repair and maintenance costs, and local taxes to pay. Even when you pay cash, you have not finished lobbing out on a regular basis for your foreign home, any more than you have with your principal home.

With a mortgage, you are paying typically a 20 per cent deposit, so much less money is being used to finance the property. If, say, you have £100,000 in the bank, and use it all to buy a property, it has gone in its entirety for the time the property is owned. But if you used £20,000 of that money for a down payment, you still have £80,000 to play around with, and maybe buy a second, third or even fourth foreign property. My own personal preference would be to pay cash whenever possible for something that is essentially a luxury item; on the other hand, if you are considering establishing a holiday home business, for example, then a mortgage might make more sense, as with any luck you will be generating income from your foreign property.

It also depends on your age. Somebody in their 30s or early 40s, with high-earning years still ahead of them, might be happy enough to buy on a mortgage. But if you're in your late 50s or beyond, with most of your earning years behind you, the prospect of a 20-year mortgage round your neck might not be so appealing. Also, by then, you may consider you don't have sufficient energy to run a rentals business, and just want to enjoy your second home for yourself.

Most lenders offering foreign mortgages stipulate that all repayments must be made in any case by the time the borrower reaches his or her 75th birthday. By then, of course, you may have accumulated enough money not to care about making anything from your holiday home. If not, it may be too late anyway, as it will be almost impossible to borrow large amounts of money for this purpose.

As mortgage lenders become ever cleverer at finding ways of lending you money, some are even starting to offer 'more than lifetime' mortgages, where your children will pay off the mortgage after you die.

The first such mortgages were introduced towards the end of 2006 and are interest-only mortgages. This type of mortgage is already well established in Switzerland and Japan, where even 80-year-olds can now be offered a 40-year mortgage on a property to be paid off after their death. What happens is that the children will then take on the mortgage after their parents' death and use the property as a holiday home or second home. The children would have to agree to it, of course, but so long as the equity in the home is larger than the mortgage your children would still be inheriting an asset rather than a liability.

What we can say is that all the traditional methods of lending money on property are being turned on their head, and we can expect ever more creativity on this in the future.

A report in the magazine *International Homes* in November 2003 made the point that the over-50s market is Europe's fastest-growing demographic, and is forecast to grow 75 per cent in the next 20 years. Ever more of the over-50s are selling up the 'big old family millstone' in the UK to buy somewhere abroad. This market is now, apparently 'respectable, sophisticated, slim and sexy'. Instead of retiring in the UK, ever more people are spending their grey pounds, or grey millions, in other countries.

A final word on mortgages: don't consider buying on a mortgage if the worry and hassle of making the place pay for itself would be too great. Either pay cash or, if you can't afford this outlay, rent holiday homes from others rather than owning one yourself.

There are a few other things it's important to know about when buying abroad. In many countries there is high VAT levied on new property, so if you are buying a brand-new home, check whether or not this is included in the price.

It often costs more to buy a property in another country, and such extras as lawyers' fees, property taxes and insurance must all be paid for in your host country. These may be more expensive than similar products in the home country. Experts reckon that extra charges must be calculated at 10 per cent, at least, of the property price.

Financial experts also believe that it is best to arrange a mortgage in the currency in which you earn, unless you are going to receive rental income from the property in the local currency. Again, there are pros and cons. A mortgage with a UK bank may be easier to set up than one in the host country, but then you will not benefit from low interest rates in the eurozone.

Is it a good idea to use a currency adviser? This is a new breed of professionals who can, theoretically at least, arrange the best method of payment to suit your particular needs. Currency advisers may be able to help you to avoid some of the foreign bank charges on your transaction, but beware: not all companies posing as currency advisers are reputable. As with so many areas where strong emotions, desires and longings are bound up in the transaction, there are unscrupulous people all too ready and willing to take money off you without giving a good service in return.

## Currency brokers

These are relatively new but already highly advertised, particularly on the internet. Many specialist brokers maintain that their currency exchange rates are cheaper than those of the main banks.

But what are currency brokers, and how do they operate? Put simply, they buy currency in large quantities so they can secure better rates than banks. As they specialize in this business, again unlike banks, which have many financial functions, they can secure preferential rates for their customers.

Specialist brokers can take time to talk to you about the best ways of financing your property purchase. Your dealer will need to know the proposed dates of the purchase, as exchange rates can vary from day to day. Then the dealer will tell you the best likely rates available at that time.

Before signing up, you can check rates with other currency dealers then, when you are satisfied, you place an order with your dealer. The rate will be confirmed in writing, and your dealer will fax a currency contract to you.

You have to sign this, complete the details requested and then fax the signed document back. The transaction will typically cost you around £20 as the broker's fee. Currency brokers make their money in exactly the same way as supermarkets, in that they buy the currency cheaper than they sell it to you, and their profits are obtained at the margin.

For instance, if a broker buys £100,000 of euros, he will pay less than that for them. But as exchange rates can change overnight, dealers will set the upper and lower exchange rates on a deal. These margins are built into your purchase order. Obviously one big advantage of using a broker is that they can advise on likely exchange rate movements as this is their sole business – something the girl at the bank might not know much about.

It sounds highly complicated and very high-finance, but ever more ordinary people are now using currency brokers rather than banks to buy property abroad. But because this industry is relatively new, just check that you are dealing with a reputable company by:

- making sure the company has at least three years of audited accounts;

- using a company that specializes in foreign exchanges only;

- making sure the broker is a trained broker and not just a telephone salesperson (high-pressure sales techniques operate in this business);

- asking about staff turnover, or how many people will be handling your account – the fewer the better;

- and finally, always get several quotes.

If you use an IFA, and they recommend a broker, ask whether they get a referral fee.

Most of all, do not sign up with a currency broker until you are absolutely clear about the service offered, and that you understand it completely. Never be afraid of asking awkward questions when there are large sums of money involved.

When buying property abroad, remember that even quite small fluctuations in exchange rates can significantly affect the purchase price of your property – and I mean total purchase price, including costs to agents, lawyers, tax advisers and so on.

# Taxation

All properties abroad are subject to local taxes, the equivalent of council tax, and there may be other taxes to pay as well, depending on the country. All this must be calculated before buying.

Any income derived from rent – even if you do not make an overall profit – must be declared and tax paid on the gain. UK residents letting out a property abroad will be liable for UK tax. Any business or income-generating activities must also be declared in the country of the property, although tax only has to be paid once. You will in any case have to make a yearly tax return to the tax authorities of the country concerned, even though you may not be liable for actual taxes in that country.

When the property is sold, it will be subject to capital gains tax unless it is your principal private home. This applies whether or not you have rented the property out, or used it to generate income by other means, during your ownership. Capital gains tax is extremely complicated, and is best calculated by an accountant, or HM Revenue and Customs, who will do it for you.

On 6 April 2008, the UK capital gains tax laws changed for investments made after April 1982, when a new flat rate of 18 per cent was introduced for all non-business assets. This has replaced the sliding scale which allowed for inflation and 'indexation', which meant that the longer you had owned a property, the less CGT you were liable to pay. But although taper relief no longer exists, there are still many costs you can set against this tax when you come to sell your property.

Because CGT laws are complicated, it is advisable to check out what you might be liable to pay, and how this tax is worked out, before you buy any property. It is common for companies selling properties abroad to hype up the capital gain by quoting the buying price and the selling price. For instance, if you buy a property at £100,000 and sell it at £200,000, you have apparently made a 100 per cent gain. But when you factor in capital gains tax, selling costs and running costs, this gain could be considerably reduced.

And don't forget that capital gains tax is payable on the sale of any property which is not your main home. Second homes, investment properties and renovation projects will all attract CGT on sale.

The UK has tax treaties with many countries, which allow for exemption from foreign tax so long as this is paid in the UK. It is a good idea to get professional advice on the tax status of any country where you are interested in buying a home, as this can vary considerably. What you need to know is whether the country where you are considering buying a second home has a double-taxation treaty with the UK. Most do – but not all. If this arrangement is not in place, you might well find yourself having to pay twice.

Whether or not you pay tax in the UK, or in the country of your property, will depend on your residence status. Generally, you are considered to be resident if you stay in the country of your second home for more than six months in any one year. There are quite strict regulations on this, so all relevant information needs to be obtained from your local tax office in advance.

## Taxation pitfalls

Whatever you do, don't try to be clever by listing a lower price at the Land Registry than you have actually paid, in order to avoid paying higher tax. This is illegal but has happened in the past, particularly in Spain. It might also be a problem in countries where there is not yet a well-established Land Registry system.

Under-declaring the price paid for the property is quite common in some countries, so that sellers can minimize capital gains liability when they come to sell, but it is not worth taking the risk.

In Spain, where this practice has been particularly common, the authorities are now clamping down hard. What has happened here in the past is that buyers have paid for part of their property in cash while the lawyer turns a blind eye, and the full price paid for the property is not declared to the tax authorities – only the amount that goes through the system.

According to a report in *The Times* in January 2006, Britons, particularly, face having to pay back taxes for previously undeclared amounts, although admittedly it will not be easy to claim back taxes on properties bought many years ago. In 2005, it became mandatory for a property registry number to be included on income tax forms. The new law will require a tax identification number to be included on documentation kept at the property registry, thus allowing authorities to keep track of homeowners who do not register their properties and therefore do not pay tax on income from renting or selling.

When it comes to declaring rental income, it is also common in Spain (and possibly other countries) for landlords to declare that a property is unoccupied when it is actually occupied, again to avoid paying tax in the foreign country. To counter this, the new Spanish legislation will require tenants to include the property registry number on electricity bills, as this will allow officials to determine which properties are occupied and which are empty.

Very many Britons now living in Spain are not registered with the authorities, but they are putting themselves at huge risk, thanks to these new laws. As immigration grows in other popular destinations, similar laws will probably be introduced elsewhere. Funnily enough, countries take a dim view of being cheated out of tax due by foreigners.

Whatever you do, never attempt to be even cleverer by trying to avoid paying taxes such as income tax, local taxes (council tax equivalent), inheritance tax, or any other taxes that you may be liable for in the host country. It is just not worth taking the risk of being found out, and then having to pay huge back taxes.

When dealing with the complex matter of taxation in another country, it is probably impossible to be aware of every ambush that lies in wait. But here is one you do need to know about. In the United States, when non-US citizens sell their US property, the Internal Revenue Service (IRS) automatically withholds 10 per cent of the selling price. This is their guesstimate of how much tax you may owe on the profit from the sale, and will always amount to a lot of money. If you sold your US house for (say) £200,000, the IRS will appropriate £20,000 – automatically.

US financial expert Mike Arman says that, if you don't know how to get this money back, the IRS will simply keep it. So when buying a US property, you really do need to retain every single receipt and documentary evidence of expenses, so that when selling you can instruct a US-based accountant to go through these and present all the figures to the IRS to prove that you made little or no profit on resale.

If the IRS is satisfied, you will be entitled to your money back, but the cheque will be in US dollars. This will mean it can take 60 days to clear and you will have to pay fees and take into account exchange rates. So the thing to do is appoint a US representative who can receive the cheque and then order a transfer through a currency converter.

Yes, it is complicated, but writing as somebody who has been on the horrendous receiving end of the IRS I would say you can't be too careful. The IRS has many ingenious methods of receiving revenue – and is very reluctant to pay any of it back.

## Inheritance tax

When you own property in another country, inevitably inheritance tax matters have to be addressed. Before buying any property abroad, consult your lawyer or accountant about whose name should go on the property contract. For instance, if your spouse is very much younger than you, it may be advisable to put the contract in his or her name rather than your own, or in joint names.

But generally speaking the home is better in joint names, because in most countries other than the UK inheritance tax is charged on property passed between spouses. In the UK, property can pass from one married partner to the other without incurring this tax.

If you wish to put your children's names on the property, or set up a limited company or a trust fund, it is a good idea to take professional advice first. It is also worth discovering in advance how inheritance laws in your host country operate, as these may be very different from those in the UK. The older you are when buying, the more crucial these issues become.

Another point: in some countries now emerging as desirable second-home locations, a woman is not allowed to own property according to local laws. This is the case in Islamic law, so if you are interested in buying into an Islamic country, discover how far these traditional laws and customs apply with regard to inheritance and ownership.

Generally speaking you have to abide by the laws of your host country, rather than those of the UK, even if you decide to remain a UK citizen.

Bear in mind, before buying, that inheritance rules can vary greatly from country to country. Although IHT has now been abolished in many US states, it still applies in most European countries, including the 'new Europeans' that have recently joined the EU.

You also need to know, in advance, whether your foreign property forms part of your UK estate. Every individual's circumstances will vary, so what applies to one buyer may not be the case with you.

Here are a few specifics: in Spain, Portugal and Italy, as a foreigner, you can normally leave your property according to the rules in your native country, but in France, Dubai and Turkey, even as a foreigner, you must abide by the laws of that country. This means, for instance, that you cannot cut out your children and there is no automatic tax-free inheritance between husband and wife.

On buying a foreign property, you must make both a new English will and a will that is valid in the host country.

## Buying to let

Increasingly, buyers of foreign properties intend to rent them out for part of the year. Although it is certainly possible to make money from renting, the standard advice is: don't buy if the rental must *always* cover *all* of your costs, including mortgage, taxes, utility bills, repairs.

Here are some figures to give an idea of what might be involved (figures in US dollars; calculate that there are around $1.96 dollars to £1 sterling):

■ If you buy an average three-bed, two-bathroom detached house with a pool in Florida for $174,740, with the intention of renting it out for at least part of the year, your running costs will include: management, $100; pool care, $75; lawn care, $65; electricity, $150; water, $75; gas, $75; cable, $30; phone, $30; pest control, $40; preventative maintenance, $25; cleaning, $120. This comes to $785 a month, but by the time you add on agents' fees for renting it could easily come to $1,000.

■ Before calculating any rental income, there are further costs, at least if you are buying on a mortgage, which most buyers of Florida properties do. On a purchase price of $174,740 and putting down a 20 per cent deposit, you would be $57,937 out of pocket by the time you had bought your furniture package ($16,000) and paid all the purchasing costs ($6,989).

■ The mortgage repayments would come to $11,729 a year. Then there are local taxes to pay at an average $2,736; insurance, $480; and HomeOwners Association dues, a particularly US idea, $300 per annum. Add on top your running costs for utilities, pool care, cleaning and so on and you will probably find it comes to a staggering $23,045 a year at least just to own and run the place. And that's before you eat, run a car, see any places of interest or cop any repair bills.

■ Supposing you manage to rent out the property for 40 weeks at $725 a week, this will bring you in a gross income of $29,000. Not bad. But by the time you have paid rental commission to the management company (as distinct from day-to-day management of your property) plus all the other costs detailed above, at $2,900, you are left with a net taxable rental income of just $3,055 a year (figures courtesy of World of Florida).

It may not sound much, but if you view it as a way of making the unaffordable affordable, it begins to take on a different hue. Even when renting the property out for most of the year, at £500 a week, you will only just about break even. *But* – all those calculations, horrible though they are, indicate you should be able to afford 12 weeks in your Florida holiday home yourself – and have a bit left over for the flights.

All this assumes, of course, that your place would rent out easily and quickly, with no void periods. But this can never be guaranteed.

In order actually to make any money from renting out, as opposed to simply helping to cover costs, you would have to rent it out all year round – and that would defeat the purpose, for most people, of owning a home abroad. Even then, the money you receive wouldn't actually amount to an income. Add to that the likelihood that your Florida home would probably not increase in value as the years went by, and you don't have to be a mathematical genius to work out that it's hardly the way to get in the rich list of *Forbes* magazine.

What you are getting, of course, from your Florida (or any other) home is fun, added lifestyle, added interest, an added frisson to life, which is just as important as hard cash. The safest way to work out the figures is to ensure, as far as humanly possible, that you are not going to be worryingly out of pocket. Any extra income you may make should be regarded as a pleasant bonus rather than anything else.

In Florida, homes are sold totally ready to rent out, equipped with furniture, appliances, curtains and carpets, all of the required standard. Management companies, pool and cleaning staff are also on hand and the whole thing can work in one smooth, although expensive, US-type operation.

In Florida, the above figures are the typical costs, expenses and likely return from rentals, and you take it or leave it. There is not much scope for individuality, although obviously there will be some variation in the purchase price, rental income and running costs.

You would have to be very rich indeed to be able to afford to run a house in Florida without renting it out, unless it is your own year-round home, which is why most foreign owners of non-rental homes in Florida are celebrities or very high earners.

It's a different matter when you are renting out a Tuscan villa or French farmhouse where the situation is much more *ad hoc* and fluid. You may not have any idea what to charge, what standard is required and whether you have to do all the cleaning and maintenance work yourself. But you do have to ask yourself: do I want to maximize income, or just cover running costs?

If maximizing income is your main objective, you will be unable to stay there yourself during the main season, when rents are at their highest. If it is your lovingly restored or blissful retreat, it may also not be suitable for renting out, not because the location is wrong but because it does not have the necessary equipment to make it a viable letting proposition.

As a general rule, kitchens must be fully equipped with dishwasher, microwave, washing machine, coffee maker and all crockery and cutlery. There should be ample hanging and storage space, and good-quality beds or sofabeds in each room. The place must be super-clean and tidy – at hotel standard – and all the furniture usable, unbroken and comfortable. If you have furnished your second home with bits and pieces from the main home, it may not present well enough to be a viable rental. You may be happy enough to put up with clapped-out sofas and sagging mattresses, but paying holidaymakers won't be.

One of the advantages of buying a brand-new property in Europe is that fully fitted kitchens and bathrooms tend to be already in place, which they might not be in your remote rustic farmhouse.

In any case, your insurance policy may have to be increased to allow for renting out. Then if you are not there yourself you will have to employ a management company to organize changes of linen, cleaning and supplies. A full-service rental agency, according to Holiday-Rentals.com, will charge between 30 and 50 per cent of the rental income, and may insist on the property being available for so many weeks of the year. If you let to a holiday package company, this will almost certainly be the case. As these agencies charge so much, it is essential to check up beforehand what they will provide, and whether they will guarantee a certain level of bookings per year, at a certain rent.

Whether you use a full-service agency, or a cheaper bookings-only agency, you will still have to employ local workpeople to maintain your place in lettable condition. Whichever method you use, it is essential to be very professional and make sure you take the whole of the rental money in advance. Doing it on an amateur basis or renting out to friends who want it for nothing is a recipe for disaster.

Irene Goodman, owner of a small studio flat in Mougins, near Cannes, in France, believes it is almost impossible actually to make money from renting out your own holiday home. The manager of a Versace boutique in London, Irene says:

I would say, in the 20-odd years I've had the French flat, I have barely covered the running costs of the place.

I have a managing agent to keep an eye on the place, and that is quite expensive, but essential if you're not there yourself all the time. The flat costs around £2,500 a year to run, with community charges, local taxes and other running costs, and we can just about get that back in rentals. But that's about it. We would have to be very much more organized than we are to make any money, and because it's only a small studio I don't think we could ever actually show a profit.

All I would say is that the rental income gives us a bit of bunce, and helps to pay some of the costs. But then, we haven't got the place for the money it can make us.

On the other hand, if you are very canny and businesslike, you *can* make money from letting out your property abroad. Here is an example of how it might be done.

Management consultant Andrew Burford owns a ski chalet in Chamonix, France, which he reckons turns in a far better profit than buying to let in the UK. Andrew says: 'We've always been keen on skiing and for many years went with top-quality operators. Then we reckoned that, if the operators were doing well, we must be able to do equally well. We chose Chamonix, as it's only 50 minutes from Geneva airport, and it also has a dual season, which increases its rental weeks.' The resort is great for snow in winter, and for rock climbing, whitewater rafting, climbing, walking and cycling in summer.

Andrew believes the rental income he gets is twice what he could obtain on a UK property, even though he lets it out for less than half the year. He and his wife have furnished and decorated the chalet to appeal to the top end of the market. In the high skiing season it rents out at £3,000 a week, and in the summer it brings in £1,000 a week. But in order to command those rents, you have to be extremely organized and concentrate on marketing.

Andrew has created his own website – www.winternational. co.uk – and he also sells a number of weeks to Indigo Lodges, a company specializing in upmarket ski properties. He reckons to make £40,000 a year gross from rentals.

Out of his rental income, Andrew Burford pays for an on-site cleaner, electricity and mortgage. He paid £400,000 for the four-bed chalet, which also has a sauna and hydrotherapy steam room, and financed his purchase with a 65 per cent French mortgage. He says: 'I generate enough money to cover the mortgage repayments, all my costs and a small profit which helps with school fees.' Plus, he says, the property is going up about 8 per cent a year. One reason for this is that there is a shortage of property in the French Alps, as building regulations have become very tight, creating a booming market.

The secret of successful letting, whether at home or abroad, is to let your head rule your heart. It's no use buying somewhere you love and then just hoping it will rent out. Hard research is needed first, if making money from your home abroad forms part of the affordability equation.

Some agents trying to sell you a property off-plan may try to seduce you with promises of 'guaranteed rent'. There is in fact no such thing, so if you are interested in renting out your property, or need to do so to make it pay, talk to other owners in the area to get an objective idea of rental possibilities before buying. Do not ever just go on what the selling agent – on a commission of between 8 and 15 per cent, don't forget – tells you.

Many owners who do rent out report dissatisfaction with management and rental companies that take too large a slice of the income. So before signing up with any agent, ask to speak to satisfied customers. Many management agents promise much and deliver little.

If you don't feel you are the type of person who would want to involve yourself with the hassle of renting out your property, you will be responsible for the entire running costs yourself. If you add on to this the mortgage repayments, local taxes, property taxes and utility bills, you will find that running your holiday home can work out very expensive indeed. If you are self-employed, there may also be income lost during the weeks you are in your holiday home and, therefore, not earning.

John Morrill, who specializes in selling properties in Florida, says: 'We always advise people never to buy a second home until they are completely ready. If it is going to stretch your finances beyond a comfortable limit, it is better to wait until you can afford it without hardship to your other, non-holiday, life.'

It is a sad fact of life that owning and running a holiday or second home in a dream country comes down to whether you can comfortably afford it, but there's no escaping it.

A London couple bought a villa in Kalamata, Greece, which came complete with an olive farm. Kalamata is famous for olives and the couple, who decided to make their permanent home in Greece, enthusiastically set about harvesting and marketing their olive crop. But it didn't, and never will, amount to a proper income, so they have to find other ways of supporting themselves.

For some people, it's an exciting challenge to try to afford a place in another country. For others, the prospect of money running dangerously short would spoil their pleasure in their foreign home. In any case, it makes sense to work out all the figures and then add on some for unexpected eventualities, before taking the plunge – especially when you may well have to sell at a considerable loss.

All international property experts say the same thing: remember that buying overseas is a long-term investment opportunity rather than a short-term income-generation scheme. Also, even those who put the most positive glow on buying abroad admit that renting out your property is *unlikely* to make you any significant money, although it can be a way of making the otherwise unaffordable affordable. You are unlikely, so the expert advice goes, to realize an overall profit from rental income alone, even in areas where demand is high for most of the year.

If buying on a mortgage, you should aim at least to cover interest repayments with the rental income, but you should bear in mind that the only way you are actually likely to make money from your property is through capital appreciation when you come to sell.

# Transportation costs

It is also essential, when buying abroad, to think well in advance about what you might want to take to the new place and how you are going to get it there. For instance, if your new foreign home is halfway up a mountain, is a huge removal lorry going to be able to tackle the terrain?

You need to budget at an early stage for how much transportation might cost. This is often something people never even think about until the last minute, when they are running dangerously short of money.

Philip Pertoldi, from Abels Moving Services, which has been moving furniture and effects abroad for 70 years, offers a few tips:

Many people never even think about removals until the last minute, yet really it is something you should consider before even buying, and talk to specialized removal firms about the best way to transport stuff from one country to another.

One of the most important things you have to consider is access to the new home. You can either pay for a 'special' which means there is nothing else on the vehicle, or you can cut costs by sharing the load with other people. Obviously it is more economic to go as a part-load, but the vehicles will be much larger and may not be able to negotiate narrow mountain tracks, for instance. Then, how many people will you need to transport the items? Costs are based on volume plus weight, and large heavy items such as a grand piano, for instance, will need an equal number of people each end to lift it.

You also have to think carefully about any electrical equipment you might want to take and whether it will work in the new country.

If you are going to a faraway place such as Australia or America, you will usually have a choice of air or sea transport. For New York, for instance, air freight will be cleared through customs in about a week, whereas shipping the goods will take three to four weeks. If going to somewhere like Australia, there will be a choice of going through either the Suez or Panama canals, with the former taking 30 days and the latter, six weeks. It can sometimes be cheaper to go by the longer route, but that depends on how quickly you will need the goods the other end.

At the time of writing, it costs around £4,000 door to door if moving to Australia, where there are also very strict quarantine and fumigation regulations. As so much is out of your control, it is advisable to choose a removal firm which is a member of FIDI – the Federation of International Furniture Removers. This ensures you are protected by insurance should the goods be lost or the firm goes into liquidation during transportation. If you want to transport your pet, you would need to use a specialist pet transporting company.

> We always say that every customer has their own Ming vase – something which is very rare and precious to them, even though it may not be of any monetary value, or interest to anybody else. With these items, it may be safer to courier them separately. Not all collections, such as those of Dinky cars for instance, may be covered by ordinary home insurance. Whatever, make sure you always get a quotation door to door, and ask whether the price includes being cleared at customs or through a bonded warehouse. Also ask whether the stuff will be professionally packed, as owner-packed stuff often comes apart in transportation.

As removal costs are high and removals to other countries can be complicated, it's something you need to budget into the overall cost of buying your new property. A company such as Abels will send you a very complicated and detailed proposal form and inventory and it is essential to read it all through very carefully. Although most UK financial services such as insurance companies are regulated by the FSA (Financial Services Authority), this only applies to the UK, so you would need to be clear about how insurance works abroad, and whether the companies used are properly regulated and monitored by a professional association.

Self-storage units, now rapidly springing up on all sorts of wasteland and industrial estates all over the world, may look like a convenient answer but they are very, very expensive. Philip Pertoldi says: 'What you are paying for with these units is easy access. It is much cheaper for the removal company to store your goods, but then you wouldn't have the easy access.'

# The different types of market

Buying abroad is now so popular that experts have identified three different types of foreign market: primary, secondary and tertiary.

Primary markets are sophisticated and long established, have a well-developed infrastructure, a proper legal basis and are places where foreigners have bought successfully for many decades. Examples of primary markets are France, Spain, Portugal, Italy and Florida.

Secondary markets are less well established, legal structures may vary or be very fragile and are places where foreigners have only just started buying. In such places, there may not be many well-established estate agents and the buying procedure may not be sophisticated or streamlined. However, in these secondary markets foreigners have already started buying and selling properties. Here, the risks of buying are necessarily higher than in the primary markets, but the returns can be correspondingly higher. Examples of secondary markets are Croatia, Turkey and Dubai. Many companies are already advertising properties there, but as yet nobody knows for sure what the future holds for these countries, or whether property values will rise significantly.

Turkish properties, for instance, are now heavily advertised in the media, but at the time of writing (2008) it is by no means certain whether Turkey will enter the EU. Turkey was very much hoping to join the EU in 2007, along with Romania and Bulgaria, but in the end this did not happen. It is a complicated issue, but Finland, which held the EU presidency at the time of the application, ran out of patience. The main problem is that Turkey refuses to recognize Southern (Greek) Cyprus as an EU member, and will not resume trade with this section of the long-divided country.

Northern Cyprus is, of course, still Turkish and the country remains divided. Another problem regarding Turkey's accession to the EU is that it is a Muslim country, although avowedly secular, and there has been a rise in fundamentalism among some citizens. There has also been concern in some quarters over human rights issues.

At the moment, it seems as though Victorian prime minister William Gladstone's vow to drive the Turks 'bag and baggage out of Europe' holds to this day.

The EU has stated that, although Turkey has been denied accession for the time being, this does not mean the door is closed completely. There is still a possibility that Turkey will be granted accession one day although no date has been given.

Turkish property experts insist that this market is still emerging fast, and the accession position should not adversely affect property investment there.

Tertiary markets are countries or areas where buying by foreigners has recently become possible, but is not at all established. Properties in tertiary markets can appear to be very cheap, but the infrastructure may be extremely fragile or unknown, and the buying process may be difficult for many reasons: the title may be disputed, nobody really knows who the property belongs to, mortgages may not be available and the paperwork may not be legally valid.

These brand-new markets represent the highest risk of all, and at this stage are only for the very brave – or foolhardy – to consider. Examples of tertiary markets, at the time of writing, include Poland, Slovakia, Russia and the Czech Republic. In tertiary markets, economies may not be well developed.

But remember: the countries now considered to be primary, sophisticated and safe were also, at one time, what are now considered tertiary markets. People buying properties in France or Spain in the 1950s would have been at as high a risk then as those considering Slovenia or Hungary now.

## SIPPs update

It was widely expected that, from April 2006, the Chancellor of the Exchequer was going to allow residential property, both in the UK and abroad, to be put into a Self-Invested Personal Pension (SIPP). This was going to have important tax-saving consequences for owners of second or investment homes.

But on 6 December 2005, four months before A-Day, the government backtracked on this, without prior warning, with the result that residential property cannot now be put into a pension fund. Or at least, it can, but there is no tax advantage, so no point whatever in wrapping your property up in this way.

So what is the situation now? SIPPs cannot buy individual property, but they will be able to buy into property funds, known as REITs (Real Estate Investment Trusts) once these become established. This is an indirect way of investing in property, and cannot be done by individuals.

At the time of writing, REITs have not become established for foreign property, but this is how they are expected to work: if you want to invest in a Spanish villa you cannot now do this directly with your SIPP, but you can – or will be able to – buy into a fund that invests in Spanish property, to be put towards your pension provision. They will work in much the same way as stocks and shares, in that you will own a share in the foreign property.

Some companies are currently working to set up such funds in a number of countries. REITs are popular and well established in the United States, the Netherlands and Australia, and look like becoming a new way of investing in property abroad. With a REIT your SIPP would not, of course, own the property as it would have done under the proposed scheme, which was dramatically scrapped after many investors had already put down deposits on properties to complete the purchase after 6 April 2006. It meant egg on face all round, especially as a whole new industry had geared itself up ready for residential property SIPPs.

You can buy commercial property and land, either in the UK or abroad, to put into a SIPP, as you have been able to do since 1989.

# French leaseback properties

France has pioneered the idea of leaseback, whereby you as the investor purchase a property to be used solely as a holiday let. You are the freehold owner, but under the terms of the deal the operating company agrees to furnish the place, rent it out and pay you a guaranteed rental income, usually between 2.5 and 5 per cent of the purchase price.

The operating company also looks after all the utilities, repairs and maintenance but the owner pays local rates, the equivalent of council tax, as this is levied on the owner – as with UK holiday properties – rather than the holidaymaker.

As the owner, you can use the property yourself for a few weeks as a holiday home, but probably not in the highest season. French leasebacks are best viewed as a long-term investment rather than something on which you can expect a quick profit, as although there is also the strong possibility of profit from resale this cannot of course be guaranteed.

Most leaseback properties are located in popular tourist areas and are new-build, rather than resale, properties. The advantage of new-builds is that in France no VAT (TVA) is levied if the property remains in the scheme for 20 years. If the property is sold, say, after 10 years, or used as a full-time holiday home by the owner, then half the VAT concession becomes payable.

An added benefit of leaseback for UK and Irish buyers is that under some circumstances it can be placed in a SIPP. This can happen only when it becomes considered a commercial rather than residential property. What happens is that the SIPP buys the property and leases it back on a French commercial lease for between 9 and 20 years for hotel use, and the management company pays the rental income into the pension fund. Many French developers are now offering leaseback properties that are suitable for SIPPs. However, in order for a property to qualify for inclusion in a SIPP, the owners must never use it themselves as a holiday home. It must be purchased as pure investment.

It is a complicated type of investment, so expert advice is necessary before taking the plunge, although it has to be said that French leaseback properties are becoming ever more popular with UK investors who feel that the UK market has possibly peaked, investment-wise.

Leaseback schemes were introduced in France as long ago as 1976 by the French government to stimulate regional economies and boost tourist trade, which by that time was rapidly growing.

These are purely investment purchases, not your dream home abroad. Typically, you as the investor would buy an off-plan property such as a ski chalet or beach apartment in a popular tourist area. As it is considered a commercial proposition you would sign a commercial rather than a residential lease, and this means you must rent out your property through a specified management company for a fixed period, usually around 10 years. When this period comes to an end, a new lease can be negotiated or the property can be sold, but if you do not renew you will most probably have to pay the developer a pre-agreed sum of money as compensation.

As the purchaser, you would have to put down an initial deposit of between 2 and 5 per cent of the property's price when you sign the reservation contract. Then you would pay, typically, 20 per cent of the purchase price in cash and borrow the rest on a mortgage. Once the project is up and running and being rented out, you will have to pay tax on the rental income, although there are generous tax allowances available on leaseback schemes. To find out more, you would need to speak to a French accountant – or an accountant who is conversant with the French tax system.

Promoters of leaseback schemes, now being heavily promoted, maintain that they are low-risk, maintenance-free and constitute a good long-term investment, possibly as part of a pension plan. But as with any other type of investment, it's important to understand and evaluate all the hidden costs, such as the management fee which can increase each year, the interest you have to pay on any borrowing, and how easy or difficult it would be to sell the property after the initial lease period is up.

# Fractional ownership

This is another relatively new scheme whereby you purchase a fraction of the title deed. Once purchased, the property acts just like any other second or holiday home in that it can appreciate in value. Fractional ownership is not the same as timeshares, or holiday clubs where membership is purchased, as these do not come with a title deed.

Fractional ownership is quickly becoming popular all over the world, and these properties can range from condominiums and hotel suites to cottages and single family homes. They are usually located in prime tourist spots and sometimes form part of a specially constructed resort complex. Such properties come fully furnished, and a property management company is retained to take care of maintenance.

Fractional ownership is best suited to holiday homes that the owners would use for perhaps four to six weeks a year. This type of ownership is typically offered in one-quarter or one-twelfth shares (13 weeks or one month). Responsibility for management fees is worked out on a pro rata basis, and they are obviously much lower than if you had to pay the entire amount yourself for the year.

As you own part of the title deed, fractional ownership can be considered a worthwhile investment; you always have something to sell. You can also benefit from rental income, should you decide to rent out the property during 'your' weeks. This type of ownership would suit somebody who wants a guaranteed bolthole, but not the fuss and bother of year-round upkeep.

These properties tend to be situated in luxury holiday complexes with sports facilities, swimming pools, restaurants and shops on site. Mostly, it is a deluxe type of operation whereby the fridge is stocked before your arrival, the car is unpacked for you, beds are made up and dinner reservations are made for you. Fractional ownership operators maintain that this option brings together the best of holiday home ownership with a first-class hotel service. Yet it is less impersonal than a hotel.

On the other hand, it is never really yours.

# 4  France

France is the nearest 'abroad' country for UK nationals, and, along with Spain, by far the most popular. In recent years, the French property-buying business has become huge, and it's getting bigger all the time. The whole industry has been given an immense push, of course, by the arrival of the Eurotunnel, and also the introduction of pet passports. The proliferation of cheap flights by airlines such as easyJet has also made the process of getting to France much easier and quicker than ever before. It is estimated that around 40 per cent of the inhabitants of Gascony are now British or North Europeans, ie, not French. Around 300,000 British people now live permanently in France, and numbers continue to increase each year.

France as an option for a second, or even permanent, home has much to recommend it, not least that, for UK citizens at least, it's by far the easiest and quickest country to get to. You don't even need to hang around at airports, as you can drive there, or take the train. Also, for most UK people, France does not present such a major culture shock as some places as, for many of us, it already feels quite familiar, even if this familiarity is a concept rather than an actuality.

Although pure investment is becoming ever more popular in many countries, the vast majority of people who buy a property in France do so to improve their lifestyle, and they are most often looking for either a holiday home or a retirement home, rather than for financial gain.

Novelist Paul Micou, who moved with his family to Provence in 1999, pondered the lifestyle options in an article in the *Author* in December 2006. He says that, although France may be a foreign culture, you can read every single UK newspaper, most US ones and most English-language news magazines online, and even

British newspapers, the same day, should you wish to. And, he adds, if you do up sticks and move to France permanently, what are you running away from? 'A grotesque, out-of-control, anti-intellectual culture of consumerism, vulgarity and materialism?' Paul Micou (whose name sounds very French, anyway) advises:

> If you're feeling the now-standard urge to get away, then close your eyes and take the leap and move to the South of France. Just do it... It's a spit away; you already know it is gloriously beautiful; it is forever not England. There are ample reasons to stay put, but I would suggest that if the urge to escape is strong enough you have already answered the question. Your future is a foreign country.

Well, you can't put it more plainly than that, and Paul Micou also confirms the received wisdom that you can get a wonderful place in France, even in the expensive South of France, even in 2008, for a fraction of the price of a similarly beautiful house in the UK.

Yet you have to bear in mind that, in a sophisticated, mature market such as France, property prices do not rise by the same annual amounts as in some of the emerging markets. In 2005, for instance, the average price of a French property rose just 10.3 per cent. France does not tend to attract the hard-nosed investors who might be considering buying in Poland or Estonia, for instance, but rather the kind of people who like mellow old farm-houses full of character, wonderful wines and cheeses, and French culture generally.

Having said that, new-builds are becoming increasingly popular with the type of foreign buyers who at one time turned up their noses at anything new, at least in France.

France is a very big, rural country and, in spite of its proximity to the UK, has a very different 'feel' about it, even though the two nations' histories have been intimately intertwined for centuries, with periods of friendship and alliance interspersed by bloody and prolonged wars. In more recent years, at least since the Second World War, the two countries have enjoyed, or maybe endured, an uneasy *entente cordiale*.

In some ways, France and Great Britain may be seen as rather like siblings who have an endless love–hate relationship with each other. Novelist Joanne Harris, author of the best-selling book *Chocolat*, who is herself half-French, observed:

> The boorishness of English footballers has done damage to our entente cordiale, as has the aggression of French farmers. The French are perceived as arrogant; the English as greedy and insular. Rural communities in Provence have been completely absorbed by the British, driving house prices high above the reach of locals… Ferries of supermarket day-trippers swamp Calais and Boulogne in search of cheap booze.
>
> The French joke that the British love France – they adore the countryside and the beaches; appreciate the wines and cheeses – it's just the people they can't stand. The British argue that they have brought trade… and boosted the rural economy. Caught as I am between both sides – always at least half-wrong – I can see both points of view.
>
> (*Sunday Telegraph*, 24 February 2002)

Perhaps the countries have always been geographically too close for comfort. And now, thanks to the Eurotunnel, they have become closer than ever. You can board a train at Waterloo and get out at Aix-en-Provence without any discomfort at all – a far cry from the 20-hour car journey and getting on and off ferries such a destination would once have entailed.

For very many British people, France has always seemed rather exotic, in a way that Holland, Belgium and Germany, for instance, have not. Whether Britain appears equally exotic to the French is another question, but certainly the French are not falling over themselves to buy property in the UK in the same way that thousands of British people are currently buying themselves homes in France.

Maybe the UK doesn't have such nice properties or, perhaps nearer to the truth, they are just too expensive to be considered as viable second or holiday homes. The average price Britons pay for a French home in 2008 is £200,000. Traditionally, also, France has always seemed to have so much more to offer than the UK in terms of enjoyable lifestyle. France is a wine-growing country, which Britain, in spite of somewhat laborious attempts in recent years, most certainly is not. And although of course it's easy enough to buy French wines at the nearest supermarket, it's not the same as looking out at vineyards from your window, and buying the local stuff from the grower.

Then France has an exciting culinary tradition, which is by no means duplicated in the UK. There are not the home-grown glorious cheeses for which France is rightly famous, and one only has to read Peter Mayle's books about Provence and France generally to appreciate how differently the two nations regard food. In France, meals are considered a religious experience almost; in the UK, it's mainly a matter of filling up at intervals.

On the artistic, literary and historical side, France's heritage is a million times more glamorous than that of the UK. France has had a Revolution; it has had left-wing intellectuals; it was the home of existentialism and very many avant-garde movements in all the arts.

Then of course France, of all countries, has had the tradition of the artist's garret – a romantic and bohemian concept no other country has managed. Artists' garrets were tiny rooms situated under the eaves of big houses, rooms where you could hardly stand up, but which provided an extremely cheap roof under which struggling artists could torture themselves to produce great and lasting works. Household names such as Modigliani, Balzac and Picasso were in their struggling days grateful for the existence of the artist's garret, and the opera *La Bohème* is, of course, set in such an interior.

Now, landlord and tenant laws have prevailed so that one of the last vestiges of romantic, bohemian France is about to disappear. New laws mean that the traditional garrets must have hot and cold water and en-suite facilities.

France was also for centuries the world leader in *haute couture*. One thinks of such names as Chanel, Dior, Yves St Laurent, Givenchy. Truly, few countries have had such a rich and diverse cultural heritage. And as its glamour becomes mythologized and fades into memory, France appears to be becoming ever more popular as a second- or holiday-home destination.

The south of France is increasingly inhabited by Russians, for instance, maybe seeking an escape from the inhospitable steppes, and many Northern Europeans are eagerly snapping up second homes in the more attractive areas of France. For as well as exciting towns and cities, there are also many quiet, unspoilt villages, wonderful beaches, the French Alps and nearness to other European countries.

Plus, property prices are cheap compared to the UK. In some ways, France may be considered to have everything to beckon the second-homer, particularly the British second-homer.

And there are practical considerations other than those of scenery, food, wine, heritage, architecture or variety to take into account. Dick Shrader, founder of the magazine *French Property News*, believes that the main reasons for France's great and growing popularity as a first choice for a second home are now those concerning lifestyle, rather than heritage, food or wine. All these play their part, of course, but Shrader says:

> From the feedback we get from readers, it seems as if UK people are choosing France mainly because they are so fed up with the stresses and strains of life in the UK. In France, trains are cheap and run on time, the roads are relatively traffic-free, the health service is excellent, schools are good and you can buy a big house for a fraction of what it would cost in the UK.
>
> Also, in many parts of France you get vastly better weather than in Northern Europe, and there is still a great attraction for foodies.
>
> But it is undoubtedly dissatisfaction with life in the UK that is leading ever more people to settle in France. France is more relaxed than the UK and there is simply not the same level of stress, hassle, dirt, noise, pollution and general wretchedness associated with life in the UK these days.

Driving across France, journalist Alexander Chancellor found that the motorways were miraculous, beautifully planted and landscaped, with surfaces as smooth as billiard tables and 'as far removed from the M1 as heaven is from hell'. Writing in the *Guardian*, he continued, 'French motorways don't need widening because they are already more than wide enough to accommodate all the traffic that wants to use them, and they do not seem to need repairing either, for their condition is perfect.'

Chancellor feels that in many ways the quality of life in the UK has worsened, while that in other countries has improved beyond all measure. He was driving across France to visit Nat Waugh, son of the late Auberon. Nat, his wife and two children decided to leave London and start a new life in France as provincial shop-keepers. And, adds Chancellor:

> For what it costs to buy a wretched flat in Hammersmith, Nat is now the owner of a fine spacious medieval stone building surrounding a courtyard entered from the main street by a broad arch, above which sways a shop sign displaying ... the name of the shop, La Perfide Albion (perfidious Albion, the traditional French insult term for Britain). Nat is about as English as can be. But there he is, a real French shopkeeper. We are witnessing European integration at the grass roots.

But before you put your horrible old expensive UK house on the market, say goodbye to horizontal rain, dirty trains and traffic-clogged motorways, and head for the relaxed, hedonistic lifestyle that beckons in France, stop and think for a moment about whether France is really the country that calls out to you. France is a very large country with much geographical variety. The French are also, perhaps, less welcoming to foreigners than natives of some other countries, particularly if you don't speak the lingo reasonably fluently.

Which part of France would you choose for your second home, and why? Would you prefer to be by the sea or inland? Near to the UK or very far away? How important is weather, bearing in mind that nowhere in France enjoys sun all the year round, and winter nights in Provence can be 16 degrees below freezing? If hot sunshine and year-round good weather are high on your wish list, then France would probably not be a wise choice, even with all its other multifarious attractions.

> Vicky Harrison, who chose the Cluny area for her French home, says:
>
> > You have to pick a place that resonates with you. After doing huge amounts of research, I decided to be near Lyons, which is a big exciting town, yet at the same time I have a view of a wonderful landscape from my window. For me, a view is important.
> >
> > The location means I am relatively near to my sister in Geneva, fairly close to my daughter in Moscow, yet close enough to visit my elderly mother in the UK. As I am half-German, I am already more European than many British people, and I also like the idea of being able to drive round Europe. I'm fed up with the insularity of living on an island, and I wanted the middle of France, which has easy access to the Alps, Italy and Germany.
> >
> > Also, it's an attractive part of France in itself. My view is that you have to be very specific indeed about where you want to be, and concentrate on that area.

Once you've hit on the area, there are other vital decisions to make. Most people buying a second, or permanent, home in France prefer old to new houses. Vicky Harrison was looking for an old house already renovated: 'I could not consider major renovations,' she says. 'Yet at the same time I would not want a modern house.' However, a few years after she moved to France, Vicky *did* embark on a major renovation of her barn. But while works were in progress she already had a habitable home and by that time was more familiar with the ways of French building workers.

> Writer Lee Langley, who with her husband Theo Richmond owned a house in the Gironde area of France for 21 years, says:
>
> > To my mind, it's essential to be fluent in French if you are considering buying a holiday or permanent home there. It's no good thinking you can get by with four words of French and gestures. There is much bureaucracy to deal with, and more or less any home you buy will need repairs sooner or later, as would your own permanent home.

Lee, who herself does speak fluent French, adds: 'We spent ages tussling with workmen when renovating our own place. You also have to remember that most lawyers and town-hall officials, with whom you eventually can't avoid at least some contact, will most probably not speak English.'

Vicky Harrison's experience is that, although many lawyers and estate agents advertise 'English spoken', when you get into their offices you discover that your French is most probably vastly better than their English. In fact, one overwhelming piece of advice I received from everybody who has bought in France is: speak the language, or learn it, as you are likely to get into terrible trouble without it. (The same goes for Italy, Spain and Portugal, although maybe to a lesser extent.)

Novelist and biographer Henrietta Garnett, a grandchild of the artists Vanessa Bell and Duncan Grant of the Bloomsbury Group, has lived in France as a permanent resident for over 25 years. As a long-term French resident, although remaining a UK citizen, Henrietta's expert advice to anybody considering spending a lot of time in the country is: first do your homework as to region, and never buy the first place you see and fall in love with. You may find you don't like it all year round; there may also be hidden snags with the place not immediately apparent:

If you think you would like to have a place in France, ideally you should take time off work and spend several months touring the country, to see it in all its aspects. Then make sure you are in France during the worst-weather months, to see if you still like it when it's cold, wet and windy and the temperature drops below freezing.

Now living in Provence, Henrietta says:

I would advise spending a February in the place where you think you would like a home. If you like it in February, you will probably like it for the rest of the year.

For me, it's essential to be able to speak the language and I don't know how I would manage otherwise. I do know of some English people, long-term French residents, who live completely expat lives here, listening to *The Archers*, watching *Sky News*, playing bridge and never speaking a word of French.

For them, I suppose, the main point of being in France is that they can afford nicer houses than in the UK, and they certainly drink more wine. In fact, the amount of wine they drink is unbelievable. But unless you speak French you are only going to be barely tolerated by the French people. If you speak their language, you are accepted by them.

If I didn't speak French when I arrived, I would make sure I learnt it.

The need to speak good French is echoed by Mike Walker, who has an old house in Montréal du Gers, Gascony. He says:

When I was buying the house, literally the only French I knew was what used to be on the HP Sauce bottles. When I was faced with the contract, and all the legal terms, I was completely at a loss, so much so that the sale was about to fall through.

The lawyers tend not to speak English, nor do the estate agents. I somehow managed to work out that they were trying to take me for a ride, and when I said I was going back to England without signing, they suddenly backed down.

Now I'm having French lessons, and getting better. But if you're buying property and negotiating with builders and planning permissions, all the French you speak is transactional French. I would love to be able to talk about history, culture, literature – but as yet I can't.

When Henrietta Garnett first moved to France, she lived in Normandy, although she was not entirely happy with her life there:

I got stuck there as I couldn't afford to move. Normandy was handy for trips back to England, but it wasn't really where I wanted to be.

But then I had a stroke of luck. I came into some money when *Aspects of Love*, a book by my father [the novelist David Garnett] was made into a musical by Andrew Lloyd Webber. I then decided to move to Provence, where I had actually always wanted to be.

Henrietta's house, an hour's drive from Marseilles, is not old, but she has made it look old:

> I put on a new roof of old curly tiles, and stone flags on the floor, so that you get an illusion of an old house, and it suits me perfectly. The house was actually built in the late 1970s, so at least I don't cop huge repair and maintenance bills. My greatest extravagance was to put in a swimming pool, as it gets so hot in summer and I'm too far away from the sea for easy journeys. That was the most expensive thing I did, but it was definitely worth it.

Henrietta is full of praise for the French health service, and believes she wouldn't be alive today but for its excellence: 'I had an exploding ulcer, with blood hitting the ceiling, and a doctor was round right away. Would that have happened in England? I doubt it. But again, I would be worried if I became ill in France and couldn't speak French to the doctors or hospital staff.'

From a cultural point of view, Henrietta feels satisfied: 'At Avignon and Aix in the summer, there is culture galore. There is a lot of painting going on, a lot of theatre and a tremendous buzz of high-level cultural activities. The trains are fantastic, so much so that when I'm in England I can't believe people will put up with such poor service.'

Any drawbacks to what sounds like an idyllic life? Yes, says Henrietta: she cannot see as much of her daughter and two grand-daughters as she would like:

> In an ideal world I would love to have a pied-à-terre in London. But I just can't afford it. I would recommend, though, that anybody who can afford it should retain a bolthole in their own country if they have friends and relatives they would like to see. I am rather in exile here, although the advantages do far outweigh the disadvantages.

Henrietta's advice to do proper research before buying is echoed by Lee Langley:

> We had friends who had bought in France and were raving about it. Theo and I realized what a good basis it would be for

family holidays to have our own place, so one Easter the two of us spent an intensive week looking round.

We first drove round the Dordogne but gave that the thumbs down because it was too expensive and too full of British people. Then we drifted into the Gironde, which was much cheaper, with some lovely old towns and far fewer English.

We saw places every day, being taken round by one estate agent or the other. We almost bought a totally run-down chateau but, in view of our later problems with workmen, had a lucky escape.

Other houses we viewed were too close to neighbours, and we wanted peace, quiet and isolation. In the end, we found the place we bought, which had woods around it, fields and vineyards and about three acres of land. The roof tiles were old and cracked but the place had – dangerous word – *possibilities*. So we bought it, although it took months to get it all settled.

What was it like for long family holidays? 'First of all,' says Lee:

it's vital to check the location. If you want sun and swimming, you must make sure the weather permits this. We had Atlantic weather, which could be cold and windy. On the other hand, the more perfect the weather, the more expensive the house.

We wanted privacy, which we got. But we had not realized when we bought that the nearest villages had no traditional bar, or indeed a bar of any kind. So there was none of that sitting at a pavement table or leaning up against a zinc bar drinking a glass of cognac with the locals. The locals were all indoors anyway, watching television. On the other hand, we didn't have that depressing thing of being surrounded by expats. Our neighbours were all French, so we were able to become part of their lives.

If you have children, advises Lee, and the sea is not close, it's essential to have somewhere they can swim:

We were lucky in that there was a large lake nearby. Once you've settled on the rough area you want, it's a very good idea to spend time sussing it out generally before jumping into decisions.

And if you buy somewhere that needs a lot of work, as we did, local artisans are crucial. We put in a new septic tank, a soakaway for kitchen waste, we built terraces, converted a barn into a huge bedroom, had the roof retiled. All this meant contacting workmen, waiting for them to come and look, waiting for the estimate, and then waiting and waiting for them to do the work.

All the work their place needed eventually proved to be a bit of a downside. 'On the upside, there is simply nothing to beat that feeling of driving the last few hundred yards, seeing the roof, unpacking, turning on the fridge, and by sunset be sitting watching the sky darken with a glass of wine in your hand,' enthuses Lee.

Theo's memories of their French home, sold when their three children grew up, are perhaps not quite as affectionate as Lee's, as the endless DIY eventually got him down. Even so, he says:

Although we bought the place with summer in mind, as winters in the Gironde can be severe, one of my best memories is of huge log fires blazing on autumn nights. We closed the shutters, and the logs crackling, plus the delicious smell of Lee's cooking accompanied by litres of local plonk, was an experience hard to beat.

Warm summer days were everything one hoped for – a hammock slung between two mature lime trees, starlit skies at night, the silence – yet looking back, I can't now think of those years, however great they were at times, without the ever-looming shadow of B and D. Black and Decker. Because we couldn't afford to have all the work done for us, I spent hours putting up shelves, painting, splashing on anti-rot liquid, repairing wire fencing, filling holes in walls.

It's OK if you're young and enjoy DIY but for me the wonderful memories are quite severely marred by all-too-vivid recollections of having to spend hours in local hardware stores searching for the right screws, nails, tools, paint.

Also, we found that the local artisans were in such demand they had to be courted like medieval princes. It was fantastic to see our old, dilapidated farmhouse come back to vibrant life, but unless you are a brilliant DIY-er, or have very deep pockets, I would now advise against buying an enchanting

> wreck going for a song and, instead, wait until you can afford something already in reasonable nick.
>
> It was definitely a great experience for the children when young, and wonderful for them to get to know another culture and another country. We had fun and we learnt a lot. But looking back, I would not recommend buying somewhere that needs loads of work every time you go.

The usual textbook advice on buying a second home is always: rent first, to get a feel of the place and ensure you really like it. But Vicky Harrison believes this can be difficult:

> It's OK if you go to a known tourist place with lots of holiday apartments. But where I've been looking there is just nothing suitable to rent. As there is little tourist trade, nobody could make a living from renting places out, so there's nothing available.
>
> I would certainly like to have rented first, to get a proper feel of the place. But it's just not possible. Another thing to bear in mind when looking is that French estate agents are a different breed from their English equivalents. They hardly give away any information in case you go away and do a secret deal with the vendor behind their backs. Also, they all have the same properties on their books. I went to two estate agents and was shown exactly the same properties twice.

However, Keith Atkinson, who has visited France every year since his teens and now, in retirement, lives for six months of the year in France, believes it's a major mistake to sell up your existing home and move to France without being absolutely sure it's the right decision for you. He says:

> You should live in France for a few months first, winter as well as summer, as only then can you be reasonably sure you are not going to make a serious mistake, both in terms of your quality of life expectations, and financially. After 6 to 12 months, decide if it's going to work, and then buy, but not before.

It seems, from talking to many second-homers, that owning your own place in another country provides a rich addition to life not easily duplicated by renting different places all the time. By returning year after year, it becomes possible to know and love a place you might forget about if you visited it only once.

There's a kind of nesting instinct that is satisfied by owning your very own place, which may not be entirely logical in terms of what it costs to maintain and how much time is spent there, but which nevertheless is so special that it comes close to being a permanently blissful experience.

This is the case anyway with writers and publishers Maureen and Tim Green. They have had a place in the Luberon, quite near the area made famous by Peter Mayle's books, since the mid-1980s, and believe that on the bliss scale their little retreat comes pretty near the top.

Maureen says:

We had been wanting to buy a place in France for many years, as we are definitely Francophiles. We both speak good French and this was the country that tugged at our heartstrings.

At first, we looked at places along the coast, but found it very concretey and crowded. Also, resorts tend to be very miserable places in winter. So then our thoughts turned inland. We wanted to be in a place where life went on 12 months of the year, rather than that awful feeling of everything shutting up when the season was over.

We first started looking in Saint-Rémy, but found it too expensive and full of German industrialists. Then we drove round the villages in the Luberon until we came to our village, or what became our village.

We fell for a 15th-century house in the Provençal village of Lauris. It actually belonged to the estate agent who showed us round, and he had done it up as the perfect bachelor pad. Then he got married and had children, for whom the steep terrace was too dangerous. So he wanted to sell it. We, of course, loved the terrace.

Tim and I looked at each other and the same thought went through our minds: this is it. And we love it. As we're both now self-employed, we can choose when we go, and we now go every six weeks, including in winter. We used to go by car, but now we go from Waterloo to Aix-en-Provence, and if we leave our London house at 8.30 we can be in our French home, sitting by the fire, by 4.30 in the afternoon.

Originally, says Maureen, they went there to rest and chill out, but now Tim finds the house an ideal place to write his books. But, much as they love it, they would not consider retiring there, or living there permanently:

I love London, and we go to the theatre every week. For us, it's wonderful to have these two separate lives. Because it's quiet in our French village, we find we read as we've never read before. For example, we're getting through huge Victorian novels we wouldn't have time to read at home.

There's not much to do in our little village but the Luberon hills are beautiful, there are interesting walks and lovely genuine markets. It's a simple life and we love it, all year round.

Maureen and Tim believe it's essential to have good neighbours: 'In summer, our plants need watering every day, otherwise they would die. Also, our neighbours will come and turn the radiators on in winter. People don't always realize that the Provençal climate can be very harsh, 95 degrees in summer, and in winter remain below freezing all day.'

Jackie Harris, whose passion is skiing, has a ski flat with her family in the popular area of Haute-Savoie, in the French Alps:

We used to rent places, or stay in hotels, but then wondered about having a place of our own.

We chose France because it's more accessible from the UK than other resorts, and this particular resort because it's on a motorway, and an easyish 13-hour run from England. As the area is mountainous, it's essential to have a 4-by-4 jeep. I don't mind the drive at all, and in fact would far rather drive to France than Cornwall.

When we drive to France, there's not a red cone in sight, we eat good food on the way, banks are open on Christmas Day and, altogether, France is far more service-oriented than the UK.

Unlike many second-homers, Jackie and her family have not chosen a place in the sun. 'It's purely for skiing,' she says. Nor have they bought their French apartment as an investment, but as a lifestyle choice. Even so, if they were to sell the place, they wouldn't lose:

Property prices are going up because of the euro, and in the year that we've had our apartment, prices have already risen.

We made up our minds to buy after being extremely disappointed with our accommodation one year, and started looking in estate agents' windows. We were lucky in that we had a sudden windfall of money, which turned out to be the exact price of the apartment – £130,000 – so we bought it with cash.

For Jackie, as for many second-home owners, the introduction of the pet passport scheme has made the impossible possible, or the unthinkable thinkable: 'If we're going for more than five days, we take our two dogs. I was part of the pilot scheme for pet passports and it's wonderful not to have to leave them in kennels when we go to France. You have to book up ages in advance to get your pets into kennels, and it's a huge hassle.'

Pet passport schemes are now available for many countries, including Australia and New Zealand, and the cost of preparing your cat or dog for a first holiday abroad is about the same as two weeks in kennels. Your pet will have to be microchipped – implanted with a permanent radio frequency device for identification, and have anti-rabies injections and blood tests. It's all quite a hassle, and worth talking to your vet well in advance, or logging on to www.petsabroad-uk.com for an information pack. Note: some breeds of dog may not be permitted pet passports.

Although much of this chapter emphasizes the need to learn to speak French and to integrate with the French people, otherwise they will give you the cold shoulder, this is not always the case, as the inhabitants of the town of Eymet in the Dordogne region of South-West France have demonstrated.

For this little medieval town in the heart of France has become known as Little England, as it has the highest proportion of Brits living there year-round of anywhere in France, and is stocked with English-style shops selling English-style products such as Branston Pickle, Tetley tea, Heinz tomato soup, Weetabix, British sausages and many other products guaranteed to give the Gauls a mighty shudder. Kevin Wells, an expat who runs a store in the little town, says his best-selling line is Walker's crisps.

Most of the (British) residents there don't speak French, and went there not looking for something typically French, more for an idyll of what England was like (in their imaginations at least) 50 years ago. In their defence, the British residents say that 15 years ago Eymet (pop: just over 2000) was run-down and lifeless, but now, thanks to the influx of foreigners, it is booming again. A family home there costs a fraction of what something similar would cost in Hampshire, Sussex or any other expensive country. The once-abandoned estates and farmhouses have been turned into desirable properties which can be snapped up for under £250,000 for a three-bedroom house with a swimming pool and an acre of land. A chateau there costs around £500,000.

In a dramatic break with tradition, non-French citizens can now stand in local council elections and, in Eymet, Brits who have made their home there are now enthusiastically serving their adopted town on the council.

The Dordogne region, which has long been popular with the Brits, now permanently houses around 20,000 fugitives from the UK, and very many are retirees who have come in search of a better life there.

Ever more people are considering retiring to France, as permanent residents.

Vicky Harrison, a language lecturer in the UK for many years, falls into this category.

Vicky, who has lived permanently in the Cluny area of France since 2003, and has completely sold up in the UK, has made sure she speaks the language fluently so as to get the most out of living in the country. Since moving, she has carried out an extensive and trendy barn conversion at her French farmhouse, which she could, if she wanted to, rent out for profit. At the moment the conversion, which cost around £60,000 and entailed much inter-action with French builders, is just used for family and friends. But it has hugely increased the value of her farmhouse which was in excellent condition when she bought it and cost just £140,000. You cannot even get a studio flat for that in the South-East of England.

Vicky has entered fully into local life and has a constant stream of visitors who arrive, usually at Geneva airport where they are met by their hostess for the two-hour drive back to the isolated but beautiful village where she lives. I have myself stayed with Vicky (who is an old school-friend) several times and marvel at her 'estate' – a large manor house, huge courtyard, massive barn, enormous cellar and wonderful views. All in all, it is idyllic, but you would certainly need to be able to speak good French to cope.

Another thing retirees need to know about is health care provision. Vicky is fully entitled to treatment on the French NHS system, which she believes is vastly superior to that in the UK. She says:

> When I retired I felt I needed a complete lifestyle change and France has provided that. My pension from teaching gives me just enough to live on and I am using up my remaining capital bit by bit. I hit on France because everywhere else is too far away and you can't always get cheap deals on flights.

Vicky spends her time in France gardening, reading books (in French!), teaching English to students and schoolchildren, enter-taining, and is also often in the UK to visit family and friends. It all works for her but then she is a talented linguist and was already bilingual (in German) before settling in France.

If you have retired and are in receipt of a state pension, this can be paid straight into your French bank account. How much you receive will depend on the current exchange rate, so it may be subject to some fluctuation. Your pension, though, could be liable to French, rather than UK, taxation. In any case, it must be declared as part of your income. Otherwise, warn financial experts, you could be accused of tax evasion. All the relevant paperwork must be done in advance of moving, but you could be in for a pleasant surprise in that you will be paying less tax in France than in the UK.

Just to make matters more complicated, anybody in receipt of a UK government pension, such as a civil servant or police officer, will definitely be required to pay UK, not French, tax. More details are available from the International Pension Centre: 0191 218 7777. Those in private pension schemes should consult their pension providers.

## The process of buying

Buying a property in France is not the same kind of transaction as in the UK. The whole process will take about two months if paying cash, three months with a mortgage.

French property transactions involve a personage with no exact equivalent in the UK: the notary. He or she is a legally qualified public servant who does not represent either the vendor or the purchaser, but both. It is absolutely essential to have a French notary, and the final deed has to be signed in the notary's office. The purchaser has to pay all the notary's costs, which amount to around 7 per cent of the purchase price.

The notary's job is to make all relevant searches, notify the authorities, draw up the draft deed of sale, look into any rights of way or planning permission and ensure there are no outstanding charges or arrears on the property. Note: most notaries do not speak English, so it is essential to be fluent in French, or have somebody fluent with you when dealing with the notary.

Purchasing a French property involves two contracts. The first is a preliminary sales contract, which can be drawn up in the UK, and can be witnessed by the estate agent. Contracts will vary depending on whether the property is finished or whether you are buying an unfinished home.

On signature of this preliminary contract, the purchaser has to pay 10 per cent of the purchase price, which will be deducted on signature of the final deed. If the purchaser changes his or her mind, the deposit is forfeited. If, by contrast, any conditions included in the agreement are not fulfilled, the deposit is refunded.

Along the way, there are certain payments to be made. Transaction fees charged by the estate agent amount to between 5 and 10 per cent of the purchase price. The notary's fees are fixed by law and range from around 8 to 14 per cent of the purchase price but exclude disbursements, duties, taxes, any searches and mortgage registry, if applicable. VAT (TVA in France) may be payable for properties under five years old not previously sold.

It is also advisable, when buying property in France, to make a French will, as inheritance laws are different from those in the UK, and apply to any property owned in mainland France.

Once you own your property, you will immediately become liable for local property taxes, plus occupancy taxes if you live in the property. You will also be liable for French tax when you sell the property, or if you derive any letting income from it. French tax may also be due if you die whilst owning a French property. As soon as you become the owner, you will need a French bank account to pay for all utilities.

It is also possible to buy a home in France by instalments from an elderly person not expecting to live much longer, by a method known as *la vente en viager*.

This type of sale is usually arranged when the elderly property owner wants to raise capital while remaining in the property, in a type of equity release situation. A potential buyer considering this type of deal must be prepared to wait and not want the property immediately.

What happens is that the buyer will pay the owner an initial lump sum known as a 'bouquet' and will then make regular prearranged payments to the owner for the rest of his or her life.

The upside of the scheme is that the new owner does not have to pay the full price of the property all at once, so it could be a useful idea for those on high salaries who do not have appreciable capital. The risk element comes with not knowing how long the existing property owner will live, of course. If he or she only lasts a year or two then the buyer gets a bargain, as payments stop on the death of the existing owner. But if the elderly owner lives for, say, another 25 years after the contract is signed and wants to occupy that property for the duration, it could work out very expensive. Was it in France that somebody lived to be 116 recently?

This type of sale is popular in France with elderly owners who have no children or close relatives to inherit – or who specifically want to prevent their heirs from inheriting according to French inheritance laws.

If, however, the worst-case scenario happens whereby the buyer dies before the elderly owner does, the payments must continue to be met by the buyer's heirs. But if the new owner dies 20 days before completion of the sale, it is regarded as null and void.

So, like all transactions that are based on longevity, this type of purchase does contain many inherent risks.

# Weather

Whilst good weather is of great importance for many second-homers, French weather is unpredictable and most probably not a huge advance on British weather, taken all year round.

Julius Caesar famously pronounced that all of Gaul is divided into three parts, and this is certainly true of French climate, although whether these are the same parts delineated by Caesar remains uncertain.

In the north of France, say above Tours or Dijon, you get similar weather to that of the south of England. In summer it may be slightly warmer, although this cannot be guaranteed. Mainly, the weather is no better than in the UK. In the south, say below Valence or Cahors, summers are vastly warmer than in Britain, but it can be very cold in winter. The middle layer of France enjoys longer summers than the UK, but winters are very similar. There is simply nowhere in France that you get good weather all year round.

Here are typical winter and summer temperatures in various areas of France, in degrees centigrade:

Marseille:     22.2 in summer, 7.2 in winter;
Bordeaux:    20.0 in summer, 6.3 in winter;

Brittany:          15.9 in summer, 7.4 in winter;
Lyon:              19.6 in summer, 2.5 in winter;
Nantes:            18.2 in summer, 5.3 in winter;
Paris:             18.1 in summer, 3.5 in winter;
Normandy:          17.0 in summer, 4.5 in winter.

## Picturesque ruin or modern home?

If interested in the romantic ruin, remember that budgets can easily run away with you and that it will probably cost far more to renovate a ruin than to buy a modern home. Unless you can do much of the work yourself, you are, as Lee Langley and Theo Richmond found, at the mercy of workmen. Or you spend your entire time wielding the dreaded B and D. Most people buying in France are, it has to be said, interested in old rather than new houses, but don't be too prejudiced in favour of the old. Although some of the holiday developments along the coast are dire, there are many modern homes on offer that are definitely worth a second look.

Skiing, like golf, is phenomenally popular, and becoming more popular all the time. Indeed, foreign-property experts are increasingly advising those after a good investment to go for a golf or ski resort, as these offer excellent rental possibilities as well as a good chance of increasing in value.

If you are not a golf or ski enthusiast, of course, then this advice will fall on deaf ears, but if you are, it's certainly worth thinking about buying somewhere in France where these sports are on offer. So far as ski resorts are concerned, France has it all – chic attractive villages, and year-round appeal. And there is major development now going on down the mountain slopes. Simon Malson of Investors in Property (020 8905 5511) says:

If I had to choose my favourite year-round resort, I'd pick the ski village of Megève, which is a proper place where people live.

People may not equate the Alps with fantastic summer weather, but they should. We have had temperatures of 30 degrees in May. The weather is perfect for golf, walking, mountain biking, swimming, tennis or downhill racing.

Arc 1950 a Canadian-backed development specializing in ski resorts, is a vast complex in the Paradiski ski area, is 80 per cent owned by British and Irish people and consists of brand-new apartments priced from around £160,000, and attracts the 'ordinary' rather than the super-rich or super-trendy skiers. Most buyers use their apartments for between two to seven weeks a year and then the developer, Intrawest, lets them out for the rest of the year.

There is such a very English atmosphere there that the area has been called 'Surrey on the slopes.'

Developer James Rodwell, who also specializes in apartments in the French Alps, believes that ski enthusiasts wanting to buy in France should look for places with year-round potential:

> At one time, skiers wanted places where skiing was on the doorstep, but now more people are considering traditional villages farther down the mountains.
>
> You have to drive to the slopes, but the advantage is that you get year-round interest, and mountain villages are now attracting investors.

Many of these villages are now being developed with chalet-style apartments suitable for year-round living. Purists may object that these will spoil the previous 'unspoilt' nature of the villages, but at least some village atmosphere remains, which may not be the case in a dedicated, utilitarian ski resort.

## New-build projects in France

When considering buying property in France, most people have in mind a building with character, whether or not it needs major renovation. But France is now entering a major new-build stage, with new properties going up all over the place. So before deciding that you just must have that 17th century farmhouse or cottage, it may be worth checking out some of the more attractive new-builds on offer. Most French towns now have well-designed apartments which can tempt the foreign as well as the local buyer.

If your time in France is likely to be limited, it may be worth considering a brand-new 'lock up and leave' apartment in a beautiful location, rather than a pretty, old house where security might be a problem.

France, though, unlike Spain, Florida and Portugal, is not predominantly an off-plan country. The weather is not good enough, year-round, for there to be a reliable rental market and in any case, most experts are of the opinion that France is saturated and not a significant growth market so far as the investor is concerned.

New-build properties tend to have a very high proportion of non-French owners, so be aware of this if you like the idea of a brand-new foreign home.

## What about renting out your home?

There is a thriving rental market in France's main tourist areas, but the season everywhere is short. Most property owners are of the opinion that it is difficult, if not impossible, actually to make money from your French property and that rental income can only, at best, help to cover some of your costs.

In any case, as many areas of France have no letting potential at all, it is essential to do thorough research on the letting market in your chosen location if you need or want to rent out your property when not in personal use.

As a general rule, old properties that have been renovated are more popular than brand-new developments. This is not the case in all countries by any means, but France is rather different from other places in that most visitors to France are Francophiles who want to experience the 'real' France when on holiday. There is little allure to Francophile foreigners in the secure, gated new developments with golf courses and tennis villages, although these do exist, and there is some demand.

Year-round lets are a different proposition if you are interested in buying an apartment in, say, Paris or Nice, which would rent out all the year round to students or professionals, and thus escape the seasonal holiday market situation. Here, you would have to find out whether you were actually allowed to rent out apartments, or whether this is not permitted.

Renting out a holiday apartment is a different matter anyway from letting a property long term and, as in the UK, different rules apply.

If interested in the holiday market, remember that the days of basic *gîtes*, when you motored to your primitive dwelling and took all your own sheets and equipment, are over. Nowadays, holidaymakers demand smartly furnished, properly equipped rentals with dishwasher, proper beds, satellite television and video. The reason? The market has become so competitive that you have to offer what everybody else is offering, and standards are going up all the time.

Internet companies such as Holiday-Rentals.com have made advertising your property easier, and this company has much useful downloadable literature and advice. There are now several internet companies specializing in French rentals, and you can learn a lot by visiting these sites before buying your French home.

As with letting property in any country, there are many rules and regulations, tax and legal matters to attend to, and these cannot be circumvented. For example, you may need a licence to rent out your property in France.

The vast majority of tenants will be wanting to rent your property for a short holiday. In such cases, the rental agreement will be relatively informal. Should you want to rent out your French property as a business, however, different rules apply.

If, for instance, you own several properties you wish to rent out, the property will be classed as a commercial venture rather than residential and under the French Commercial Code you will be classified as a tradesperson. Before advertising such properties, it is essential to seek legal and financial advice from a French property lawyer and accountant. It is simply not worth risking falling foul of the authorities. You may also need to obtain planning permission from the local town hall or *mairie*. In fact, any potential alterations will need planning permission.

French property expert Jacquie Clavey advises: 'If you buy a holiday home which brings in some rental income, that is one thing,

but as an income-producing investment it is hard to make it pay.'
Also, as with the UK, if you have only one investment property in
France, you may well find that a large percentage of your lovely
rental income is swallowed up in fees and taxes. The more properties
you have, the more money you are likely to make from renting.

If considering letting out your property, you will have to
complete a French income tax return, for which you will need a
French accountant. Also take advice from your local UK tax office
as to whether tax on rental income should be paid in the UK or in
France; you won't have to pay it twice, but will have to have a
double-taxation agreement stamped by your local tax office.

As ever, research rental demand before buying with rental
income in mind. In many areas of France, supply well outstrips
demand for holiday rental properties.

## A word of warning

When buying a property in France, beware of those places that
can only be reached by a budget airline, as these small airlines are
always vulnerable and liable to disappear for one reason or
another. But apart from that, buying any French property is a
decision that has to be approached with extreme care.

Many French websites have properties on offer for £10,000 or
less. The price of an average French house (in 2008) is £100,000,
compared with the £200,000 that is now average for the UK. So
they sound cheap, but as always with something that appears to
be an amazing bargain, there are several catches.

Firstly, the picturesque barn or cottage on offer at an absurdly
low price will almost always need complete rebuilding. Because
France is a large country, with plenty of building land (rather like
Florida) there is little value in a tumbledown property. There are
around 2 million empty homes in France, compared to just
150,000 in the UK. Then French property prices do not rise by
anything like the same degree as UK properties. In 2007, prices
rose by just 4 per cent in France.

# Earning a living

Most people buying second homes in France will probably not be thinking of earning a living there, at least initially. But circumstances may change as time goes on, and you may find you need, or want, to get a job or earn money whilst at your French home, or you may decide to relocate permanently.

UK citizens are allowed to work in France, but unemployment is high, and preference will usually be given to a French national. The ability to speak good French is, of course, a must for anybody seeking work or gainful employment. Much illegal work, known as 'on the black', takes place in France, but the best advice for incomers is: always play it straight. Never try to beat or buck the system, as you end up tying yourself in terrible bureaucratic and legal knots. For some people – young people maybe – casual, seasonal work may be available at resorts or in hotels.

If you live in France for more than six months in the year, you will become liable for French taxation. Long-term French resident Henrietta Garnett pays her taxes in the UK, which is an option for most UK nationals, as there is a reciprocal arrangement between the countries. In any case, make sure you don't pay income tax twice.

In France, income tax is high, rising to 56.8 per cent (at the time of writing) and is assessed on all sources of income including investments and 'unearned' – ie rental – income. If you are employed, social security contributions are paid by your employer, which is one reason why it may be difficult to get formal employment in France.

By far the great majority of incomers will be self-employed, and there are few restrictions on this. If self-employed as a craftsperson, tradesperson, writer, translator, etc, you have to register as a *travailleur indépendant* and pay a monthly sum to social security. Very many UK nationals, for instance, have moved permanently to France where they have set themselves up as IT consultants, website designers and so on. But be careful here: a number of IT workers have discovered that when in a foreign country you can become ever more remote from your clients and, before long, they start to forget about you. Although theoretically it is possible to work through e-mail and the internet, once the real contact is lost virtual contact is no substitute. Other incomers have ideas to run a bed-and-breakfast, small hotel or riding school, for instance. Builders and manual workers may be able to get work in France, but the *gîte* and B and B market, which many incomers dream about, is becoming overcrowded, and it is getting difficult to make a living in this way. Average French wages are around the same as in the UK – around £20,000 a year is standard, with managerial salaries starting at around £27,000.

France is a highly bureaucratic country and there is much red tape involved in setting up your own business. Again, fluent French is a necessity. The French economy encourages small businesses and the country is littered with them: even more so since the advent of the internet. Most experts advise taking legal advice before setting up any kind of business, as regulations should never be ignored. You may, for instance, be required to register for French VAT (TVA).

## Owning and running a French *gîte*

If you are interested in owning and running a real French *gîte,* first make sure there is a ready rental market for what you are offering. There is already considerable oversupply in the Dordogne, Brittany and Normandy areas – all regions popular with British second-homers.

In all areas, though, competition is hotting up, so such properties have to be comfortable, stylish and well equipped to stand a chance. These days, holidaymakers often look for a house with a pool – and this is rapidly becoming standard. Then you have to decide whether to advertise your property individually, or work through a tour operator. Individual advertising often means higher profits, but then tour operators do all the work for you – for a suitable fee, of course. Tour operators insist on certain standards, so holidaymakers are more likely to book with confidence through a recognized operator than with an unknown self-advertiser.

If you are going it alone, you need to have a well-designed, up-to-date website that will attract viewers. This has become an essential aspect of marketing, and Tim Williams, who runs a course called 'How to Buy and Run a *Gîte* Complex', believes that a personal website is the secret to success in this endeavour. Then you have to look after your guests properly. In other words, you have to be thoroughly businesslike to make the *gîte* pay – or even just to tick over.

Chris Taylor and Jenny Appleton have two *gîtes* in the Gers region of Southwest France and, speaking from experience, they believe it is essential to greet guests with a welcome pack of basic groceries and also to stock the bathrooms with toiletries and towels. They offer satellite television, a stock of DVDs, children's games and, round the pool area, towels and children's toys are provided.

Chris and Jenny have their own personal website as well as advertising across a range of other websites, but say it's still hard work making a go of it.

# Health and social security

Many people agree that the French health service is the best in the world; this has been recently endorsed by the World Health Organization. The French are often known as the hypochondriacs of Europe, and anybody who has spent time in France counting up the number of pharmacies, apothecaries, complementary practitioners, spas and health clubs will probably agree with that remark. The French love homeopathic medicine, and this is available on their health service.

The French health system consists of a private–public partnership whereby part of the cost of medical treatment is paid by social security and the remainder by the individual. In France, these private and public aspects work in harmony rather than against each other, as in the UK.

In order to make the system work efficiently, French social security contributions are high. For somebody on a managerial salary, they could be as much as 18 to 20 per cent of net income. Retired UK citizens living permanently in France can receive the same benefits as French nationals, so long as they have worked in an EU country. The form E121, available from the pensions office in Newcastle upon Tyne, is necessary in order to register.

Those who are not French residents, but staying temporarily in the country, will have to pay first and then apply for reimbursement through their own country's social security system. Having said that, anybody requiring emergency treatment must be accorded this regardless of ability to pay. Those living in France permanently should strongly consider taking out suitable private health insurance.

For short stays in France, the form E111, stamped and signed by your local post office, enables you to obtain medical treatment under a reciprocal agreement with the UK. It lasts for three months. Although hospitals in France must by law treat emergency patients, it is advisable to have private health insurance cover. The older you are, the more sensible it becomes to make sure you are covered for health problems that may arise. If on chronic medication, you need to know whether your prescription pills or treatments are readily available in France, and how much, if anything, they will cost over there. In most cases, the same treatments are available, although certain drugs and treatments may go by different names.

## Pros and cons of buying a property in France

Pros:

- easy distance from the UK;
- properties generally cheaper than in the UK, like for like;
- a wide choice of regions and lifestyles, from quiet little villages to highly sophisticated cities;
- wonderful architecture and charming rural scenery;
- easy access to the rest of Europe;
- good health service;
- fabulous cuisine, wines, cheeses, breads;
- a language many UK residents are at least half-familiar with;
- a romantic, exotic country with a glamorous heritage.

Cons:

- unreliable weather;
- cold winters in all regions;
- short season for letting and renting.

*Top Tips*

1. Don't take things for granted: the estate agent, the notary, and others work to different and usually more restricted rules than in England.

2. Don't sign blind: seek legal advice from a British-based or British-speaking lawyer; any Frenchman would consult their lawyer, so should you.

3. Don't misunderstand the role of the notary: he is not a solicitor, he is a public law official, technically impartial. Do not expect any advice from him.

4. Don't use an offshore company unless you are sure that it is the right thing for you: the notary or yourself may not understand the implications, but you can be sure that the taxation authorities will.

5. Don't get involved in tax evasion: the main beneficiary will be the seller, not you. 'Under the table' payments are a thing of the past and must be resisted. It is not a local tradition, it is tax evasion and it is against the law!

Top Tips courtesy of Hamptons' France office

# Spain

Spain is, and has been for many years, the most popular choice in the world for second-homers, and there are good reasons for this:

■ a wide choice of new, second-hand and old properties;

■ guaranteed sunshine in most parts of the country for much of the year;

■ easy access and cheap flights;

■ enclaves of expats who mingle only with each other and have as little to do with the Spanish as possible (mind, this puts some people off, but it attracts far more);

■ reasonably certain rental possibilities if in the right location;

■ an unsnobbish, welcoming attitude to incomers on the part of the Spanish that you don't find in every part of the world.

It is for these reasons that every year upwards of 60,000 Britons buy a property in Spain – more than in any other country. In 2006, around 750,000 British families owned property in Spain, as a holiday home, main home or – increasingly – as an investment. Over the past 20 years, property prices have grown faster in Spain than anywhere else in the world.

The overwhelming reason why second-homers choose Spain, though, is undoubtedly the weather. Many second-homers I spoke to said they loved France, and enjoyed driving through France on their way to their Spanish villas or apartments, but would not have a holiday home in France simply because of the unreliable weather.

Not all parts of Spain are warm all the year round, of course, but the further south you go, the better chance there is of year-round sun.

Nowadays, not all foreign buyers head for the famous costas. There are now nearly 210,000 foreign residents in Andalucia, of which the vast majority are British, and many are known disparagingly as the *por favores*, which means that in spite of living in Spain for maybe many years, they speak hardly any Spanish and show no signs whatever of integrating.

Many of the new migrants have come to Spain because of low property prices, in addition to the guaranteed sun, although water shortages have begun to be a problem with many new developments.

There are now 39 international airports in Spain and, although the emerging markets are starting to have a negative impact on price rises at the lower end of the market, the climate, accessibility and fantastic network of motorways combined with a huge continuing tourist industry – there were 50 million tourists in 2005 – still make it difficult to go wrong in Spain. Prices have risen by 48 per cent since 2004 generally, and although some areas, such as the Costa del Sol, have cooled off slightly, Spain remains one of the safest options for rental yields owing to the very well-established tourist industry.

Spain is, and always has been, the country for new developments, and the pace is hardly slacking, as ever more apartments and villas are being bought off-plan and paid for by instalments. Another advantage of buying off-plan is that any profit comes free of capital gains tax if the property is sold on before completion.

But whatever the problems might be, there is no sign of our love affair with Spain abating, and ever more UK citizens are heading for Spain – permanently. They will use the Spanish health system, their children will attend Spanish schools, and even if the parents find it difficult to integrate and learn the language, their children have no such problems.

Before the 1960s, very few people had ever been to Spain on holiday, or had ever considered going. But the concept of Spain being far away, unknowable and irredeemably foreign changed for ever with the advent of the cheap package holiday.

From the moment cheap flights began to be arranged to places like Benidorm, Marbella and Majorca – locations that have become almost joke destinations over the years – Spain started to throng with foreign holidaymakers. These early package tourists loved what they discovered – cheap booze, endless sun, guaranteed hot weather, no rain, the exotic appeal of being abroad for the same price as a fortnight at a cold, windy, rainy British resort – and they kept coming back for more.

By the early 1970s, the British, Dutch, Germans and Scandinavians had started to settle in Spain, mainly along the costas. The Spanish authorities didn't much mind, because all these tourists and lovely foreign money – even if some of it was ill-gotten gains – were enabling previously poverty-stricken Spain to become a modern, developed, affluent country.

But before long, tripping over itself in the Gadarene rush to accommodate the foreign tourists and settlers who were suddenly flocking to the country, Spain gained itself a bad reputation for nasty unfinished hotels, grim apartment blocks and hastily erected villas. One early visitor, surveying all the building sites, remarked: 'It will probably be nice when it's finished.'

But Spain never has been 'finished'. Although the authorities long ago stepped in to control the type and number of apartments going up to be sold to foreign buyers, there is still a lot of building going on in Spain, much of it heavily pushed at property fairs and exhibitions. Spain has always, at least to the snobbish or elitist traveller, seemed 'cheaper' and more downmarket than France.

But what is the reality?

Geoff Sadler's love affair with Spain goes back a long way – right back to 1962, when he bought his first apartment in Javea. Geoff, an artist and graphic designer, says:

This was right on the beach, and in those days there was nothing there except vineyards and orange groves. They were just starting to build holiday apartments there and blasting rock to put in fully grown palm trees. They were building a Parador, a state-run hotel, and I bought a flat in the second block to be built, on pure impulse.

The way it happened was the sort of thing sensible people advise you against these days. I had been with the family to France a couple of times, and to Spain, which we loved. We hadn't really thought about buying a place until we came back to England from one such holiday and saw an ad in the *Sunday Times*, where this property company offered to put you up in a hotel for a week to view properties being built.

This is common practice nowadays, but Geoff had never come across such an offer before:

I said to my wife: I'll go out there and have a look. When I got there I met this Spanish girl aged 21 who had just started an estate agency. She hardly spoke English and in those days I didn't speak Spanish, so we got on extremely well. I went up and down the coast with her, but Javea turned out to be the nicest place I saw. She showed me this four-bedroom flat with a vast L-shaped terrace, right on the beach, and I bought it on the spot for £4,500.

Back in England though I got horrible cold feet and managed to change my mind. I bought a cheaper flat in the same block for £3,500 and it all worked brilliantly. We drove out there every year until 1973 when I decided to sell it and build my own house nearby.

I bought some land in the mountains and had my own villa built. In those days access was difficult, but I always drove and we enjoyed the journey. We would spend about two months out there every summer, and two weeks at Christmas. If I had to get back to work, I used to fly back.

The main advantage of owning a home there, says Geoff, was that when his two sons were young, they were able to have much longer holidays than would have been possible otherwise. It is a remark made by many people who actually own foreign homes, rather than just renting them. Once there, you can stay as long as you like, just supposing nobody is coming to rent it and take it off you:

Holidays in hotels are not easy with small children but in Spain we had plenty of room and the boys loved it. Once you put out the initial outlay, you can have much longer, cheaper holidays than any other way. The villa cost me £7,500 altogether.

And once it was built, I hardly spent anything more on it until recently. At first we didn't have mains water, but facilities were laid on later.

Why Spain? 'I had always loved France,' says Geoff:

but for me Spain was the first place to present itself. Also in Spain the weather is incomparably better and there's no getting around that. At one time we considered moving there permanently, and took up Spanish residency for five years. They were crazy times, involving getting into the Spanish tax system, which was extremely bureaucratic. In the end, it was the complications of the tax system which prevented me from moving out there as a permanent resident. Technically, I'm not supposed to spend more than six months in the year in Spain, because of the tax laws.

But Geoff's story also illustrates what can happen to foreign property owners when they get old or infirm. Geoff's beautiful villa is very isolated, up a mountain track and not near any shops or public transport. This was absolutely fine when he was in good health but Geoff now suffers from macular degeneration and can no longer see well enough to drive.

This means that he can only visit his villa when one of his sons is able to drive him there, and then he is more or less stuck unless they are around to shop for provisions and to take him out and about. Although Geoff has decided to hang on to his villa for the time being – his two sons will inherit the property – he can no longer get to it on his own. This is something which has to be very much considered by anybody buying in another country, and very often, an aspect which is ignored or minimized.

The couple who had to watch their house being bulldozed to the ground were already in poor health, suffering from heart problems and arthritis, and many people who retire to Spain find that their health gives out after a few years.

The fact is that, eventually, everybody will need medical treatment in their old age, and although nobody ever likes to anticipate being in poor health, it is something which happens to us all eventually.

Geoff continues:

Although it is a good idea to have somebody to keep an eye on the place when you're not there, I have never had this luxury. I've been broken into once in 30 years, which I don't believe is bad. I've never attempted gardening there, as the place is very rough and wild, but just recently I put in a swimming pool, bowing to pressure from my now grown-up family. But I've never been in it once, myself.

Eileen Daniels has owned a villa near Mojácar, southern Spain, since 1973. She says:

My husband had recently died, and I didn't feel like going on holiday alone with my nine-year-old son. I just didn't fancy being with him alone in hotels or rented places, so I told him I would buy somewhere instead.

I already knew the north of Spain and, for me, the south was the only possibility. I love Italy, but my sister had lived in Positano for several years and I knew it had cold winters. I discovered that the part of Spain I liked didn't have cold winters, so I booked a flight with my son and we went out to have a look. I was sitting in a beach bar when I got talking to this American who said, 'I've got just the thing for you.'

We got into his jeep and went up a dirt track until we came to a valley, which looked like Shangri-La, full of orange and lemon groves. It was Easter, and the weather was very hot. I knew I didn't want to be in Mojácar itself, but we found this glorious place that was half-built.

I loved it so much because of the wonderful views, and felt I had to have it. At the time, water came from the reservoir and there was no electricity, but I couldn't wait to buy it even so. I started asking this American – with whom I'm still friendly – how I could pay, and I got it for £11,000, which was quite expensive in those days.

We had to wait for it to be finished, and it was everything we dreamt of. We still have it. Nowadays, buying and selling in Spain has become big business, but in those days it was easy, so long as you had the money. My husband had left me quite well off, so I could afford it. In the event, my son and I used to go twice a year and it was all very carefree, very happy.

> We would spend two weeks there at Easter, and two weeks in October. I would let the villa for August, and that money paid for the gardener and the maintenance. We never went in August ourselves, but the letting money paid for all the expenses, so although we didn't make anything, it became self-supporting.
>
> After Geoff was widowed, he met Eileen, and they have been together since 1982. But they retain their separate villas, which, they say, are not ideal for retirement because of their location. 'We really ought to sell them or join forces,' Geoff says. 'But every time the subject crops up, our sons look horrified. And the 21-year-old Spanish girl, now a grandmother, is still my agent out there.'
>
> Over the years, both Geoff and Eileen have bought other Spanish properties, as investments, and have enjoyed the experience. The country has altered dramatically, they say, since they first started going there. 'In the early days, Spain was a relatively poor, backward country,' remarks Geoff. 'But in recent years it has become affluent, with the result that the Spanish themselves are buying second homes in Spain. Also, the country is full of many nationalities – not just British, but all kinds of Northern Europeans and even French and Italians.'

And almost everybody gives, as their main reason for being in Spain, the weather. It is the one glorious natural asset the country possesses that few second-home destinations can equal or better – at least, within reasonable distance for other Europeans.

> Olive Braman has owned an old house in a Spanish village near Marbella since the early 1990s.
>
> Olive says:
>
> My house is in Frigiliana, a large Andalucian village. I think I chose Spain for a holiday home because I've always been attracted to the country, and visited it first in my youth. In those days it seemed a very mysterious country, wild and unknowable. It was also so very different from England.

Apart from that, my experiences of the Spaniards have all been very positive. To me, they are nicer than the French or British, who can be extremely judgemental of foreigners. In Spain, foreigners were welcomed from the start. I just think they're very nice people and that has certainly influenced my choice of a second-home destination. I have also thought for a long time that if I retired to anywhere outside England it would be Spain.

For me, the weather is of paramount importance. I hate English weather so much, and am convinced that for most people who live part or all of the year in Spain the weather is the main reason.

Most people who have bought places in France keep reiterating the need for fluency in the language before you can really enjoy the country, or get the most out of it. In Spain, that doesn't seem so much of a necessity. 'I speak very poor Spanish,' admits Olive, 'But I keep trying to improve.'

My present home is actually the second place I have bought in Spain. The first one was a very rustic farmhouse 25 miles from Benidorm. I had that for six or seven years, then realized it needed a lot of work and that I didn't have the time or energy it really needed.

I had friends who had built their own house and invited me to go and have a look. I saw this lovely old house, which is now mine. It has had problems of damp and leaks, but eventually I managed to dry it out.

Now that I am on the point of retirement, my intention is to spend at least two months at my Spanish place every winter. The winters are pleasant, not hot enough to sunbathe, and we are sometimes deluged by rain. But the winters are a far cry from the dreadful British winters. The air is wonderful and as I'm in a mountainous region the scenery is very beautiful as well. There are silver-green olive trees, avocado trees, and it can be breathtaking. I take wonderful walks across very wild land.

Olive travels in Spain by public transport:

It's cheap, punctual and easy, so much so that it's easy enough to manage without a car. From the airport I have to take three buses but I don't mind as I'm sitting in the sun and it's not wet or miserable. I do it in a relaxed way and don't get bad-tempered, as you would if you had to get three buses in England, plus humping your luggage on and off.

Olive has to pay local taxes on top of utility bills, and also a special Spanish tax levied on foreign home owners in case they rent their place out, which she does not. Every foreigner who has a home in Spain is liable for this tax, amounting to around £170 a year if the place is not rented, and there is no way of wriggling out of this payment, even if you have no intention whatever of letting out your apartment.

Interior designer Jane Cumberbatch and her husband Alastair ended up, like Geoff Sadler, building their own home in Sierra Morena, southern Spain, after they had failed to find anything that suited them. The Cumberbatches and their children now spend four months a year at their Spanish home and reckon it suits them perfectly.
Jane says:

We used to stay with an English family who did B and B, and we just kept coming back. I have always been drawn to the sun. We were in Spain celebrating our 10th wedding anniversary when we were offered a small farm with a tiny derelict hut on it. The asking price was £60,000 and, although I'm sure we could have haggled and got it for less, we wanted it so much we paid the asking price.

Then we set about building and creating the house we wanted. The one concession we made to modern living was to have Swedish underfloor heating, as the local houses are freezing in winter. Families huddle round the kitchen table wearing charcoal-fired foot warmers.

Here are Jane Cumberbatch's tips when building your own home or looking for properties:

▌ Make sure you have all necessary planning permissions, and talk to the council before starting to build.
▌ It may be better to use a local builder than a smart modern architect who can impose his own ideas on you.

> ▮ Old buildings may seem charming, but may need much reno-
> vation and can also be dark and vulnerable to prevailing winds.
> ▮ Many estate agents are now offering rural properties in Spain,
> but nothing beats driving round looking for 'For Sale' boards
> and talking to local people.
>
> (Interview in *Evening Standard*)

Note: both Jane Cumberbatch and Geoff Sadler, who you may remember also built his own house, are professional designers. If you do not have a strong design sense, it would probably be better to go for a home already built, or in the process of being built. Designing your own can lead to many problems if you don't really know what you are doing.

For those who are really brave, uninhibited and totally determined to develop an all-over tan, Spain now offers naturist enclaves and villages where it is possible to go without clothes when the weather permits. Indeed, on some Spanish naturist beaches, you are likely to be turned off if caught wearing anything.

France also has a number of naturist villages, most notably Cap d'Agde near Montpellier, but as with most of France the season is short and lasts at best from May to September. Outside these times, naturist resorts are closed.

Costa Natura, near Malaga, is a totally naturist development, with about 200 apartments owned and occupied year-round by nationals of many countries. Very many people have bought apartments there to retire to, but others continue to earn a living. One occupant works as a legal secretary in nearby Gibraltar, for instance – one wonders whether she has ever invited her colleagues back to dinner!

One British couple have owned a studio apartment at Costa Natura since the mid-1980s. As businesspeople, they do not want to be identified, but say: 'The kind of freedom we have here is unobtainable elsewhere. We usually come here in the spring, once it is hot enough to sunbathe, and rent the apartment out for the rest of the season. We never have any trouble getting completely full occupancy. Neither of our families know that we have a naturist apartment, nor do our friends.'

This is maybe not an option that would appeal to everybody, but for genuine sun worshippers who have lost all their inhibitions Spain is the place to be. At Vera Playa, near Mojácar, a naturist village of apartments is also rapidly being established. It has to be said that the vast majority of people who buy these apartments, of all nationalities, are elderly retired couples who, probably, feel they have nothing to lose by taking all their clothes off and indulging in a freedom not enjoyed since early childhood.

These apartments do rent out successfully, though, and most home owners rent their places for at least part of the year. In some enclaves, service and maintenance charges are quite high, which makes the possibility of renting even more attractive.

Hilary and Michèle Sadler have recently bought an apartment in Spain on a mortgage, with the initial intention of renting it out. Hilary is Geoff Sadler's son, and the many holidays he spent in Spain as a child and teenager gave him the confidence to proceed. Also, he speaks fluent Spanish, which he believes has made the whole transaction far easier than it would otherwise have been:

So far as I'm concerned, Spain is a personal thing. As I've been going to Spain regularly since I was one year old, Spain is not foreign to me. In fact, I feel more alien in the UK. Michèle was brought up in South Africa, where the scenery and weather are similar to Spain.

We feel that our eventual future lies in Spain, and that it was time to get a foothold in the country. Eventually we would like to move out there permanently, but at the moment I'm not certain of being able to generate enough income to make a living there.

When first considering buying into Spain, Hilary and Michèle did wonder whether they could earn a living out there. Michèle says:

We looked at B and Bs, campsites, but soon realized everything was going to be extremely hard work for very little financial return. On the other hand, most people who make real money out there seem to have done it through property.

For us, the sun is absolutely vital. We are sun people and as I'm from South Africa I pine for heat. Spain was an obvious choice as it has become an affluent country, and has so much to offer. We bought an apartment we could live in ourselves, but at the moment, its purpose is 100 per cent to let.

Hilary and Michèle already knew the area very well, and also have a pretty good idea of the kind of people who like to spend holidays there: 'We knew we needed to have a place with an infrastructure of a tourist industry if our apartment was going to let successfully, and Javea, near where my father has his villa, seemed ideal.'

They found the place by scouring local (British) papers, pestering local (Spanish) estate agents and making visits to research suitable properties. The apartment they finally bought was built in the early 1990s, has two bedrooms and can sleep six. 'We are 100 yards from the beach, and there are plenty of bars and restaurants in the area,' says Hilary. 'We looked at new developments miles away, but felt they were too far away from the beach to let easily.'

Their apartment cost £70,000, which they felt was quite expensive, and they obtained a 70 per cent euro mortgage. 'It was quite a high price,' admits Michèle, 'but at the same time it doesn't need any renovation. There is a huge pool, and communal gardens for which we pay a community charge. We've gone for a smart block of the type that would appeal to our friends. As it has to pay its way, we had to choose very carefully indeed.'

For Hilary, as a freelance graphic designer, it is seen as his pension: 'And even if we don't make a profit, at least other people will be paying our mortgage. We have worked out that if we can let it for the peak three months only the property will still pay for itself.'

The legalities, they found, were very easy indeed. As soon as the Sadlers had hit on the property they wanted, Hilary went to see a bank manager in Javea.

'You put yourself immediately several notches up if you speak the language,' he says.

Because I speak fluent Spanish, we've done everything in Spanish with a Spanish bank. I took four years' tax returns with me, and a reference from my accountant. I made sure I had all the relevant paperwork with me so that we could get a mortgage right away. It's not an official buy-to-let mortgage, and it is designated as a holiday home. When we are ready to buy our third place, we will set up a special Spanish business.

The local Spanish bank organized the survey and checked that there were no outstanding debts on the property. As in many other European countries, the purchaser inherits and is responsible for any unpaid accounts connected with the property. The British vendor of the apartment wanted 10 per cent of the deposit in sterling, which he got.

After making an offer, the next step was for the Spanish estate agent to contact a fiscal representative who met them in a bar with the *notario*, to deal with necessary paperwork and bureaucracy. It was necessary for the Sadlers to have a Spanish tax number. The whole transaction took one month and two journeys to the property to finalize.

They drew up a Spanish will – highly advisable when buying property in a country with different inheritance laws from your own.

The Sadlers bought their apartment fully furnished, which is quite common in Spain, but decided to refit the kitchen anyway. They also bought all new linen – 16 sets of sheets and pillowcases. 'We didn't want the fitted peach nylon that you tend to get in all Spanish rental apartments,' shudders Hilary. 'Once we had completed the deal, our estate agent put us in touch with a letting agent, and the property is now in her hands.'

What advice would the Sadlers pass on? Hilary says:

You need to look very carefully indeed before making such a major purchase as a home. I would advise spending at least two weeks there on holiday, at least, and look around, poking your nose in everything. Walk to the beach. See how long it takes, and use the bars and restaurants. Check out whether there is an English video library nearby – holidaymakers now love to watch videos, and may not take an apartment without this facility.

My own feeling is that self-catering is now becoming more popular than hotels. We are 40 miles from Benidorm, but there are no hotels or huge blocks in our area. We are one hour from Alicante, the nearest airport. All this kind of thing needs to be checked out.

Chris Stewart, author of the best-selling book *Driving Over Lemons*, has lived in Andalucia since the mid-1980s. He describes what he feels are the attractions of living in Spain:

First of all, there is a relaxed and flexible attitude towards work. Punctuality is emphatically not the same virtue as with Northern Europeans, and projects are rarely completed on time. Nothing will make the Spanish miss their siesta, and I have to say the siesta is one of the most beneficial and civilized institutions known to man. A couple of hours in the sack after lunch on a summer's day dramatically reduces the incidence of heart attacks, strokes and thromboses, stress-related diseases and dyspepsia.

If you live in a hot climate, you must adapt or your life becomes a misery. It's no good going to live in Spain or anywhere else and expecting to remain the same person you were back where you started. You must be a reed and bend with the wind. You learn new habits; your diet undergoes a change; you dress differently; you learn to express yourself in a new idiom, which gives you a new persona. And a new Spanish you is an exciting prospect.

There is a profound sense of mystery to the land which is baked into the landscape by the relentless summer sun. There's orange trees and jasmine and hot nights scented by Mediterranean pine. There's cool, clear sherry and fresh fish – and the simple pleasure of Spanish sunshine.

(*Daily Mail*, 20 January 2003)

# The process of buying

British people are often amazed at how quickly a Spanish home can be bought. Spanish people do not always use a solicitor, but rely totally on the notary public, who is involved in all property transactions in most European countries. The notary is not quite a solicitor but is there to ensure that Spanish property laws have been complied with.

Although Spanish property transactions tend to take place more quickly than those in the UK, they are also more expensive. The usual advice is that around 12 per cent of the purchase price should be set aside for legal and other costs and expenses. As well as the usual costs incurred when buying or selling a property in the UK, in Spain you have to add on the notary's fees, purchase tax charged at 6 to 7 per cent, and on development land 15 per cent VAT. Estate agents may take as much as 10 to 15 per cent, as opposed to around 2 per cent in the UK.

There is also ongoing paperwork. You have to complete a Spanish tax return each year, the amount being assessed on whether the property owner is classed as a resident. Anybody resident in Spain for more than six months in the year becomes liable for Spanish taxation on worldwide income and investments. Non-resident owners become liable for income tax if the property is rented out. Then there are local taxes to pay for sewage, roads and so on.

Under Spanish law, a purchaser may be asked to pay a preliminary deposit of between £2,000 and £4,000 to secure the property. Once the conveyancing process starts, the buyer should receive a copy of the vendor's title deed, and the seller must be registered as the owner in the Spanish land registry.

It may also be advisable, before doing anything irrevocable, to visit the local town hall to check out planning permission, unpaid local taxes or any other potential or actual problems.

In Spain, even more than France, a swimming pool is essential if you want to make money from rentals. Even if you're not interested in swimming yourself, most holidaymakers will be, and for children a holiday tends not to be a holiday unless they can splash about in a pool.

Also, it is important to note that in Spain, agents and developers tend to quote the built size of a property in squared metres together with the plot area if it is a villa.

Here is a cautionary tale (from the *Sunday Telegraph*, 2 November 2003). In 1999, Peter and Joyce Pickett decided to buy a retirement villa in Spain. They flew out on an inspection tour and saw a new development they liked, two miles inland from the resort of Torrevieja, 60 miles south of Benidorm.

They returned to the UK to think about it, decided to go ahead and paid a deposit of £2,000 to the agent. They chose a corner plot with views towards the sea where they could have a three-bedroom villa built. They then paid a second cheque into their solicitor's client account for £33,150 as the first instalment.

In February 2000 Peter Pickett returned to the development, and was horrified to discover that a house had been built right in front of their plot, obstructing the view. Peter made enquiries and discovered that the developer did not have planning permission, and there were also problems with water and electricity. Peter wanted out, but was threatened with legal action if he did not go ahead and complete the transaction.

'Because we had never bought abroad before, we were extremely stressed and also lost in a sea of terrifying paperwork and threats,' said Joyce. Then, tragically, Peter Pickett suffered a heart attack and died. Joyce went over herself to see what could be done, and told the lawyer it was all her fault. The female lawyer apologized and persuaded the builders to agree to return all her money if planning permission was not obtained by the end of the year.

Planning permission was not obtained by the cut-off date, and Joyce did get most of her money back, apart from the £2,000 non-returnable initial deposit. Joyce consulted FOPDAC, the Federation of Overseas Property Developers, Agents and Consultants, which helped her with the refund. She now blames the agent, based in the UK, for not carrying out the proper checks before allowing them to pay out so much money.

Adrian Medd of FOPDAC says, 'FOPDAC can intervene in such cases, but only if the agents concerned are members. There are now thousands of agents in the UK and Spain offering properties for sale, and you can't be too careful.'

## What do you want from your Spanish home?

There are wonderful villas and character houses inland, but on the coast you will have to have a modern type of home. Old houses can be romantic but they almost always need a lot of renovation and upkeep, all of which costs money.

Along the coast you will tend to meet the Costa Brits – plus the Costa Germans, Scandinavians, Dutch and Belgians. Because Spain has become such a very popular second-home destination, there are now whole complexes that have been taken over by these nationalities. If you like, you can choose somewhere totally British, with added sun.

If you prefer to go native, it's essential to head inland, where it may be difficult or even impossible to rent out your home for profit.

# Pure investment in Spain

Ever more people are buying properties in Spain purely for investment purposes, rather than as holiday homes to use for themselves. These are almost always people buying off-plan at property fairs and then hoping to net a considerable profit when they sell their now-completed and fully landscaped apartment or villa.

Although, as we saw earlier, Spain constitutes a 'primary market', this does not mean there are no risks involved in investing in this country. We have all by now heard of land grab, where the Spanish government appropriates your land for itself, but this is confined to certain areas. Make sure it is not your area!

Spain is popular with investors because it has so much to offer. Economic growth is continuing, there is a seemingly never-ending programme of building and development going on, there are very many cheap flights available, and also many sporting activities on offer. The climate is usually reliably hot, which is always a potent attraction. Spanish properties, of the right type to attract buyers, are still increasing in value at around 20 per cent a year.

Those considering an investment-only purchase in Spain should bear in mind location (of course!). The property has to be near airports, swimming pools and beaches, and have good road access. It is also essential to look at your potential investment from the point of view of a buyer. Is it well finished? Does it have damp – as many hastily erected Spanish properties do? What will it look like in five years' time? What are the service charges like? Are they liable to rise steeply when the development is finished?

Property developers point out that there is currently around 17 per cent growth per annum on properties in Spain, plus strong rental opportunities. But there are also ongoing running costs, local taxes and maintenance costs to bear in mind.

A word of warning: do not ever be tempted to go on a fly 'n' buy trip to Spain believing it to be a cheap holiday. Reps of the developers will not only meet you at the airport, they will stick to you at all times, and woe betide you if you try to sneak off for an afternoon on the beach. You will be summarily put on the next flight home, which you will have to pay for yourself. An inspection trip is just what it says, and you can expect high-pressure sales techniques from commission-hungry reps, who are often expats recruited for that very purpose.

Remember the cautionary tale of the naive buyer on a hard-sell inspection trip and be very aware that the whole purpose of these trips is to sell you something there and then, rather than to generously offer you a cut-price holiday. If you do plan to take advantage of an inspection trip to see a new development, bear in mind the following tips:

1. Make sure you go for an established, rather than a new or virgin, developer. Ask to look at other developments by the same company and also ask questions about how long the company has been in existence and how many units it has sold.
2. If buying for pure investment rather than for a holiday or retirement home, make sure there is an exit strategy – in other words, that the property has a good resale value. If the area cools off, is there still going to be a good market?
3. What other developments are planned for the area? Is it going to be a victim of that awful blight, overbuilding?
4. Are you buying the property at its true value or could you do a better deal? The expert advice is that you should always base your decision on professional, independent valuations and not just go by what the developers say. Always bear in mind that, when you are on an inspection trip, you are in their hands. They are making all the running and you are the passive consumer.
5. Of course, these strictures all apply to any off-plan development or inspection trip in any country, but such trips are far more common in Spain than other countries, where the

dreaded inspection trip has become a well-organized business in itself.

# Renting out your holiday home

A word on rentals: the Spanish market is completely different from the French market. Whereas holidaymakers renting in France tend to prefer old properties with some character, most tourists in Spain like brand-new apartments with satellite TV, DVD players, a kitchen full of new appliances and – essential – a terrace or balcony.

# Health and social security

It's important to know about your entitlements on the Spanish health service, especially if you are planning to live there permanently or retire there.

Retirement homes and developments are becoming extremely popular in Spain. They are available to those over 70, and they usually have medical and dental clinics within the complex, plus nursing care and shopping facilities. For these, there will be a monthly extra charge to pay.

Free health care is generally available to those who pay into Spanish social security. Otherwise, it's essential to have private health insurance, and if planning to live in Spain permanently you may not qualify for a resident's permit without it.

Very many people are now retiring to Spain for health reasons, and if this is what you are planning it's essential to check out hospital and medical facilities in your preferred area before making any irrevocable decisions.

According to a story in the *Daily Mail* in December 2006, Britons who move permanently to Spain, particularly if they are retirees, can if they are not very careful fall into a nasty health care black hole.

Many Britons retire to Spain – the most popular country for retirement – in the belief that, as EU citizens, they will be entitled to the same kind of health care they would receive back at home. But this is not always the case. They may be ineligible for medical treatment in Spain but too ill to qualify for full private insurance. In any case, they will not be entitled to free health care unless they make sure they fill in the right forms beforehand.

Christine and Ken Chiarello, for instance, took early retirement, moved to Murcia, the number one area for British people moving to Spain, and for two years everything was wonderful. As neither was in particularly good health – Christine suffers from rheumatoid arthritis and Ken had taken early retirement from work following a serious accident – they needed to know they would be looked after in Spain before deciding to move there permanently.

They were assured this would be the case and that, as soon as they had filled in an E121 form, they would be entitled to the same health care as a Spanish national. This form is only applicable if you are of UK pensionable age, which the Chiarellos were not, at the time of going. But before going, they made sure they filled in all the right forms, including those for taxation. They spent four weeks registering as Spanish citizens, as they had sold up their home in Milton Keynes and were not intending to return to the UK. They filled in an E106 form, which gives British citizens not of pensionable age who have moved to Spain 'residual care' on the Spanish health service for up to two years of living in Spain. It is complicated, but the actual length of time you are covered depends on your UK tax and NI contributions.

But when Ken became ill in early 2006, he was told at the surgery where he had already registered as a patient that he was not eligible for Spanish health service care and would have to find a private doctor, as his E106 had run out. In fact he would not qualify for free health care until he reached the age of 65, three years away at the time.

Christine and Ken found a private doctor, and tests confirmed he had prostate cancer, far worse than they had feared. But as they had been abroad for more than three months, they could not return to the UK for free treatment. Private insurers would not accept him either, as he was already ill, and the upshot was that the couple had to pay £10,000 out of their savings for initial treatment.

They regard themselves as lucky that they had the money to pay for treatment, although the eventual cost of the treatment will come to more than £10,000.

Sheila Tyrrell, who also moved to Murcia, from Bedfordshire, after taking early retirement in her 50s, suffered a brain haemorrhage and had good treatment on the Spanish health service through the E106, but once this runs out she will have no health cover until she becomes a pensioner at 60.

Retirees who are already of UK pensionable age should obtain an E121 form from the Department for Work and Pensions to transfer their health entitlement from the NHS to the Spanish system, as this allows a British pensioner to register for health on the same basis as a Spanish pensioner. Early retirees can get an E106 from the Department for Work and Pensions once in Spain, and this provides for free health care in Spain, funded by the UK, for a period of up to two years.

Although nobody expects to become seriously ill the minute they set foot on Spanish soil, it is sensible to prepare for all eventualities – especially if you are at or coming up to retirement and intend to settle in Spain permanently. There are reports that, in some popular retirement areas, the Spanish health services simply can't cope with the demand from elderly incomers.

If you are semi-resident in Spain, living there for, say, six months of the year, you should be aware that you can domicile your health care in one country only and would have to arrange private health insurance in the other country, informing the insurer of any pre-existing conditions.

Although there have been dark warnings about the Spanish property market being overheated causing the value of properties to plummet, in 2008 Spain is still by far the most popular place for Brits to buy holiday, investment or retirement homes.

It seems that, even with all the new and hopeful entrants vying with each other to attract foreign buyers, Spain remains the number one choice due to its mix of good weather, beautiful coastline (when not ruined by cheap developments of course) and rich culture. It is a combination that many people, and not just the British, but Germans, Scandinavians and Dutch, still find hard to beat.

There are big regional differences in property prices and of course all values are liable to fluctuate, but the property portal kyero.com gives a quarterly house price index. Barcelona is the most expensive, and Cordoba the cheapest.

# The Canaries

Anybody who insists on year-round sun above every other consideration will find they don't get it in Spain itself. The Canary Islands, which come under Spanish mainland law, are the only places where there is even a hope of year-round sun, and then it's not absolutely guaranteed. The Canaries are usually windy and can be overcast.

Most of the habitable islands have long been villa-ified by foreigners, who have gone there 100 per cent for the weather. Iris Murdoch's widower, John Bayley, now married to Audi Villiers, writes in his book *Iris* about Audi's home in Lanzarote: 'Lanzarote is a nice place if you avoid the beaches, which are black not only with lava, but with German and British tourists.'

Bayley also wonders how onions and garlic can grow there as it never rains. In the Canaries, water for washing and watering crops comes from desalination plants, which makes water a very expensive commodity indeed. As this water cannot be drunk, all residents have to rely on bottled water, which has to be lugged in very large, heavy plastic demijohns from the local supermarkets. And even the largest container of water that it's possible to buy lasts only a few days. The lack of water is a distinct drawback to enjoyable life in the Canaries; on the other hand, it's a wonderful treat for UK nationals not to have any rain.

Over the past two decades, the Canaries have earned themselves a reputation for being overdeveloped, and a mass of coastal concrete Costa-type high-rise monstrosities. Is this reputation justified today – or is it an outdated prejudice?

The *Lonely Planet Guide*, not known for being mealy-mouthed, has this to say about the seven inhabited Canary Islands:

> The Canaries are a seething mass of oiled flesh jiggling in the lap
> of the waves and to the beat of discos, bars and gay nightclubs.
> They offer the worst of mass tourism: concreted shorelines, tacky
> apartment block after tacky apartment block, and bars where you
> can pretend you've never left home.
>   It's not all mass tourism, though. Beyond the mega resorts you
> can still find tiny fishing villages, whitewashed hamlets perched
> on hilltops and even a few wild places within the dull roar of a
> volcano or with mist dripping through primeval forests. You
> certainly won't be treading where no-one has trod before, but The
> Canaries pack enough into seven islands to satisfy most tastes.

The overall capital is Las Palmas de Gran Canaria, and the major
industry (by far) is tourism. Apartments and villas, mainly
modern or new-build, are on sale in all the seven islands and
would suit a purchaser who needs constant dry heat; alternatively, if your major obsession is windsurfing, the Canaries could
fulfil your second-home dream. All the Canary Islands are of
volcanic origin, although most of the volcanoes were spent many
years ago, leaving lava fields that give a black appearance to many
of the islands.

Gran Canaria is the most developed of all the islands and has
many, many beaches. The southern tip, arid and desert-like, is,
even according to its official website, 'very touristy'. The northern
part is more humid and has green valleys, but there's nothing
much to do there.

Tenerife, the biggest of the seven islands, also has an arid,
sunny, dry south and more lush and humid north. Like Gran
Canaria, it has many, many beaches and is very built up. Tenerife,
by all accounts, is reinventing itself and trying to reverse its downmarket image of nasty high-rise flats and cheap package tours.

In recent years, the government has invested heavily in roads,
golf courses and marinas, all aimed at attracting a more upmarket
type of buyer. There are now trendy shopping precincts and five-
star hotels, and high-spec new developments are being built
around the island's many golf courses. A typical two-bedroom
high-spec apartment costs around 300,000 euros, while detached

and semi-detached villas within easy reach of top-quality golf courses are priced at around 600,000 euros – a far cry from the cheap flats of yesteryear.

La Palma is the most humid and luxuriously landscaped of all the islands, being green and full of woodlands. La Gomera, near the equator, has trade winds and cool currents. Its official website maintains that it has vast areas of 'wild beauty'.

Fuerteventura is one of the most interesting of the Canary Islands because it is vastly less developed than the others. Seeing how many parts of the other Canary Islands had been all but ruined by cheap concrete apartment blocks, the Spanish government stepped in to protect it from overdevelopment – just in time, according to some commentators. As a result, there are no high-rise Costa-type buildings, and the island has become a magnet for serious surfers and windsurfers.

There is virtually no rainfall at all in Fuerteventura, and there is almost always a strong wind: hence its name, which means 'windy island'. In the hot summer, the wind is strong enough to slam doors, and means that even in high summer the sea can be choppy. All domestic water on Fuerteventura is desalinated seawater. Apart from windsurfing, there is little to do on the island, but the villas and apartments are generally of a higher standard than in some of the Canaries.

By far the biggest attraction of the Canaries, for most settlers, is the dry heat. For this reason many Northern Europeans suffering from health conditions that respond to this type of climate obtain much relief and vastly better health. For serious watersport enthusiasts and those longing to escape from cold, wet, dark winters, the Canaries have much to offer.

There is also no real winter although, as with anywhere else in the world, good weather is not 100 per cent guaranteed. In order to decide whether the Canaries might be for you, it's important to ask whether you would enjoy being on an island rather than the mainland. Most of the islands are fairly small, and could be fully explored in a week or two.

All of the inhabitable islands of the Canaries are currently undergoing an ambitious development programme. You just choose your favourite island and you can be sure that you will find something to suit. The Canary Islands are categorized as the Zona Especial Canarias by the EU, which makes them a low-taxation area, with only 5 per cent VAT and 18 per cent capital gains tax to pay.

It is very easy for foreigners to obtain mortgages, so long as you can raise 50 per cent of the purchase price in cash.

### Pros and cons of buying a property in Spain

Pros:

■ cheap price of property compared to UK;

■ easy and cheap flights;

■ possible to drive there from UK;

■ wide choice of properties, from brand-new apartments to rural farmhouses;

■ friendly welcoming natives;

■ much English spoken;

■ good rental possibilities;

■ hot weather most of the year.

Cons:

■ a coastline all but ruined by cheap hotels and apartments;

■ many British enclaves;

■ original culture spoilt by half a century of foreign invasion;

■ little rain, therefore water tends to be expensive.

*Frequently Asked Questions*

Q. How much does it cost to buy a property in Spain?

A. Allow 10 per cent of the purchase price to cover stamp duty, land registration and legal fees.

Q. Can I get a mortgage?

A. Yes, most Spanish banks will lend up to 75 per cent of the valuation price to non-residents.

Q. Can I rent out my property?

A. Yes, long-term rentals should be no more than 11 months and short-term rentals can be weekly upwards. Seek professional advice.

Q. Should I get a survey?

A. Yes, it is possible to get a survey or homebuyers report by a UK-qualified chartered surveyor and we strongly recommend this.

Q. Is the property freehold or leasehold?

A. All residential properties are sold freehold in Spain.

Courtesy of Hamptons' Spain office

# 6 Portugal

After Spain and France, Portugal has become the third most popular European country for second-homers. Former DJ Chris Evans has a £2 million luxury complex in the Algarve, and the demand for luxury homes in the £1 million-plus bracket is increasing all the time. Many celebrities have bought expensive homes in the prized areas of Portugal, and this of course has pushed up the general price of a holiday or second home there.

What attracts second-homers to Portugal? For UK buyers, it's only a two-and-a-half-hour flight away, its climate is similar to Spain, but it hasn't been so spoilt by hasty, cheap overdevelopment and nasty hotels along the coast. Also, say contented second-home owners, there is a slower, more relaxed pace of life than in nearby Spain, which has become hectic, frenetic and competitive. It's as if Portugal hasn't quite caught up with Spain in terms of tourism and holiday homes, and has learnt some lessons about what not to do along the way. For some reason, Portugal remains more upmarket than Spain, although of course Spain has its £2 million villas, its luxury golf developments and its sports villages.

There is a British population in Portugal of about 200,000 people and the living costs are relatively low. Portugal also has the inestimable advantage, unique in Europe, of having no inheritance tax. Portugal is less well developed as a second-home destination than Spain, but big players such as Barclays Bank are currently investing heavily in this country.

Portugal, popularly known as 'Sportugal', is popular with sports fanatics. Golf there has become a huge industry, with villas backing on to championship golf courses being the most prized and expensive of all homes there. Private estates surrounded by championship golf courses are popular with expats, and in the 'golden triangle' of Quinta do Lago, Vale do Lobo and Vila Sol, all within an hour's drive of Faro airport, new villas go for over £1 million. In many of these new developments, around 90 per cent of the owners are British, which means you get a familiar way of life with added weather and year-round golf.

Obviously such developments are only going to be available to the super-rich, but many, many villa complexes are now being built by major construction companies and sold off-plan. A high proportion of these developments are being built with golf fanatics in mind – the present author had no idea how very popular golf was until she started researching this book – and these homes are sold along with life membership of a golf club and discount on green fees. If you hate golf, then this kind of second home, where golf is almost the sole reason for being there, would not appeal.

If interested in Portugal, you have to decide whether buying into a complex is an attractive way of life for you, or whether you would prefer the peace and quiet of an authentic Portuguese village. Prices are obviously lower the further inland and the further away from the golf developments you go, but at the same time they are harder work to find, buy, maintain and get to.

Mike Carr and his wife, Sam, moved out to Portugal permanently in 1999, although they had owned a villa there since 1995. Both former City workers, they became tired of the stress of their lives and longed for something simpler and more relaxed. Now, they say, they wouldn't go back to their former lives for anything. Although not earning the vast sums they could command in the City, they tick over reasonably comfortably and please themselves over what they do.

Mike has a word of advice for anybody seeking a simpler life in the sun: don't, if you can possibly help it, borrow money to achieve this dream. Instead, sell your UK home and buy for cash whenever possible. This is what he and his wife did, and he believes it delivers a worry-free life where you don't have to think about making the place pay through rental income to cover the mortgage.

Mike has moved to Portugal permanently, and cut all property ties with the UK. After working in the City for many years, he has become totally debt-averse and therefore, for him, it was more important to rid himself of all debt than to keep even a tiny toehold in the UK.

He explains how moving permanently to Portugal all came about:

I came out here in 1985 with the intention of buying a holiday villa, but ended up buying a plot of land instead, when the government suddenly became strict about what you could build.

I've been back and forth ever since, and have always loved Portugal. For me, being Irish, there is a certain similarity to Ireland, and so it feels familiar in a way. Portugal is smaller than Spain, rather like England and Ireland, and the Portuguese have a simpler way of life. For some reason, Spain has never appealed to me and I couldn't bear the thought of being somewhere like Benidorm, which seems full of dodgy people.

Luckily, Portugal doesn't have an equivalent of Benidorm and, although a potent magnet for tourists, has managed to retain an element of quality, which has been lost in much of the frenetic building programmes in Spain.

Another reason for choosing Portugal, so far as we were concerned, is that it's only a two-and-a-half-hour flight from the UK. Florida, for instance, is an eight-hour flight away, and I didn't fancy doing that four times a year when we were still working and maintaining our English home. But above all, it's a personal thing. Either you like France and that's your choice, or you like Spain or Italy. In our case, Portugal has retained a certain charm and is still a little bit behind in terms of development, although I have to say that is changing fast. It offers a slowness which is not common anywhere else in the world. And after our hectic lives in the City, getting up at half past five in order to be at our desks by seven, this slow pace is total bliss to us.

Choice of country is one's own call but, for us, there could be nowhere but Portugal.

I used to work in the stock market, and became keen to slow down. By 1998 I had bought two villas here, and thought to myself: maybe I can earn enough from renting out these two villas to give up my City job. My own feeling is that a career in the City has a definite time limit. Although it paid very well, it was no longer exciting, and I made a decision in September 2000 to sell my UK house and move out here permanently.

My wife is Finnish and, although coming from a cold country, appreciates the hotter weather here. It's around 20 degrees every day, and I can walk around in shorts for most of the year. Also, we now get up at 7.30 to 8, instead of 5.30.

We are in Carvoeiro, which is the mid-Algarve, and to my mind the perfect spot. We are close to the beach and in a good residential area. We eat and drink better and cheaper than in the UK, and friends who've come out here say I look 10 years younger.

Why does he recommend a debt-free life in the sun?

To me, this is the most important thing of all. Most people who buy places abroad do so on a mortgage, and they then have the continual worry of making it pay. Also, maybe they have another mortgage on their main home. To us, the debt-free way of securing our present life was to sell our home in Surrey, and I would recommend it as you have so few worries once the financial ones have gone.

When I got my first mortgage 20 years ago, I was told it was the best form of borrowing. And that may be true, so long as your job is 100 per cent safe. But when I got fired from my job in 1998 just after the stock market crash, I couldn't sell my house. Your life goes down the pan when you have debts you can't meet and I never want to be in that situation again. Stocks and shares go up and down but property comes up trumps most of the time, and in Portugal it's recently gone through the roof. Debt never goes away, but keeps reminding you of itself.

Mind, we're not sitting around here doing nothing. Since moving out here I have become a managing agent, and now manage six properties altogether. When we came here, we noticed that the places were not being well managed, with hedges not cut and so on. We felt we could do better, and this is what we now do. I also search properties for other people interested either in moving out here or buying a holiday home. I've now both established a business and I'm having a good time.

Economy-wise, Mike reckons Portugal has had a similar recent history to Ireland: 'The country was struggling, but it had money from Europe just like Ireland and because there is a thriving tourist industry now it is back on its feet. The euro has been great for Portugal. Two days after we got rid of the escudo and the euro was introduced, things were running as smoothly as ever.'

Those who have broken their links with the UK, as the Carrs have, must have private health insurance. The country's own health service does not have a high reputation, so insurance is necessary. Although nobody expects to become ill when in their paradise home, it does happen. At least with reliable private health insurance, that worry is also removed.

Getting to Portugal is now extremely easy. Flights have become cheap and highly competitive, with cut-price airlines such as easyJet offering extremely economical deals to Faro and Lisbon airports.

# Mortgages

For those not in the Carrs' position, or who are not debt-averse, to use the current phrase, mortgages on Portuguese property are arranged on exactly the same lines as those for Spain.

Many lenders insist that Portuguese properties must be bought through the medium of an offshore company. This is not some-thing the borrower has to worry about at all, as it is taken care of by the mortgage lender. So long as you satisfy the mortgage requirements, which are exactly the same as for Spain, you can borrow the money. As with most other European countries, mort-gages are available in either euros or sterling.

Mortgages are available on any kind of property, for up to 75 per cent of the property's value as estimated by the mortgage company's valuer.

In order to satisfy the lender's requirements as to your financial status, you will need to submit two recent utility bills giving proof of address; some form of photographic ID such as a copy of a passport; six months' bank statements; three months' payslips; budget planner; and latest mortgage statements for any current mortgages.

Additional information may be required on request, if the lenders are not satisfied with what is provided. Self-employed people would need to provide four years' worth of audited accounts.

Portugal would suit you if you like the idea of Spain but are put off by the massive urbanization programmes and building developments still going on all over the place. Portugal remains slightly classier and more upmarket than Spain, yet offers more or less everything that attracts people to Spain, such as wonderful weather (except for January and February, when it can be cold, windy and rainy and downright miserable), lovely beaches, beautiful inland scenery, easy and cheap flights, lots of fellow countrymen and women (if that's what you want), cheap wine and plenty of fresh vegetables.

So far as health care goes, Portugal has a national health service, but the general advice is: don't rely on it too much as it has a widespread reputation for inefficiency. For this reason, most foreign nationals prefer to use private health insurance, although British nationals are entitled to free emergency state medical cover, so long as they have filled out form E111, available from post offices.

Those who have retired to Portugal and are in receipt of a state pension are entitled to the same level of state health care as native Portuguese. Doctors are trained to the same standards as UK doctors, but tend to be far less efficient. Those relying on the state system should present their resident's permit, social security number and proof of address at the nearest local health centre, where they will be allocated a doctor.

In any case, it's a good idea to research health care provisions thoroughly before taking the plunge to move to Portugal, especially for those who are near retirement age or have existing health conditions.

## Pure investment in Portugal

Those considering investing in property in Portugal should pay close attention to the sporting facilities on offer in the chosen location, as this is perhaps the overwhelming reason for buying and renting in Portugal.

Golf is particularly popular and some developments offer discounted green fees, which may be important for people who play a lot. If considering investing, look for championship-quality golf courses, as Portugal tends to attract golfers who not only want to play year-round, but who are also discerning players rather than beginners.

There is always potential rental income from the property, particularly if you can attract sports obsessives. Most property experts believe that Portugal still has a long way to go, and that the huge developments now being built on the Algarve and in the Greater Lisbon area mean that property prices have nowhere reached their peak. Portugal expats also report that there are now many designer outlets in the country, making it an international shopping location.

# Madeira

Although Madeira has many charms, such as fertile volcanic soil, good weather year-round and beautiful scenery and plant life, it has only very recently become a second-home spot.

The island has not, for some reason, been as sought-after by second-homers as other parts of Portugal, but now at last, the place looks set to follow the Algarve, which has been phenomenally popular for many years.

Maybe, according to property developer Roger Still, Madeira's image has remained relatively downmarket, but this looks set to change as upmarket developments are being constructed in the Palheiro Village area.

Also, EU grants and other investment mean that there are new marinas being built, plus, as ever, golf courses – and much thought is being put into landscaping, so that the island can become an upmarket haven for those who feel that places like Cyprus and Spain are over-subscribed.

## Pros and cons of buying a property in Portugal

Pros:

- 'classier' than Spain – less spoilt by hasty overbuilding;
- a slower, more relaxed way of life than Spain;
- great emphasis on sports activities in second-home developments;
- beautiful countryside;
- easy and cheap flights;
- luxury hotels;
- less 'yobbish' element than Spain.

Cons:

- many all-British (plus Dutch, German, etc) enclaves;
- many artificial environments created by construction companies – emphasis on secure, gated, manicured developments;
- cold, rainy weather in January and February.

### Top Tips

1. Set yourself a realistic budget allowing for added purchase costs.

2. Contact a reputable estate agent preferably with offices at home and overseas and obtain as much information as possible from them about the different areas and prices.

3. Plan a property inspection visit via the agent who will guide you all the way.

4. Arrange a meeting during your visit with a reputable lawyer and arrange for him/her to have your powers of attorney to act for you in your absence.

5. Leave a 10 per cent deposit with your lawyer so he/she can exchange contracts once the searches are completed.

Top Tips courtesy of Hamptons' Portugal office

**Italy**

As with France, UK nationals who have decamped to Italy tend to become lyrical about the place. The sheer beauty of the country, the shimmering summer heat, the landscape, the art galleries, the architecture, the food, the music, the olive groves and vineyards, all provide their seductive, irresistible appeal. Italy seems especially magical to those used to cold grey weather, flat fields of potatoes and oilseed rape, grimy polluted towns and traffic-clogged motorways.

And as books such as Peter Mayle's *A Year in Provence* have beguiled readers with their descriptions of marvellous feasts, beautiful scenery and the funny antics of French foreigners, so sojourns in Italy have given rise to similar outpourings. One thinks of a book such as *Extra Virgin*, the best-selling account of innocents abroad in Italy, a land of surprising foreignness, it seems, if you try to live there and become one of them. And the appeal of the funny Italian foreigners can also be hard to resist, according to Annie Hawes, author of *Extra Virgin*. She went with her sister to Liguria for a vacation job, was offered a tumbledown shack for around £500, bought it on impulse and fell totally in love with the place and the people in spite of all their idiosyncrasies.

In fact, she loved it all so much that she was still there some 15 years later, although the tumbledown shack has moved on somewhat in terms of mod cons.

Rather like France, Italy has always seemed romantic and exotic to Northern Europeans. This has been the case from the time of Shakespeare and his contemporaries, who liked to set their plays in a kind of poetic, unreal Italy, probably because in those days it was safely very far away from most British people's direct experience.

Italy is the home of the Romans, the Renaissance, Catholicism, much great art and music, and wondrous cities and buildings. It

**IDealBox**
Italian Deal Box

IDealBox is a London-based company specialising
in exclusive investment opportunities, all in rigorously
selected locations in Italy

We offer:

1) Prestigious properties, such as villas and "palazzos"
   (prices from €800,000 to €8 million)

2) Development projects, ranging from boutique hotels
   to spas and golf clubs
   (prices from €5 million to €50 million)

With the majority of our properties enjoying exclusivity rights,
IDealBox can offer a truly unique investment opportunity

Check out our website at www.idealbox.co.uk or contact us
at info@idealbox.co.uk or phone at +44-(0)2070344482

IDealBox stands for Italian Deal Box: a 'box' offering exclusive business opportunities associated with the style, quality and passion of Italian people, as well as the beauty and appeal of the country.

Unfortunately, it is not always easy to buy and invest in foreign countries. The difficulties arise from cultural differences, language barriers, peculiarities of local administrative and legal systems, and different working practices. Perhaps, nowhere else is this true than in Italy and, as a consequence, these factors have to be taken into account. Unless potential buyers/investors have already gained a lot of experience through living and working in Italy, it becomes extremely difficult to deal with all these obstacles efficiently.

On the basis of these considerations, IDealBox was set up as a UK company with its headquarters in London. Its management is Italian and, therefore, well positioned to deal effectively and efficiently with local administrative authorities, building companies, notaries, surveyors, architects and the like, as well as the Italian real estate administrative system. Having had a long experience of living and working outside Italy, IDealBox staff know the different cultural and working practices of major European countries – more specifically, the ones pertaining to real estate – allowing them to effectively help clients achieve their objectives and fulfill their desires.

The properties IDealbox have to offer are of two types, each aimed at a specific group of buyers (sc. www.idealbox.co.uk). In the first category are properties such as villas and homes in the most beautiful parts of the Italian peninsula, properties designed on the basis of local architectural features and in harmony with local landscape. Typically, these are aimed at individuals looking for a prestigious second home where they can spend their holidays or retreat from the stresses of urban life. In some cases, these properties will be in need of renovation thus allowing buyers to become involved in the design and finish of their future homes.

Over time, IDealBox has gained trust from its several business partners and this is reflected in the exclusivity rights that most of IDealBox's properties enjoy: these homes are indeed unique and clients have an unrestricted freedom of choice.

The second category, named "projects" on our website, is aimed at professional investors, such as real estate funds, building companies and entrepreneurs. These are exclusive development projects in sought-after Italian locations. Normally, what is being sold is a plot of land together with planning permission granted by local authorities, in order to renovate existing buildings or develop new ones.

Typical projects include the following:

- Development of exclusive residential complexes, often with on-site leisure facilities such as hotels, golf clubs or spas.
- Restructuring of prestigious and historical properties, such as convents and castles, or upgrading of boutique hotels.

Thanks to direct relationships with sellers, IDealBox projects are often not available on the open market. This enables us to enjoy more personal relationships with our clients, work with them more efficiently, and assists us in delivering a first class service.

Even though IDealBox's real estate properties are, in general, rather expensive and, as such, not affordable to everyone, the team is willing to use its local network throughout Italy to help potential clients to identify those properties that best match their requirements and financial means.

In addition to real estate and property, Idealbox also works to constantly provide exclusive new business opportunities. Fervently scouting for small companies in sectors where Italy has a history of quality and excellence, such as fashion, textiles and food and wine production, Idealbox upholds its' reputation for providing a consistent, high quality service by considering and carefully selecting every deal on the basis of product quality, business profitability and value.

Idealbox is the ideal business partner for whoever shares this passion in Italy and a similar approach in doing business.

Idealbox Ltd
First floor, 27 Gloucester Place
London W1U 8HU
Tel: **+44 (0)20 7034 4482**
Fax: **+44 (0)20 7486 2589**
**www.idealbox.co.uk**
**info@idealbox.co.uk**

used to be said, 'See Rome and die' – in the days, probably, when very few people would have the chance to view Rome, Florence, Naples, Venice or Milan for themselves.

Italy has also been home to many expatriate poets, aesthetes and art historians. One thinks of Robert Browning and Elizabeth Barrett, who eloped one dark night to Italy and lived the rest of their lives there; of Keats and Shelley, who died there; of Harold Acton and his fabulous villa; and of US art critic Bernard Berenson and his famous Italian villa I Tatti. Many contemporary British novelists and writers have, famously, had second homes in Italy, most notably Tuscany, which has become known as Chiantishire for the number of UK nationals who have bought stone farmhouses or other desirable properties there for their long summer holidays. John Mortimer has even written a 'Tuscan novel', *Summer's Lease*, about the three months a year that successful British people spend in their Tuscan paradises.

John Mortimer believes that one of the main attractions of Italy – at least in the Tuscan region – is the fact that Italian cities, unlike those in the UK with their pedestrian precincts and edge-of-town supermarkets, have been allowed to remain intact. As such, they vibrate with ancient history and modern life, unlike our soulless concrete walkways and chain stores. Also, each city is very individual, every one quite unlike another.

The novelist Lisa St Aubin de Terán has made her home in Umbria, and Muriel Spark also lived in Italy for very many years. For centuries, Italy has been a natural home for artists, writers and all those in love with literature, music or painting.

In her book, *A Valley in Italy*, the story of acquiring and renovating an Umbrian dream house, Lisa St Aubin de Terán writes:

> I worshipped Italy as a pilgrim might worship Mecca from afar, determined some day to go there. As a girl, I had married for the chance to live in Italy. I can hardly remember a time when I wasn't in love with the idea of it. Sitting out on the Corso Vanucci, with the pastel pink and ivory Umbrian marble warming in the morning sun, surrounded by palatial banks and offices, with grey-green hills at one end and the great Medieval Fontana Maggiore at the other, I fell in love with Umbria.

Modern Italy may no longer be home to world-shattering philosophical, religious or esoteric movements, but it retains a world reputation for style, glamour, designer goods and chic. In fact, it could be said that *haute couture* has now moved from France to Italy, and world-famous designer names such as Versace, Armani, Ferragamo, Emilio Pucci are all Italian. Italian shoes and leather goods are also greatly prized, and Milan has in recent years become the fashion capital of the world, ousting Paris.

How important are any of these aspects to the second-home buyer? The cities, architecture, art galleries, scenery and designer goods can be appreciated during a holiday; there is no need to buy a permanent home there to take advantage of these. No, those seeking a second home in Italy are people for whom no other place will do, for whom no other country has the right level of magic, appeal, ambience, lifestyle, aura. You have to fall totally, utterly and passionately in love with Italy, as Lisa St Aubin de Terán did, to buy a home there, as it is an uphill struggle not recommended for the faint-hearted or for those who merely want a sunny place to spend their holidays. For people whose main requirement is for a little easy-care away-from-it-all bolthole, Italy would not represent the ideal destination.

Unlike France and Spain, Italy has, in spite of a vast influx of Northern Europeans since the 1960s, retained an aloof, elitist and upmarket air which can put off potential buyers, believing they have to have lots of money and/or be very arty or literary to be able to have a place in Italy. And there is certainly some truth in this belief.

Italy as a holiday destination is emphatically not associated with lager louts, karaoke nights, Irish pubs, drunken 18–30 carousers, unfinished hotels, cheap holiday developments or any of the other elements that, for extra-sensitive souls, have all but ruined countries such as Greece and Spain.

Most second-homers would, though, not choose Italy for its climate alone. As with France, weather can be uncertain and, although extremely hot in the south in summer, winters in all parts of Italy can be very cold indeed. Typical summer temperatures in degrees centigrade are: Rome, 24.1; Milan, 22.8; Naples, 23.5; Venice, 22.5; Pescara, 22.9. In winter these go down to:

Rome, 8.3; Milan, 2.5; Naples, 8.6; Venice, 3.6; Pescara, 7.2. Lisa St Aubin de Terán speaks of winter snows in Tuscany, and the 'arctic microclimate' of Siena in winter. Winters in romantic Umbria can be bitter, with frost, snow, blizzards and bitingly cold winds from December until March, at least. Although the sun continues to shine throughout the winter, most parts of Italy are at least as cold as in the UK, although maybe for a shorter part of the year. And certainly the spring, summer and early autumn have guaranteed good weather.

Nowhere in Italy guarantees winter warmth. In April, it can be snowing in Rome, and the temperature in Milan in early April is hardly likely to be much above freezing. In fact, it can be far colder in Milan in March than in London.

Also, many parts of the country are prone to earthquakes, flooding and, in the winter, dense fog. Snow and ice can also be hazards during the winter months in northern Italy. In the summer, there can be severe droughts and water shortages. Droughts are a constant problem in Italy, one of the prices paid for all that sunshine.

It is very pleasant to sit outside your Tuscan farmhouse or splash about in your Italian-tiled Tuscan pool in June, July and August, but the high season in Italy does not extend much beyond these three months. For most second-homers, their Italian house would probably be shut up in the winter, unless they are considering becoming permanent residents, which is a different matter altogether.

Most experts advise renting a place in Italy before deciding where or whether to buy, and doing research in a number of different places to see which, if any, exotic location appeals. Italy has a huge and thriving holiday rentals market, as a quick internet search will reveal. Also, Sunday newspapers are always full of private ads for holiday villas in the Tuscan 'golden triangle' of Italy.

I would advise anybody contemplating buying somewhere in Italy to read Barry Unsworth's brilliant novel *After Hannibal*, before they go. This short novel rips open the reality of moving to Italy and although exaggerated, or maybe dramatized, with some novelist's licence, probably eventually paints a more realistic picture of life there for expats than all the turgid guide books.

In this novel, an English couple who have relocated to Italy to save their relationship (some hopes) have to tussle with wily natives determined to wreck their dreams of paradise. The calculating lawyer advising the expats also has a continuous beady eye on all the money he's making from these innocents abroad. Unsworth, who himself lives in Italy, is well acquainted with all the multifarious ways in which Italians can make life difficult for incomers. A builder on the make continually rips off an innocent abroad American couple, with the result that their house eventually falls down.

Sebastian Cresswell-Turner, writing in the *Sunday Telegraph*, warns of Tuscan properties that might or might not be for sale, depending on who wants to buy them, and what sort of deal can be struck with the owners. Parts of many Italian estates, he says, have been altered illegally and without planning permission.

Although there is no actual shortage of properties available in Tuscany, many are not offered for sale on the open market. People with lots of money, or of 'high net worth' in the current phrase, can do complicated private deals with landowners, but picking your way through the tax, local council, legal, planning and ownership issues is not for the ordinary buyer, or the person of ordinary means.

The appeal of Spain is obvious: sun, sun and sun; and the appeal of France, at least for UK nationals, is also obvious: proximity, some level of familiarity and a language that is not too strange – most British people learn at least a smattering of French at school.

The appeal of Italy, for UK second-homers, is less clear. There is not a guaranteed climate, and it's further away and more difficult to get to, and more expensive to reach, than France. There are not the same number of apartments and villas on offer for foreigners as in Spain, Portugal or Greece, and in any case most people who buy homes in Italy are looking for something characterful, old, charming, Italianate, rather than an anonymous modern villa or apartment in a block.

Those who are less enamoured of the enduring romance of Italy tend to speak darkly of another side to the place – interminable bureaucracy, endless politicking, corruption built into the very fabric of society, incomprehensible tax systems, hundreds of petty rules and regulations to untangle and the impossibility of getting any repairs or renovations done.

So what's it really like to have a second home in this most romantic and artistic of countries? Italy has never attracted the huge influx of Northern Europeans who have flocked to France, nor has it lent itself to the innumerable second-home developments that have gone up all over Spain since the 1960s. There are no golf developments or sporting complexes for holidaymakers, no holiday parks or blocks of beach apartments. And yet there is, as there has been for centuries, a booming tourist industry.

It seems that most foreigners who have bought second homes in Italy are the rich or educated upper-middle-class people who do not have to worry overmuch about money. The Tuscan farmhouse has become a cliché, almost, for well-heeled foreigners, with the result that much Tuscan property has become very expensive indeed. Italy, unlike Spain, has not been subjected to cheap ribbon development along the coast – partly, it has to be said, because the weather is simply not as good or reliable as it is in Spain.

It is also more difficult for foreigners actually to buy property in Italy than in most other countries, for strange reasons that will be explained later in the chapter.

On the other hand, Italy has a buzz and an ambience that is unique, and if this tugs at your heartstrings then probably no other country will do. At one time, the food and wine were potent attractants. Nowadays of course it is possible to enjoy wonderful Italian meals in more or less any large British town. But Italian cuisine is, rightly, considered among the best in the world, and there is little to beat a superb Italian meal.

For those who live in Italy, or have second homes there, locally grown olive oil or wine, and exotic vegetables that have just been trundled down from the next village, are a huge advance on the British supermarket varieties. The Italian produce available in supermarkets or the nearest Italian restaurant most probably does not even begin to compare with the locally grown or locally prepared ingredients for taste and lusciousness.

If you fancy Italy as your first and only choice for a second home, this will probably be because you have already become totally passionate about the country. Maybe you have had wonderful holidays in Italy. Maybe the Italian way of life suits you. Perhaps you are fluent in the language. Perhaps you have studied Italian art or music. There are many good reasons for choosing Italy as your second-home destination – and some equally good reasons for avoiding this country, if it does not meet your holiday home requirements.

Firstly, there is the matter of the distance. Italy is further away than France and therefore less accessible for weekend or impulse visits. Although cheap flights are becoming increasingly available, it still takes much longer actually to get to Italy than to France. Secondly, the process of choosing, buying and renovating a home is vastly more difficult and expensive than it has now become in most European countries.

However, it appears that ever more British people are rising to the often expensive and difficult challenge of renovating a derelict or abandoned Italian villa, often situated in a deserted village long abandoned by the original native Italian population. There are around 340 such abandoned villages, and some Italian property companies are now working at selling off entire villages for development to foreign buyers.

One leading property company, Gruppo Norman, will negotiate the often complex ownership situation, ensure that the buildings in the villages are suitable for renovation and that, in fact, the village itself is suitable for being brought back to vibrant life. The main reason for these villages being abandoned in the past was poor communication with the rest of the country. It was mainly their sheer isolation that led the original inhabitants to find somewhere else to live.

As with much of the second-home business in Italy, the scheme is not that easy to operate, and James Price of international estate agents Knight Frank, believes there are many traps for the unwary: 'Local authorities are encouraging these restorations but at the same time, there are many rules on what you are allowed to do, and it could take four or five years to obtain planning permission. Also, these projects are not cheap and restorers are always upping their prices.'

One successful renovation of an entire Italian village is the development at Colletta di Castelbianco in Liguria, formerly completely derelict. It was bought by some young idealistic architects who restored the stone houses and narrow streets, with the addition of broadband, digital TV and other high-tech attractions. Lovers of Italy can buy into this restored village at prices starting at around £100,000. Details from www.collettadicastelbianco.com.

If you go to an overseas homes exhibition, you will almost certainly *not* come across a stand for new-build or off-plan Italian homes. You will probably even find that Italy is not represented at all. Spain, Portugal, Cyprus, Greece and Florida will be well represented, but not Italy. This is because Italy does not attract foreign investors or big property developers. And in foreign property, the big profits are in the off-plan bulk sales rather than one-off, expensive, customized, renovated farmhouses.

There are several reasons why big developers have avoided Italy. One is that many local councils are still controlled by Communists, who emphatically do not want gated, manicured, high-security golf developments on their wonderful farmland. Nor do they want foreigners, if at all possible. Their view is that farmland should stay farmland, and also remain in the hands of Italians rather than being used for the swimming pools and third bathrooms of fat-cat foreigners.

Local government in Italy is in any case in the hands of thousands of tiny little councils all at constant loggerheads with each other and all with their own ideas on planning and development. You might get planning permission from one council, for instance, yet be ordered to pull down an identical construction by the next-door council. Even the biggest construction companies in the world have found that the prospect of building second or holiday homes in Italy is too much of an uphill struggle for them to manage. So they go where the pickings are easier.

This is all great news for those who want something really individual, upmarket, expensive and hard to attain, but no good for second-homers who simply want to choose their sunny plot, their style of apartment and let the developers do the rest.

One small town in Italy may have nothing whatever to do with an identical small town a couple of miles away. All towns are mired in their own closed systems, and the kind of efficiency with which the British buy their homes (even if it doesn't always seem like that) is simply unknown to Italians. There is no common ground, and likely to be a total lack of communication between two different councils, should your plot of land fall in between the two authorities' jurisdictions.

For people who can cope with all this, the lack of efficiency and the eccentric rules and regulations can be part of Italy's charm. But if all you want is a simple second home in the sun, Italy cannot be a front runner.

You will also be lost without totally fluent Italian, or at the very least a handy bilingual friend to help you through the maze of bureaucracy associated with buying an Italian home.

Lorna and Trevor Roberts bought a small house in Umbria in 1998. The first problem was that under Italian law all documentation uses only the maiden name of the wife. As Lorna and Trevor bought the house in joint names, they wanted it to be in Lorna's married name, but no amount of arguing would persuade the notary to agree with this. As a result, the house is in Lorna's name, with that of her husband tagged on. And as Trevor could not speak Italian, it seems he had little choice but to go along with it.

Secondly, the estate agent involved in the purchase told them to anticipate a fee of 2 million lire – about £600. However, when the deal was being concluded, they discovered the fee had mysteriously gone up to 6 million lire. When Trevor tried to query this (in his non-existent Italian) the agent said they had better not complain, otherwise he would increase the bill even more. So they decided to cough up. This is just an example of what can happen in Italy for those foreigners rash enough to try to buy a home there. There is much dinner-party folklore about this kind of thing happening, and it seems it's not such an urban myth, after all.

What made Trevor and Lorna choose Italy? Trevor is Australian and Lorna is British. When Trevor retired from his job in Hong Kong, their first thought was to retire to Australia. But it proved impossible for Lorna to get Australian residency, so they sold their house there and thought about Europe.

'First of all,' says Trevor:

we looked around Portugal. But the mad driving, language problem and political uncertainties about the place put us off. I would have been happy to buy a place in Ireland, but it has become a land of immigrants rather than emigrants, and in any case house prices were far too high. Ditto the UK.

With Italy, we had the great advantage that Lorna spoke the language. Also, we already had an Italian friend there who was able to help us enormously over the purchase.

Trevor and Lorna bought a semi-detached house in a rural setting six kilometres from Gubbio. The house, which cost around £50,000, has three bedrooms, two bathrooms, kitchen, balconies and garden. Their other reason for choosing Italy was that their Italian friend, Piero Musini, was running a spiritual retreat centre, Casa Sangam, in Umbria, and asked Lorna and Trevor to help run it with him.

Trevor now says: 'Our service at the centre keeps us happily occupied, but those choosing to live here without any particular purpose in life might find there was not enough to interest them or satisfy their needs. Many Germans live in the area around us, and there are also very many British people.' Most, if not all, of the permanent foreign residents are retired people.

There has for a long time been a general feeling in Italy that second-home developments such as exist in Spain and Portugal would ruin this beautiful country. This means that it is almost impossible for incomers to buy a modern or even habitable flat or villa unless, like Trevor and Lorna, you have a handy Italian on hand to help you through the many problems and pitfalls. So for most people it's either the 17th-century Tuscan farmhouse or nothing. Mind, most of the kind of people who want an Italian second home would not want a modern villa or anonymous apartment in a faceless block.

When Lisa St Aubin de Terán and her third husband, artist Robbie Duff-Scott, bought their dream villa in Umbria it was almost a total ruin with two tractors, a combine harvester and a transport van rusting in the downstairs hall. However, with not enough money to buy the place and no idea where the money might come from, they put down a 20 per cent deposit and were given six months to pay the rest.

It's the kind of thing that can happen to people when in Italy: buy now; worry about paying later. But, as the author of *A Valley in*

*Italy* points out, it is a criminal offence in Italy to be overdrawn at the bank, with immediate penalties. As work progressed on St Aubin de Terán's expensive ruin, 'windfalls were all instantly signed over to them [the workmen], royalties and advances and all kinds of sales sank into that bottomless pit. I felt despair and elation mix with the truckloads of cement.'

The intricate bureaucracy surrounding every transaction in Italy, the armed guards at the bank and the impenetrability of the Italian banking system, to outsiders at least, added to the stress and strain of buying something that would, undoubtedly, be very beautiful when finished.

But was it worth it? For a writer, probably yes. Both St Aubin de Terán and Annie Hawes were able to extract mountains of copy from their experiences, enough to write entertaining books and maybe with the proceeds pay for some more plumbing or electrical work in the process. But buying a romantic ruin in Italy is not, as everybody who has done it attests, an easy task. Also, for St Aubin de Terán, writing her way out of debt did not come easy: 'Our debts were getting out of hand, and the bank at Città di Castello turned nasty. We borrowed money at inflationary rates and faced the fact that I would not be able to write my way out of my dilemma.'

Of course, wholly practical or prosaic people might snort that St Aubin de Terán's dilemma was totally self-imposed, and she could, if she wanted, have lived in a neat semi in Milton Keynes, and saved herself the time, trouble and effort of restoring an expensive Umbrian ruin. But, if Italy takes hold, Italy takes hold, and there is, it seems, no release, no alternative. For those who are passionate about Italy, it has to be Italy and no other place will do, however hard the struggle, however expensive the undertaking.

Marco and Deborah Vigni are a husband-and-wife team who search and renovate suitable Italian properties for second-homers, and guide their clients through each difficult process. Marco is a *geometra*, a peculiarly Italian profession that is a cross between an architect and a chartered surveyor. Without a *geometra* on your team, renovation can be a lifetime's work – and cost a lifetime's income. Even *with* a *geometra*, it's hardly likely to be cheap or quick.

'Buying property in Italy is expensive, partly because there is no standardization of doors, windows and so on,' says Deborah Vigni:

> If you are going to restore a house, it's likely to be a project for life, simply because the starting point is so bad. Planning permission is extremely difficult to obtain and takes for ever. Because every council has its own ideas, it's all too easy to get lost in a morass of paperwork, toing and froing, and plans that are initially approved then rejected for no reason that you can see.
>
> The initial reaction of local councils to building plans is to close up. They are extremely suspicious of foreigners wanting their smart second homes, and take the view that they want to have space for their farmers, not encourage even more tourists.
>
> Our company, Tuscany Now, specializes in restoration and renovation of old houses. About 97 per cent of people who want to buy a second home in Italy want an old house; hardly anybody is interested in a modern flat.
>
> Some books give the impression that you can go to Italy and buy a property for £50,000 as you can in some parts of France. But even if that was true once, it is almost impossible now. Tuscany is expensive and getting more expensive all the time. But Tuscany and Umbria are the most popular areas of Italy for second-homers, simply because they are the nicest parts of the country.

Naples can be cheap, but the main problem there is that there is no infrastructure or easy way to buy. All the fiscal and bureaucratic problems of central and northern Italy are multiplied tenfold in southern Italy, which is why very few foreigners venture to these parts for their second homes.

'Really you should only buy in Italy if no other country will do,' advises Deborah Vigni:

> If you are not hopelessly in love with Italy, don't do it, as it's far too difficult. Italy is popular because of its lifestyle and culture, and that's why it attracts upmarket people. If all you want is a sunny holiday, you are better off going somewhere else.

Unlike Spain, foreign companies are worried about investing in Italy. The political situation, the volatility of the government, the many political parties, all these factors put big developers off.

Italy remains a traditional country, a place where you can make your own organic olive oil from the olive trees on your land, or watch aubergines and tomatoes ripening by the minute. Annie Hawes points out, in *Extra Virgin*, that whereas in England gardeners have immense difficulty in persuading tomatoes to grow, even with the most intense loving care, in Italy the problem is to prevent them growing, as they seem to shoot up about a foot each night.

'Italy is the *crème de la crème* for second-homers,' points out Deborah Vigni. 'There are presently around 100,000 Britons in Chiantishire and all have come there for the culture, the way of life. They are there for the same reason that poets such as Shelley and Byron sought out Italy – for the Renaissance, the art galleries, the music, the food, the wine, the relaxed way of living.'

# New developments in Italy

Since the first edition of this book was published, the Italians have become slightly less snooty about new developments, and these are starting to be advertised in much the same way as those in Spain or Cyprus. Although Italy remains problematical in many ways, and the country will never be as welcoming to investment and tourism as Spain, for many its lure is irresistible.

The new developments presently being constructed are mainly in the Calabria region (not Tuscany, perish the thought!) and tend to be golf, ski and beach apartments. There are even golf apartments near Venice, and all along the coast front-line beach developments are being constructed.

Although Italy is beginning to succumb to the off-plan and new-build frenzy in line with the rest of Europe (and, it has to be said, the rest of the world which is fast beginning to look like one vast construction site) the main focus of interest for buyers remains in conversions and renovations, in old, character properties lavishly supplied with all mod cons without sacrificing the original features of the place.

For instance, a medieval castle in Campiglia Marittima in the Alta Maremma region is (at the time of writing) being converted into luxury apartments with an indoor pool. The developers are focusing on preserving the original character of the castle, and this is just one example of the many renovation and conversion projects being undertaken in the more attractive areas of Italy, with a view to attracting foreign investors.

With most of these properties, rental schemes are available to enable owners to gain an income from the place when they are not there, but these converted, upscale apartments are not cheap – in 2008 they start at around £350,000 – and there will also be a hefty annual maintenance charge on top of the purchase price.

Obviously, some areas are more expensive than others, with Tuscany coming out way on top as ever. Lombardy, which includes Lake Como, is slightly cheaper, and attracts walkers, cyclists and skiers, so again could be good for rental possibilities.

Other areas becoming popular with foreign buyers include Venice and the South Tyrol, Sicily and Sardinia, where prices can start from as little as 28,000 euros for an old mill in need of complete renovation. But – as all those who have undertaken renovation keep pointing out – the purchase price is only the start of a project which can easily eat up all your cash and more before it is finished.

# The process of buying

If you are interested in an old house, it will cost around £160,000 in Tuscany for a total wreck. The house may not even have a roof, and may well have been uninhabited for 60 years or more. St Aubin de Terán says in her book that she almost wouldn't look at any possible house that did have a roof; with a roof, an Italian villa didn't really count as a genuine ruin. Many such houses will not have basic services such as electricity or water, and these will have to be piped in.

The next stage, after you have chosen your noble ruin, will be to get together with a *geometra* who will draw up plans for restoration and renovation. Most of the houses will be totally uninhabitable when first bought. And don't expect the precise, detailed plans that you have come to expect from a British or US architect. The plans will be fluid, sketchy, maybe even drawn on the back of an old envelope.

The *geometra* will know what he is doing, although the customer might remain bewildered. At this stage it is essential to have somebody with you who is not only totally bilingual but also well versed in Italian technical building terms.

The plans have to be approved by the appropriate local council before you can proceed, otherwise you may be ordered to remove the construction. 'My parents, who bought a house in Italy over 20 years ago, wanted to raise the roof,' said Deborah Vigni. 'But this was completely forbidden by the local council, so it was back to the drawing board.'

Restoration is likely to come to around £350,000, making the total outlay something in the region of £500,000, which is a lot to pay for a second home. Renovation can also take around 10 years to complete if you attempt to do it yourself, because there is so much stop–start about it.

It is extremely difficult to get estimates out of Italian builders. They say they will let you have an estimate, and months later they haven't even started to think about your home. Nor are they likely to give the kind of detailed estimates that Anglo-Saxons are used to, when they do eventually get round to the stage of licking their pencils and sucking their teeth. You will be lucky to be given a vague estimate of what it's *probably* going to cost, which means that budgeting is almost impossible.

'There is no possibility of buying into Italy on the cheap,' says Deborah Vigni, 'at least if you want a real Italian home':

You are buying a customized villa, which is completely individual. There will not be another one like it in the whole of Italy. This is in direct contrast to somewhere like Florida where all the villas look exactly the same.

> There are no holiday complexes in Italy, so you are emphatically buying a second home, a proper home rather than a holiday home. You are buying into a funny, eccentric country, but most of all you are buying quality when you buy in Italy. You have to be in love with the place to overcome all the problems, and you have to be dedicated to restoring the house properly.
>
> Renovated farmhouses in Italy look stunning, but they take a lot of time and effort. In my view, Italy has a more refined taste than Spain: nicer ceramic tiles, nicer designs, a more beautiful finished product.

The actual legal process of purchasing a home in Italy is very similar to that in France. You will need a notary to make sure the preliminary agreement is what it says it is. In Italy, most purchasing problems occur from the preliminary contract. The notary could find that there is an old, unpaid mortgage or other debts, or that there is a right of way right through the middle of your villa.

With old properties, everything needs to be checked very carefully. It sometimes happens that two different sets of people are trying to buy exactly the same property, without either party knowing of this.

It is vital to employ a bilingual solicitor, preferably an Italian who is well versed in the labyrinthine Italian ways of doing things. The system seems extremely chaotic to Britons, but it's the time-honoured Latin method, and it works (up to a point) with the Italians.

Italy is a law unto itself when it comes to closing a property deal, although now that they have the euro the likelihood is that before long they will come into line with the rest of Europe. 'Italy has had to change and come in line to some extent already,' says Marco Vigni:

> For instance, 10 years ago you weren't allowed to have a swimming pool in many Tuscan homes. But most of our customers insist on a pool, especially if they are not near enough to the sea. Rental companies may well insist on a pool, as your lovely Tuscan villa will be virtually unlettable in the summer without one.

> The Communists controlling so many local councils impeded progress for very many years, and they have been a big part of the problem as regards foreigners buying farmhouses.

Generally speaking, it will cost more actually to buy a house in Italy than in the UK, because you need the services and expertise of two professionals without an exact equivalent in the UK: the notary (essential) and the *geometra* (advisable). Also, there may be a solicitor and estate agent to pay, plus the cost of a survey and valuation, on top of everything else. In fact, purchasing costs can come to around 20 per cent of the purchase price, by the time you've finished.

## Buy to let

Most people who buy half-million-pound Tuscan farmhouses will need to rent them out in order to make them pay. And this is where Italy really comes into its own. Although the rental markets in France and Florida can be tricky and not guaranteed – partly because there are just so many holiday homes and modern villas available to rent – the demand in Italy well outstrips supply.

The rentals in Italy are mainly restored farmhouses, rather than new villas or holiday apartments, and the most popular areas by far are Tuscany and Umbria. The summer rental market for Tuscan farmhouses is huge, because the properties are so delightful, and living in them is such a heady aesthetic experience. Then you have the landscape, the little villages, the home-made olive oil and home-grown wine, plus all the wonderful vegetables and herbs, right on your doorstep and as fresh as could be.

There is also the attraction for holidaymakers that you are embedded in a genuine environment, rather than one artificially created by construction companies.

'In Florida, the market is so saturated that you can hardly make any money from rentals,' says Deborah Vigni. 'My parents bought a villa in Florida mainly on the promise of good rental income, which they have not been able to get. They were promised 25 weeks of rental income a year, but have never managed to get anything like that. In Italy, by contrast, you can rent out your villa for 25 weeks in the year, easily.'

Although it is unlikely that anybody owning an expensive farmhouse would be able to make serious money from rentals, it is certainly possible to more than cover costs.

Suppose you spent a total of £500,000 on your ancient wreck, including renovation costs. You could expect to get around £40,000 a year in rental income, provided the villa has a swimming pool, four bedrooms and two bathrooms – which is what all US buyers and renters insist on. If you take out a mortgage for 10 years, this rental income will go a long way to covering your mortgage and running costs, and within a decade you will have yourself a handy investment.

Most developers selling new-build and off-plan holiday homes in other countries make the point that these homes cannot be considered as a financial investment. The more villas and apartments that are being built, the more likely your second home is to go *down* in value.

The exact opposite happens in Italy. Because Tuscany and Umbria are fast running out of medieval farmhouses and beautiful ruins, there is a definite limit to the supply. And because no more will ever be built, they will increase steadily in value. Unlike the London market, which is subject to huge upswings and downswings, in both owned and rental properties, the Tuscan market is steady, and remains impervious to economic upturns and downturns.

Also, Italians are now buying old Tuscan farmhouses for themselves, or as rental investments, now that they have seen what the foreigners are doing. All this is pushing prices up relentlessly.

If you decide to rent out your Italian villa through a recognized rental company, they may well insist that the property is available for certain weeks of the year. Should you want to use it yourself during high season, you will have to extract those two weeks or so for yourself. Many rental companies only operate during the summer, so it would be difficult, if not impossible, to rent out your villa in the winter.

Most Tuscan properties owned by foreigners are shut up in the winter, although it is essential to have somebody to keep an eye on the property when unoccupied. This is again something that has to be thought about, as most Italian farmhouses are fairly isolated from each other.

## Living and working

For incomers from EU member states, there should be no problems over residency. Obviously, if you intend to settle in Italy permanently, it is advisable to go to your local tax office to be apprised of your exact tax position, and which taxes you will be liable for in which country. Italy broadly follows the same pattern as regards tax, health care and social security for foreign nationals as Spain and France. There is a reciprocal tax arrangement in place, so that you will not have to pay tax in both countries.

The cost of living is vastly cheaper than in the UK; the usual estimate puts it at around 35 to 40 per cent cheaper. Italians maintain that their health service is superior to that of France, which is itself often considered to be the best in the world. Italy, even more than France, is a nation of hypochondriacs and every Italian's medicine chest is stuffed with all kinds of orthodox and alternative remedies.

Italy has many spas that offer both orthodox and complementary treatments. Italian doctors tend to be more holistic in their approach than UK doctors, and will tend to prescribe a mixture of standard and alternative treatments, particularly for chronic complaints such as arthritis and high blood pressure. There are very many doctors in Italy; some may say that the country is vastly over-doctored. Their plastic surgeons are among the best in the world, and much medical research carried out in Italian universities is right at the cutting edge.

The Italian medical profession, unlike its UK equivalent, is very much into looks and appearance, which they consider an integral part of standard health care. Italians do not consider a preoccupation with appearance frivolous, and incorporate it into their medical treatments. Massage, mud baths, anti-cellulite treatments and facials are as much a part of medical treatment as hypertension or angina pills.

Life in Italy is vastly more relaxed than in the UK, and two-hour lunches are not uncommon. Whilst workers are on a lunch break, do not expect the telephone to be answered. Lunch is far more important than work, which can be completed at any time, according to Italians.

There are now around 60,000 Britons living in Italy and, for the reasons given, it will never attract the massive numbers that Spain and Florida do. Nor is it an off-plan country. But it remains something special.

## Pure investment in Italy?

Not really. Although more websites are now offering new developments, golf apartments and villas that sound very similar to off-plan developments in other countries, Italy is not primarily an 'investment' country, and probably never will be. By far the great majority of Italian properties that are offered for sale are ancient and character buildings that need extensive renovation. Even 1960s houses in Italy probably require extensive renovation.

In August 2003, Cathy Rogers and Jason Gibb, former TV producers, bought a 1960s house in the Le Marche region for 210,000 euros and then spent another 150,000-plus euros on renovation.

It would probably not be sensible to buy even a modern property for pure profit, as renovation would take too long and be too expensive to make the effort worthwhile. Even the websites that are offering cheap Calabrian off-plan properties are not promoting them as investments, but as holiday or second homes, in contrast to Spain, where most websites advertising properties for sale now have an 'investment' section.

Raising the finance to buy your Italian dream should not be too difficult. Most people borrow against their UK property but you can also take out an Italian mortgage in euros, and this can work out cheaper than a sterling mortgage. Loans are usually available for up to 80 per cent of the purchase price of the property and there will also be Italian bank fees to pay. These usually work out at around 1 per cent of the sum borrowed.

There will also be costs for the mortgage valuation (in 2008 this is about £500) and stamp duty, which comes in at 11 per cent of an urban property or 17 per cent if buying agricultural land. And we complain about a maximum of 4 per cent in the UK!

Once you have agreed to buy a property, you have to sign a promise to buy known as a *compromesco*. This is a binding legal document on both parties, and obliges you to complete the purchase by a certain date. This document must be signed and witnessed by the local notary.

If you pull out of the deal at this stage you stand to lose your deposit, which could be as much as 30 per cent of the purchase price, so you need to be very sure about both the property and your ability to pay for and maintain it. When ownership is transferred from seller to buyer, a document known as the *rogito* comes into force.

And don't forget, as Lisa St Aubin de Terán has pointed out, that you cannot be overdrawn at an Italian bank without heavy penalties.

Fractional ownership is also becoming popular in Italy, and there are schemes whereby you can buy into a project for a set number of years, or for life. Estate agents Chesterton have details of such schemes.

## Pros and cons of buying a property in Italy

Pros:

■ beautiful country with fabulous food and wine;

■ unspoilt by over-development, cheap hotels, holiday parks;

■ upmarket appeal;

■ cheap and easy flights increasingly available;

■ excellent rental market;

■ no exclusive enclaves of British, German or Dutch second-homers;

■ no artificially created holiday communities;

■ art galleries, buildings, landscapes that are among the wonders of the world;

■ designer goods, chic shops;

■ heady, romantic appeal;

■ secure market – prices rising all the time;

■ good financial investment, at least in the long term.

Cons:

■ difficult and expensive to buy a home;

■ bitterly cold in winter;

■ daunting bureaucracy;

■ very important to be fluent in Italian, or have Italian friends to help out;

■ budgets tend to run away with you;

■ unhelpful, obstructive local councils.

# 8 Switzerland

Although very many celebrities, such as Roger Moore and former racing driver Jackie Stewart, own wonderful homes in Switzerland, and of course Charlie Chaplin famously lived there with his vast family, it is not easy for the ordinary person to buy a property in Switzerland, at least if this is for the purposes of a second, holiday or investment home. If you want to move permanently to Switzerland, and you hold a residential permit, that is a different matter.

Foreign ownership is very restricted and for good reasons, as the country has a stable, high-performing property market and an enviable lifestyle. Also, the country is quite small and the Swiss government wants to preserve its expensive, exclusive qualities. For these reasons, far more people would like to buy there than the country feels it has room for. However, although restrictions are still in place, the process has now become slightly easier, although Switzerland, it has to be said, very much favours the very rich or celebrity entrant over the ordinary, undistinguished buyer.

Before you can buy, you would need a special permit to purchase and the more popular the area, the longer the wait for the permit. Every canton has its own permit quota, and the time taken to process this permit varies greatly. In Vaud, for instance, 300 permits for foreign buyers are issued annually, and these are then split up between the various communes or subdivisions. The waiting time will depend on how long it takes for the commune of your potential property to use up its allocation.

The average wait is 12 to 18 months, but could be much longer.

However, Simon Malster of Investors in Property says that there are other, quicker ways to buy rather than go through the daunting process of waiting for a permit to come through. One way is to buy from another foreigner and take over their permit rather than waiting for yours to come through. Another possibility is to buy off-plan, where the chances are that your permit will have come through by the time the property is built. Investors in Property are selling off-plan apartments in Le Matin Calme, a new-build chalet development near Villars. But they are not cheap, with prices starting at £380,490 in 2008.

Another answer is to buy in a less popular area where there is lower demand and where permits are more likely to be available. The German-speaking Bernese Oberland or Italian-speaking Ticino have cheaper properties than those in the most desired areas, and if you go for a German-speaking canton, you would probably hardly have to wait for a permit at all.

But it has to be said that it is not legal in all areas for foreigners to buy in Switzerland, and in Geneva, Lausanne and Zurich, you would not be able to buy anything at all. An ancient Swiss law, the Lex Friedrich, now renamed the Lex Koller, restricts foreigners who do not hold a residential permit to buying properties in certain designated areas, although there have been reports that some Swiss nationals will offer to buy you an apartment in their name. This, however, is illegal and if you are caught the property will be confiscated and you will go to jail. In any case as a foreigner you would only be allowed to buy one property. It is not possible to amass an investment property portfolio in Switzerland as it is in some other countries.

If you buy a Swiss property as your main residence you would not be allowed to rent it out so, again, you would need to be rich to be able to afford the property year round, unless you are moving permanently to the country.

The buying process itself is similar to that in most European countries in that it has to be overseen by the notary public. First of all you would need to sign a binding document with the seller at the same time as paying a cash deposit, then request the government to issue a notice of confirmation that you can proceed with the purchase. Once this document is received, you pay the balance of the purchase price plus any taxes. The whole process is said to take less than two months, and mortgages are available, in this country famous for its financial institutions, for up to 80 per cent of the purchase price. There is also a 4 per cent stamp duty tax which you pay direct to the notary.

Buildings insurance is compulsory on all Swiss residential properties, and if you want to sell, this has to be to somebody who has the right to buy. If there is capital gains tax to pay, this comes in at around 18 per cent on the gain.

What about language problems? Switzerland has three languages, which are French, Italian and German, although English is widely spoken as well.

# Greece and Cyprus

## Greece

Greece and Cyprus have long been extremely popular as holiday resorts. Greece, along with Spain, was one of the first countries to welcome package holidaymakers, and as a result much of Greece's economy is now based more or less on tourism. And it's growing all the time as ever more people discover for themselves the glories that are still Greece.

At one time, it was extremely difficult to get to Greece unless you were an exceptionally dedicated and hardened traveller, but since the days when Freddie Laker opened up the country to ordinary people with his cheap flights the demand for cheap, easy access has grown and grown. Nowadays flights to Athens take three and a half hours from Heathrow, and many cut-price airlines have regular flights there.

So now that it's both easy and cheap to get to Greece, ever more Europeans are wanting to buy holiday homes there. Greece has for many years attracted new-age, hippy types, but as new developments are being built this ancient country is also fast becoming a holiday home magnet to rival France and Spain.

Vastly hotter than France, less built up than Spain, Greece still retains much of its traditional charm, even though big construction companies are now building luxury developments there. Although hot compared with most European countries, Greece is still in the northern hemisphere, which means it can be cold in winter.

The beautiful island of Corfu, for instance, is still very cold at Easter, far too cold for swimming or sunbathing, and you would have to put on a woolly jumper or fleece in the evenings. In the spring, Greece is very beautiful with carpets of wild flowers, but warm it ain't. Another problem connected with Greece is that the sea is full of huge jellyfish at certain times of the year, which can wrap themselves round you and cause, in some cases, serious skin problems.

As against that, there is nowhere more magical for snorkelling or just sitting on the beach, when weather permits, which it does for a far longer summer than in the UK.

There is also in Greece not only the language problem but also the alphabet difficulty, which can deter some people. Although it is true that English and German are now widely spoken in Greece, thanks to intensive tourism over the past half-century, the language still remains a mystery for most people. Also, modern Greek bears about as much relation to classical or ancient Greek as Anglo-Saxon bears to present-day English.

In Greece, there is a choice of two distinct types of property for second-homers. There are the old village homes, usually built of stone and in dire need of renovation, and the smart new developments, which are going up fast all over the place.

Whilst many, if not most, Greeks prefer the modern homes for themselves, having tired of crumbling cottages without sanitation or electricity, incomers tend to fall in love with the ancient stone cottages, many derelict or falling into ruin. The problem is that, although they are cheap to buy and can be had in some cases for as little as £10,000, the sky's the limit when it comes to renovation.

Modern villas and apartments are more expensive, although a brand-new townhouse can be bought for around £50,000. And, with any luck, it won't need to have anything done to it.

Greece, which for a long time lagged behind in the luxury new development department, has now entered the glossy brochure era with a vengeance, with a growing number of large construction companies offering new-build and off-plan villas and apartments to incomers.

As with Italy, if Greece beckons, nowhere else will do, and those who fall in love with the country would not dream of having a second home anywhere else. Remember that island locations tend to be more expensive than properties on the mainland, and that island prices are often inflated.

## The process of buying

Although property prices in Greece are generally cheap compared to the UK, there are many costs associated with purchase that can put up to 20 per cent on the cost of the transaction. The purchase of real estate in Greece broadly follows that of Spain and Portugal, where a notary is needed to make sure all the papers are in order and the property can actually be sold without encumbrances.

If buying an old house in Greece, the first thing to sort out is whether it belongs to several family members, rather than just one owner. If so, all these owners will have to be contacted and their permission obtained. This means that a lawyer well versed in Greek property matters will have to be instructed – it's no use leaving it to chance.

You also have to obtain a Greek tax number from the local tax office to satisfy the authorities that you do not owe any income tax in Greece. Buyers also have to pay a transfer tax levied on the size of the property.

As with buying property in all foreign countries, it is essential to have a Greek bank account, which must always be in credit. The lawyer's and notary's fees will amount to around 4 or 5 per cent of the purchase price of the property, and transfer taxes between 9 and 13 per cent, on average.

One problem with buying property in Greece is that there is no national land registry. This is in the process of being set up and will in future make property transactions far easier than before. To acquire a title to a property, a number of steps are required:

1. The purchaser must first secure copies of the title held by the vendor.
2. The purchaser must then instruct a lawyer to search the titles.
3. The purchaser or the vendor must approach a public notary who will work with the lawyers to draft the contract deed.

Once the contract deed is signed, filed at the notary's office and transferred at the Registry of Mortgages (as the municipal land registry is known), the document becomes the official title of the property.

The purchaser's lawyer must ensure that all property taxes have been paid and if the building is new or being bought off-plan that the required planning permission has been obtained.

Greece has, in common with many other countries, entered the euro age, which simplifies transactions considerably. But it is still extremely advisable, if not a necessity, to instruct a Greek-speaking lawyer to minimize any misunderstandings where there may be legal or real-estate jargon peculiar to Greece.

In some areas, non-EU nationals will require special permission by the relevant local council to purchase property. To quote a Greek pamphlet on the matter: 'this permission tends to be a formality for non-controversial nations'.

Greece has not been subject to the same level of development as, say, Spain, and the market is more fragmented. Most new properties in Greece are either individually built, or are part of a small complex of typically fewer than 10 units. You do not get the mass-development look that you might have to settle for in Spain or Florida, but by the same token, the second-home and holiday property market is far less streamlined and professional.

Agents in Greece tend to be very small and local, and websites are often not very helpful, either. There is also a perception among the Greeks that foreign buyers are all extremely rich and can pay anything that is asked. The expert advice is to do your homework and make sure you bargain and are prepared to negotiate. This, of course, might be difficult in a language like modern Greek, so it's essential to make sure you know what you are doing.

To give an example of what can now be bought in Greece, the Cybarco SA construction company has exclusive villas on the island of Rhodes, which now exists 100 per cent on tourism. These villas, all architect-designed, have two to three bedrooms, an optional swimming pool (highly recommended for all hot countries), balconies and terraces, all set in beautifully landscaped surroundings.

## Renting your property

Renting out your property in Greece is not quite the easy, laid-back business that may be imagined, as there is a lot of bureaucracy involved. The main thing is that if you are renting out your property to holidaymakers you will first need an EOT (Ellikinos Organismos Tourismou) licence from the Greek Tourist Office. These licences cost 5,000 euros, last for five years and are absolutely compulsory.

There are EOT offices in most towns, and before you even advertise your property to rent you have to put in an application for this licence. The next thing is that an official will come round and inspect your property to make sure it is up to required letting standards. If the property is not passed for renting you will be given a list of requirements to bring it up to scratch, all of which must be carried out before the licence is granted. All in all, the process can take many months to complete.

In the past, most people did not bother with an EOT licence but in recent years the government has clamped down heavily on holiday-home owners, with the result that without the licence you could face a heavy fine or even deportation. If you have a swimming pool, you will need an additional licence to 'operate' it and there are strict laws as to how wide or deep the swimming pool can be. Most of today's developers are fully cognisant with the EOT restrictions and will build to the required standard, but this may not be the case with older properties, so be warned if you are interested in buying an older villa. Note: you will need an EOT licence even if you are only intending to rent out your property to family members or friends, in fact whenever it is being occupied by anybody except the person whose name appears on the title deeds. The licence is not required, though, for longer-term lets, such as those for more than three months at a stretch. It is aimed purely at the holiday market.

The holiday season in Greece lasts from April to November and in 2008, the most popular holiday home is a three-bedroom villa with its own swimming pool. Apartments or villas which have community pools are much less popular and only command about half the rent of those with their own pool – something else to bear in mind if you are interested in pure investment in Greece.

# Cyprus

Increasingly, Britons are buying up holiday homes or retiring permanently to this island rich in mythology and archaeological interest.

Cyprus first came to the attention of the British public in a major way in 1925, when it became a British Crown Colony. In the 1950s Greek Cypriots, who made up 80 per cent of the population, sought union with Greece and guerillas (EOKA) attacked the British; nevertheless, very many British servicemen were posted to Cyprus, and considered it a 'dream posting'. Cyprus gained its independence in 1960, but the British kept service bases there, which they retain to this day. There are currently three service bases on Cyprus, two Army and one Air Force, all in the Greek part of the island.

On attaining independence, the island's constitution stated that a Greek Cypriot should be president, and a Turkish Cypriot vice-president. This move was designed to make the Turkish minority – then just 18 per cent of the population – feel secure and democratic. The popular Archbishop Makarios became president and Kukuk, a Turk, was elected vice-president. But after three years, unrest started to build up between the Greek and Turkish Cypriots, whereby the Turkish Cypriots withdrew into armed enclaves and set up a separate government.

In 1974 a coup was launched against Archbishop Makarios, and for the next few years Cyprus dominated the British press much as Bosnia, Kosovo and Afghanistan were to do later. Mainland Turkey invaded, and the Turkish army came to occupy 38 per cent of the island. This led to an effective partition of the island, which remains to this day, with the Greeks being concentrated in the south and the Turks in the north.

However, Cyprus enthusiasts maintain that this division, which runs through the middle of the capital, Nicosia, has not adversely affected either tourism or the economy. There is now much building development going on in the Greek part of Cyprus, aimed at attracting holiday-home buyers and retirees. Over the past few years, Cyprus has become an enormously popular location for second homes, holiday homes and even permanent homes, and its popularity is growing all the time. At a

Homes Overseas exhibition at Olympia in 2002 there were at least half a dozen stands promoting Cyprus as a first-choice holiday home destination, yet only one for Greece.

As incomers are not allowed to earn money in Cyprus, anybody who settles there has to satisfy the authorities that they have enough money to support themselves. It is currently the case that around 80 per cent of incomers are British, as the island has retained much 'Britishness' since the days of UK occupation.

In May 2004, Cyprus joined the EU, which brings it in line with other EU countries, and makes everything easier and more uniform, even if by doing so, the island inevitably loses some of its long-term British feel. But beware! Although Cyprus is now a member of the EU, it will not be fully harmonized into Europe until 2009.

At the time of writing (2008), a non-Cypriot is allowed to buy a flat, house or plot of land not exceeding 2,676 square metres. Written permission must also be obtained beforehand from the Council of Ministers. But the amount of permitted land is not a hard-and-fast rule and you may well be allowed to buy or own more than the law strictly states. But don't, warn Cyprus property experts, ever try to buy property or land without the requisite permissions being in place.

One good aspect of Cyprus is that all property, including apartment blocks, is freehold, so that you buy a flat in perpetuity in exactly the same way as a house. There is, though, a legally enforceable community statement in place, and eviction or repossession can occur for breaches of this statement. Service and maintenance charges apply on freehold flats in exactly the same way as on leasehold flats.

It is also important to bear in mind that, since accession to the EU, VAT is chargeable on all property purchases. Capital gains tax applies on selling, but there is no inheritance tax payable in Cyprus, which is very good news for buyers who want to retire there.

It is safe enough to buy property in Southern Cyprus, but it is still the case that some properties in Northern Cyprus have a disputed title. For the moment, the expert advice is that such purchases are best avoided.

Since Cyprus joined the EU, visitors have had freer access to the North and some are excited by the possibilities, considering that tourism in this part hardly exists as yet. The North, though, has a long way to go before it is completely integrated with the South.

Property experts warn that Cyprus's membership of the EU will inevitably cause property prices to rise, and encourage investors to move in. Some commentators have drawn attention to cowboy developers appearing on the island, knowing that people easily fall in love with Cyprus.

At the moment, around 90 per cent of foreign buyers in Cyprus are British. About 30,000 British expats have now settled permanently in Cyprus, and this figure is expected to rise sharply following membership of the EU. Cars drive on the left-hand side of the road, and road signs are in English as well as Greek. The legal and real-estate systems are all based on the British model, so for British second-homers Cyprus can seem less foreign than France, as well as much hotter, of course.

Now that Cyprus has entered the low-cost airline market with easyJet and Monarch flying there with cut-price fares, it is expected that both tourism and property purchases will increase sharply. It is always the case that buying properties as investments to rent out becomes more profitable when there is easy, cheap access to a country. Another plus is that now that Cyprus has adopted the euro, which currently represents 15 per cent of the world's GDP, its low interest and inflation rates will also boost property ownership by foreigners.

As a holiday home or retirement destination, Cyprus has much to offer. Its climate is warm most of the year and very hot in summer. The cost of living is extremely low, and residents say that it's possible to live well on an annual income of just £7,500 a year, which would certainly not be the case in the UK. One of the reasons for this, although not the only one, is that virtually nothing has to be spent on heating. Then food and wine are cheap, transport is cheap and restaurants are extremely cheap as well, compared to the UK.

Another attraction for holidaymakers is that most sports are available, plus walking and skiing in the mountains in winter, and watersports in summer. Watersports of all kinds – jet-skiing, water-skiing, snorkelling – are highly popular in both Greece and Cyprus.

Gloria Aubery first became enamoured of Cyprus when she visited it with her 14-year-old daughter who was on a school exchange visit with a family in Paphos. She says:

At the time we totally fell in love with Cyprus, and went again the following year. By that time we were in a position to buy a holiday home there, and we acquired a three-bedroom terraced townhouse in Paphos, which we kept for seven years. Then we looked for something bigger, and bought a villa in the village of Tala, a few miles out of town.

In Cyprus, says Gloria Aubery, it's not possible to buy a charming old house or cottage, as in France or even in Greece:

You can't buy a village house as locals rarely move, and in any case village houses stay in the same family for many generations. Everything an incomer can buy will be either new or second-hand, purchased from somebody British, and built most probably within the last 10 or 20 years.

Now that my two children are grown up, my husband and myself are divorced, and I have made my love of Cyprus my business by running Cyprus Property Services, which puts potential buyers in touch with builders and sellers.

There are currently four distinct markets of incomers in Cyprus. The first is for those seeking a holiday home. These people mainly go for the one- or two-bedroom apartments in a small complex. The second market is for the retirement home, where people go to live on the island as permanent residents. The third element is the growing second-home market, where buyers are seeking somewhere that is more than just a seasonal holiday home, but are not yet ready to retire, and the fourth is the growing number of 'jet-to-letters' who are looking for an investment property, rather than something to use themselves.

As it is not possible for incomers to work or earn a living on the island, all must have adequate finances to support themselves already, and this is carefully checked out before they are allowed to settle. As Cyprus is a fairly small island, the authorities do not want any unemployment, which could be a risk if incomers took jobs away from natives.

Although very few incomers speak Greek or Turkish, this is hardly a problem as English is a widely adopted second language.

People who are interested in retiring permanently in Cyprus must have an immigration permit issued by the Minister of the Interior of the Republic of Cyprus. Cars and household goods from other countries are allowed into the country, but left-hand-drive cars are allowed to circulate on the island for six months only. Petrol is extremely cheap, costing only a fraction of its price in the UK.

Tax would normally be paid in the UK. The former restrictions which allowed incomers to buy only one property have now been lifted in Southern Cyprus.

Mortgages are available on Cyprus properties on production of the usual documents. Obviously the authorities will have to be satisfied that there are sufficient funds for the loan to be paid back monthly by standing order.

Sheila and Neville Mantle retired permanently to Cyprus in 2000. Neville, a policeman, and Sheila, who worked in the British health service, decided to take early retirement when both were in their early 50s. They say they 'love every minute' of their life in Cyprus and have no plans to return to the UK to live.

Sheila says:

It all came about when we read an article about living permanently in Cyprus in the *Sunday Times*, one wet Sunday afternoon. We both read it and were very excited by the prospect. At the time, neither of us had thoughts of retiring early, although we were becoming very tired of the political situation at home.

After reading the article, we both kept a diary of reasons for going to Cyprus, listing all the pros and cons that we could think of. We asked ourselves what we would miss about life in the UK, and what we would gain if we took early retirement and went out there to live.

Sheila and Neville were already seasoned travellers, and had been to most places, so they were not exactly naive about abroad: 'We had already been to Greece many times, and Majorca many times, so we knew for a start that we liked the sun.'

They discovered that they would not be allowed to work or earn money in Cyprus, so had to work out very exact figures as to whether they could actually afford to spend the rest of their lives there without any extra money coming in. They thought about making an inspection visit to Cyprus, to which they had never previously been, but were worried about possible high-pressure sales techniques and their ability to resist them:

Then we were put in touch with Gloria and Tony, her then husband. Tony met us at the airport and showed us round a variety of sites. All of them were new developments, and most of the type where the builder won't start work on your house until the plot is sold to you. The development we liked was different from this in that the builder liked to start the work and then sell the property.

He preferred his clients to see something tangible, rather than just plans. The inspection trip lasted for two days; then for the rest of the fortnight we had a holiday, and a good look round.

Our first impressions of Cyprus were of friendliness and hospitality. There was also a very British feel to the place so that we felt comfortable from the start. And it didn't take either of us long to realize that this was the place we wanted to be. We had travelled all over the world, and felt more at home here than anywhere.

Neville and Sheila went back to the UK, where they made the momentous decision to sell their house. 'For us, it was not financially viable to keep two places going, especially if we were going to retire and live off our pensions,' Sheila says.

We also thought that if we didn't do it now, we never would. If we waited until we were in our sixties, we would probably feel that we were too old to uproot ourselves. In our early 50s, we were just young enough to do something as drastic as this. If it doesn't work out, we can pack our bags and go back – but somehow I don't think we will.

So what do they like about it?

The weather is wonderful. The winters are colder than we expected, but they only last two months at most and by March the temperature is in the mid-70s.

All our friends back in England ask us what we do all day. The domestic details, such as shopping and cleaning, take up some of the time. Then we belong to a walking group, we have our own swimming pool and we socialize all the time. We have good neighbours, have a wide circle of friends and are out most nights.

Cyprus is also a superb base for travel to other places. We've had a week in Dubai, which we would not have considered from the UK. Also, we have constant streams of visitors, friends and family members from the UK, which keeps us busy. Our former colleagues at work are amazed at what we've done. It's been the biggest upheaval of our lives, but why not?

The health care, says Sheila, is extremely good, although incomers must have private health insurance. Dental care is bang up to date, state of the art, and most modern operations and surgical procedures are available: 'We are aware that the island is divided, but this doesn't impinge on our lives at all. It seems likely that the Turks and Greeks will finally come together. We would certainly recommend it to anybody wanting somewhere hot, sunny, relaxing and also stimulating to retire.'

One thing that does concern the Mantles is whether the level of development will eventually replicate that of Spain: 'We didn't want to retire to Spain because in our view it's been ruined by the level of development. The water situation in Cyprus is also starting to worry us, because if the population increases by much more there simply won't be enough water for everybody.'

In common with most hot, dry, sunny countries popular with tourists and second-homers, there is always the threat of a water shortage. There are already desalination plants in Nicosia, and the government is closely monitoring the water situation in Paphos. Desalination plants mean that water rates are extremely expensive, and also that bottled water has to be constantly bought for drinking. This not only adds to the expense but also means you constantly have to hump huge jerrycans of water from the super-market to your home, and however huge and heavy the can it only lasts a few days.

But nothing is ever 100 per cent perfect. The Mantles say they have not started to worry about their health, but believe they will have to increase their private health insurance premiums as time goes on.

Writer Josephine Cox, author of more than 30 romantic novels, also enthuses over Paphos:

> There's a sense of timelessness about Cyprus, which takes hold of you and won't let you go. I ended up there by chance with my husband Ken for a holiday nine years ago. After four years of repeat visits we bought a little place in Paphos, on the west coast of the island. It's bliss. The best thing is the harbour. It's quaint and pretty and has a smattering of fish taverns, cafés and shopping bazaars. A short walk away is Tea for Two, where they do chips and cheese and pineapple toasties. You are always aware of the British connection on the island. Our military base is still there and they even drive on the left.
>
> If you're looking for rowdy nightlife, you'll be disappointed. But if you appreciate landscapes and beautiful views, Paphos is the place. It's a family resort with a lazy pace of life.
>
> (*Guardian*, 2 March 2002)

David and Liz Grandage bought their first holiday home in Cyprus in 1994. David, a former marketing director, describes how it came about:

> You could say it was serendipity, or Aphrodite, taking a hand in our fate. In 1994 I had a heart bypass operation, and promised my family that if I recovered I would raid the building society account and take them on the holiday of a lifetime. As we have five children, that was quite a commitment, but on recovery I decided to do it.
>
> We chose Turkey as an ideal destination, but there were some fundamentalist problems at the time and my wife became anxious. So we looked for somewhere else to go, and hit on Cyprus, which was not far away.
>
> Anyway, the seven of us went, and we absolutely loved the place. I loved the archaeology, the younger kids loved the discos, and my middle son loved the diving. There was something for everybody. My wife really enjoyed it as well, and when we came back we started thinking about having a holiday home there.

We got in touch with Gloria Aubery, and went on another visit, just my wife and myself this time. My middle son was by now studying geology at Manchester University, and asked if he could do his field studies in Cyprus. His tutors contacted Nicosia University, and the upshot was that he went there for six weeks.

Liz and I were approaching retirement, and thinking about having a bolthole in the sun anyway. We ended up buying a two-bed terrace house in a small complex. The house cost around £37,000 in 1995 and I spent my 60th birthday there, holding a big party for my family and all the neighbours in the development.

My eldest son fell in love with a Greek Cypriot girl whilst on this holiday and they ended up getting married, and spending two years in Cyprus. We now have a half-Cypriot granddaughter.

Over the years, the two-bed holiday home has become too small, so we are now having a much larger house with its own swimming pool built.

David says he has never once regretted his decision to buy a holiday home in Cyprus, and will be spending three or four months at a time in his new home. 'I would totally recommend it,' he says. 'Everybody has their own favourites, and we've travelled all over the world. When we went to Cyprus, it just gelled with us, and we have stayed in love with it for all these years.'

The 'British' element to the place was, David and Liz admit, part of the attraction:

English is the second language there, so it never felt foreign to us. We are trying to learn Greek, and finding it very difficult indeed. Our daughter-in-law speaks good English, but her parents speak about as much English as we speak Greek, so there's not much communication there.

We love the climate of Cyprus, and the actual buying of our homes has been completely hassle-free, compared with buying property in the UK. I just put down a deposit with my Visa card, and they trusted me to pay the rest. Also, although we never bought our first home with a view to its being an investment, it has actually gone up in value, and is now worth £60,000. So that's a bonus as well.

As Cyprus becomes ever more popular, the price of land will rise, so we feel that now, 2008, is a good time to buy. Certainly the cost of living is vastly lower than in the UK, and it's true that you can live well on around £7,000 a year. VAT, at 10 per cent, is also much lower than in the UK.

The remaining British service bases are, say the Grandages, very much like the last outposts of Empire, with policemen dressed as UK policemen, and a totally insular British way of life. That's also, they say, part of the strange attraction of this fairest isle.

## The process of buying

Buying a home in Cyprus is more or less the same as buying a home in the UK, although there are a number of bureaucratic steps to be taken to satisfy the authorities.

Non-Cypriots are permitted to buy an existing house or apartment, a house currently being built on a development site, or a plot of land for the sole purpose of erecting a residential home.

The first step is to secure permission from the Council of Ministers. This has to be by written application, after the agreement to purchase a property has been signed. Most developers assure potential purchasers that this permission is granted more or less as a matter of course; there is just the matter of ensuring that the purchaser has no intention of running a business from the property.

Otherwise, the process of buying a home is exactly the same as in the UK, whereby a solicitor must be instructed, and transfer of ownership from vendor to purchaser is made through the Cyprus Land Registry Office. Where the purchaser is a non-Cypriot, evidence of sufficient funds to buy the property must be produced. This can either be in cash or through a mortgage.

The title deed will then be issued in the name of the new buyer and recorded in the government archives. Stamp duty is payable on a sliding scale, as in the UK, and transfer fees of between 3 and 8 per cent of the purchase price are also payable to the relevant Land Registry Office.

Once the property has changed hands, there is an annual ownership tax levied by the government. Municipal authorities also levy an annual tax, depending on the value of the property. There may also be a sewage tax levied in some areas.

Capital gains tax will be payable when the property is sold; there is no inheritance tax. As the government is keen to encourage property sales to foreign buyers, there are plenty of safeguards to make sure that the investment is not at risk. Taxes are also low, compared to those in many countries.

Once the property has been transferred, owners have to pay for utilities such as water and electricity. Once that has all been done, and there is enough money in the kitty, life in Cyprus is easy, cheap and relaxing.

And hot. And dry.

Now that Cyprus is part of the EU, the government has decided to relax, to some extent, its formerly strict rules on property ownership by foreigners. As a result, property developers are sniffing around the most exclusive spots, with a view to marketing these as ideal holiday or second-home locations.

Beachfront properties in Cyprus are by far the most desirable, as well as being the most expensive. And the canniest developers are now targeting the richer second-home buyer, with a view to maintaining exclusivity and attracting those with high disposable income.

There remain many restrictions on development, which should ensure that Cyprus never becomes a second Spain. Cypriot properties cannot be built closer than 100 metres to the water's edge and height restrictions also apply, so the high-rise concrete block will never happen. It is not easy to obtain planning permission, so building density along the beachfront remains low.

As yet, though, Cypriot properties remain relatively cheap. They are, on average, 30 per cent less than Spain, 20 per cent less than Portugal and 50 per cent less than Italy. Because the market is relatively new, and has not yet fully matured, properties in Cyprus should represent a good investment.

Since January 2008, the currency has converted to the euro, making transactions even easier than before.

# Buy to let

It used to be the case that non-Cypriots could not be seen to make a business from renting out a Cyprus holiday home, as this might take valuable income away from nationals and out of the country.

However, the law has now changed so that non-residents are allowed to rent out properties for commercial gain, so long as they abide by the country's tax laws. Cyprus expert Chris Hill says: 'At one time, non-nationals couldn't be seen to be making money from property but now you can buy to let quite openly and without any restrictions.'

There remain, however, tight restrictions on how many properties non-nationals are allowed to own. The 'square metre' rule explained on page 186 applies to pure investors, although you are now allowed to overcome this by setting up a business in Cyprus. Chris Hill adds:

> Nowadays, non-nationals and non-residents can enjoy the same benefits as nationals. The government belatedly realized it was losing out by placing these restrictions on non-Cypriots and, as a result, around 60 per cent of people buying property in Southern Cyprus can be considered pure investors. There has been some overbuilding in Cyprus, and there are now some 3,700 builders operating in the South. These are of all types from tiny one-man operations to big international companies, so the investor has to be very sure when being offered what sound like wonderful deals.

There is still plenty of demand for the right product, but, if you are offered a guaranteed rental from a developer, because of the over-building in some areas and consequent lack of demand you must make absolutely sure that there is a genuine demand so that you will be able to rent out the property for the same kind of money when the guarantee period ends.

All the same strictures about renting apply in Greece and Cyprus as anywhere else: make sure you take all the money up front, and keep all bills and invoices relating to holiday lettings for the tax inspector. Although both Greece and Cyprus are fairly laid-back countries, it is not a good idea to be relaxed and casual about transient occupants of your lovely holiday home. And, as with any other holiday rental, the villa or apartment must be clean and smart, and have plenty of linen and all necessary appliances and utensils to appeal to the increasingly sophisticated self-catering holiday market.

## Pure investment in Southern and Northern Cyprus

There is currently a massive building and development programme going on in both Southern and Northern Cyprus, all aimed at the foreign investor.

Investors have usually been advised to buy in Southern, Greek, Cyprus rather than the Northern, Turkish part, although this is now starting to change and Northern Cyprus is rapidly becoming popular with foreign buyers as well.

In the past, investors were warned away from Northern Cyprus because it was assumed their title deeds were not safe, liable to be disputed, and their entire investment could be wiped out by Greek owners alleging that the property was, in fact, theirs.

A test case involving this exact scenario went to the British High Court in September 2006. Retired couple David and Linda Orams spent £160,000 buying land near Kyrenia in Northern Cyprus on which they built a villa and swimming pool in 2003.

Soon after completing this project, they were sued by Meletios Apostolides, a Greek Cypriot who maintained he had owned this land when Turkish forces invaded in 1974 and he was forced to flee south. One of the couple's lawyers in this high-profile case was Cherie Booth, the QC wife of Tony Blair. Three other expensive barristers were also involved.

What happened here was that in 2004, soon after Greek Cypriots were allowed to cross the island's ceasefire line patrolled by UN forces, Mr Apostolides travelled north and found the Oramses' house built on what he claimed later was his land. He took immediate action and won an order from the Nicosia district court ordering the couple to demolish their home and give him back the land.

But, as legal editor Joshua Rozenberg wrote in the *Daily Telegraph*, rulings by the Southern Cyprus courts are not recognized in the Turkish-occupied North, and so the indefatigable Mr Apostolides had the judgment registered in the High Court in London under an EU regulation governing foreign judgments.

Mr Justice Jack allowed the Oramses' appeal against that registration, after finding that EU law did not extend to Northern Cyprus. The upshot was that the judgment was set aside and the Oramses won the right to keep their holiday home, but the costs of the case amounted to £863,000, which Mr Apostolides has been ordered to pay.

After the case, Mrs Orams said: 'We are delighted that this judgment has been set aside. It has been very stressful for a large number of people in Northern Cyprus, both British people and Turkish Cypriots, and we hope that this judgment will mean that these people are safe to live in the Turkish Republic of Northern Cyprus.'

The results of this highly complicated case, added Joshua Rozenberg, will be welcomed by investors and others living in the Turkish-occupied North of the island.

There is speculation that this case has been funded for the Oramses by Turkish property developers and that Mr Apostolides in his turn was supported by Greek-Cypriot interests. In any event, it was a highly political as well as extremely expensive and convoluted case, and underlines the continuing hostility between South and North Cyprus.

Northern Cyprus does not have such a comprehensive Land Registry system as the South, so buyers must ensure that all necessary searches are carried out so that nobody can suddenly reclaim your land.

Northern Cyprus is now well represented at property shows and is being heavily marketed. Each year, there is greater representation of the North, which is marketed completely separately from the South and, usually, by different development companies.

Capital growth in Southern Cyprus has been between 15 and 20 per cent per annum in recent years and there are no immediate signs of this abating. Growth in the North could be even higher, although reliable figures are hard to obtain.

Since Southern Cyprus was admitted to the eurozone in 2008, interest rates have been reduced at the same time as 100 per cent mortgages have become available from some lenders. Demand for property continues to outstrip supply, and the signs are that fewer investors are now 'flipping' – that is, selling on an off-plan property before completion – but are holding on to their properties because of impressive rental yields, standing at the time of writing at 8 per cent. This has mainly happened because more cut-price airlines are now flying to Cyprus, increasing tourism. In the past, Cyprus was seen as an expensive and difficult holiday destination, but this is now all changing, which means that pure investment in Cyprus is looking good.

So far as buying in the North goes, the big plus is that property prices are cheaper there than anywhere else in the Mediterranean. Also, diplomatic sanctions and trade embargoes are set to be lifted and there is much euro investment in the infrastructure. However, investing in the Turkish North still remains riskier than buying property in the now totally EU-harmonized and very British South.

Although it is always possible to make a terrible mistake wherever you go, buying in Cyprus appears to represent a relatively safe investment, so long as reputable, well-established companies are used. The governments in both Southern and Northern Cyprus are keen to encourage foreign investors and, as such, make every effort to encourage such people to buy with confidence.

Just make sure every aspect of the investment, such as buying, selling, renting and the payment of local taxes and utilities is thoroughly understood beforehand – and that there is a ready sales market as well as buying market. In any area or country being heavily targeted by developers, there is always a risk that buyers will want brand-new properties, rather than those that are just a few years old and already showing signs of wear or beginning to look just a little old-fashioned.

The result of the Orams case should make investors slightly less nervous of investing or buying in Northern Cyprus, but it is still a risk and there is no guarantee that another such case will have the same result.

However, it has to be said that this is the only such case that has been brought, in spite of widespread fears that this would happen on a large scale once foreigners started to invest in Northern Cyprus.

For the time being the South and North parts of the island must be treated as completely different countries. Here is an overview of the current situation in the North at the time of writing (2008). Northern Cyprus experts warn that these details may be subject to sudden change, so here goes.

If you have a British passport with at least six months to run, you are allowed to enter Northern Cyprus. It has been said that if you have a stamp from Northern Cyprus in your passport you will not be allowed to enter Southern Cyprus, but there are no instances of this actually happening. Nationalities outside the EU may require a visa to enter Northern Cyprus. Up-to-date information can be obtained from the office of the Turkish Republic of Northern Cyprus in London (tel: 020 7631 1930).

The currency is the Turkish lira. In 2005, Turkey and Northern Cyprus issued the new Turkish lira, with a lot of zeros knocked off. Sterling, US dollars and even euros are welcome in most business outlets.

There are several places where you can cross the infamous Green Line, such as Famagusta, Ledra Palace and Mehetan in Nicosia. EU passport holders can enter the South with a valid passport but others will have to contact their own consulate.

There are strict limits to the amount of goods you can carry across the borders, and these include duty-attracting products such as cigarettes and alcohol, although you are allowed to do shopping and sightseeing. The country is officially Muslim, but is reported as being Muslim-lite, which means you can drink alcohol and sunbathe topless should you want to, and that women are treated in exactly the same way as men. Women are, for instance, allowed to drive cars, buy and inherit property and generally behave as full adult citizens.

Broadband, internet and British TV are now all available in Northern Cyprus. This has only happened recently and is an indication of how much the North is trying to encourage foreign investment. There are no restrictions on owning, letting or investing as in the South.

The usual advice when considering buying in Northern Cyprus is to appoint a lawyer well versed in Northern Cyprus laws and who is qualified to handle all the relevant applications regarding the purchase of real estate.

There is no doubt that a huge Northern Cyprus second-home industry is under way in this beautiful but complicated country, but there are no visible signs of Turkish occupation ceasing in the foreseeable future. The continuing Turkish occupation of the Northern part of the island is one of the main reasons why Turkey continues to be excluded from membership of the EU, which it would dearly like.

What is the answer? So far, nobody knows, although from a property point of view Northern Cyprus is becoming ever safer and more desirable as a place for property investment.

## Pros and cons of buying a property in Greece and Cyprus

Pros:

- beautiful, ancient countries with much of historical and archaeological interest;
- easy and cheap flights;
- cheap price of property;
- relaxed way of life;
- friendly natives;
- many sporting activities available;
- hot for most of the year;
- good rental markets;
- cheap food and wine.

Cons:

- many new developments continually under construction;
- at least three and a half hours away by air;
- incomers not allowed to work (Cyprus);
- certain yobbish holiday element in some parts of Greece;
- enclaves of foreigners;
- very many British (Cyprus);
- language problem.

# Malta and Gibraltar

## Malta

With their strategic position in the centre of the Mediterranean, the Maltese islands have had a chequered, and at times bloody, history. But now, peace and calm reign and, with no natural resources, the islands' main industry is tourism. Between 1 and 2 million tourists visit the islands each year for holidays, with the result that Malta is now being targeted as a desirable second-home location.

A former British colony, Malta gained its independence in 1969 and its last foreign naval base closed in 1979. But 150 years of British rule have left their mark, and Malta remains very 'British', albeit with traces of Moorish, Spanish, Islamic and French influences remaining in its culture.

For second- or holiday-home seekers, Malta has a lot to offer. It's easy for foreign nationals to buy a property there, the cost of living and taxation are low and there are reciprocal health agreements with the UK. (Remember the dramatic Siamese twins story, which led to a high court case when one had to be sacrificed to save the other? The parents of these twins came to the UK from Gozo, on a reciprocal arrangement.)

For sports enthusiasts, Malta and Gozo offer diving, yachting and all watersports. In addition, the islands are crime-free and safe, there are no religious or racial problems and the country is now politically stable. The weather is good, ice and snow are unknown, and the natives are extremely friendly and welcoming to foreign nationals buying real estate in their land.

The main language is English, although there is also an official Maltese language, which retains traces of Arabic.

## The process of buying

Once an offer has been made and accepted, a preliminary agreement, known as a 'convenium', is signed between the vendor and purchaser. This is a binding contract on both parties. In all cases, the agreements and contracts are written in English. Once the agreement has been signed, a 10 per cent deposit is lodged with the agent or notary public who acts as stakeholder. Should the purchaser pull out at this stage, the deposit will be forfeited in favour of the vendor.

Once the agreement has been signed, the notary public, acting on behalf of the purchaser, will carry out the researches and submit any necessary applications to the appropriate government departments. Once all this has been done, a deed of sale will be drawn up by the purchaser's notary. At this stage the balance of the purchase price, plus legal expenses and stamp duty, if applicable, will be paid.

There are a number of unavoidable expenses incurred when buying property in Malta: there is a 5 per cent duty on documents; notary fees of around 1 per cent of the purchase price; fees for searches and registration; plus a Ministry of Finance fee. All these expenses are borne by the purchaser. Non-Maltese purchasers must satisfy the Ministry of Finance that adequate funds are available to buy the property, and the property acquired must be for the owner's own use or for family members only.

If the property is to be let, or is bought as an investment, permission must be sought to rent out to third parties. Usually, this is a formality and, in practice, renting out properties is encouraged, as it increases tourism. Apartments and villas can be rented out as holiday lets or long lets, and there is a thriving rentals industry.

It is theoretically the case that property purchased by a non-national must be sold back to a Maltese. However, in many cases this has proved impossible to achieve, and so in reality this condition is almost always waived.

Generally, foreign nationals are allowed to buy only one property in Malta. Anybody wishing to buy a second property must sell the existing one first.

All types of property are available, from new apartments, town-houses and villas, to converted and unconverted character properties and farmhouses. However, non-Maltese may be refused permission to buy a property considered to be of historical interest. Mortgages are easily available to non-Maltese. Capital gains tax may be charged on the sale of the property. As with Cyprus, membership of the EU since 2004 has lifted former restrictions applying to incomers on property ownership and employment.

Average prices in Malta and Gozo are between £73,000 and £147,000, although you could pay up to £800,000 for a really swish Maltese coastal apartment. Malta has wonderful hotels, some with state-of-the-art spas and health clubs, and is rapidly upmarketing itself.

Malta is now being enthusiastically developed and marketed as an ideal second-home location or, indeed, somewhere to move to permanently. Malta is a non-aligned country, which means it no longer gets embroiled in political conflict, as in the past.

Because Malta has such a British feel, around 90 per cent of incomers are British, although there is no discrimination; all are welcome. Malta is considered to have one of the lowest costs of living in Europe, at the same time as life on the island is relatively sophisticated.

EU membership has already had a major impact on the property market in Malta, where a large number of upmarket marina developments have been offered for sale. Although the majority of purchases were for holiday homes, increasing numbers of British people are also now buying to take up permanent residence. It is with this market in mind that the swish new developments along the harbour have been designed.

Financially, moving to Malta could make a lot of sense. The 1988 Residence Scheme entitled people to remain in Malta with the freedom to come and go as they please. Alternatively, incomers may obtain an extended tourist permit which enables them to stay for longer than the three months allowed to an ordinary tourist. This permit is renewable at fixed periods, but all who wish to stay longer than three months must satisfy the government they have enough income or capital not to become a burden on the state.

Former *Daily Mirror* journalist Revel Barker explains why – and how – he came to live permanently in Gozo:

> I came out to a job in Gozo, Malta, in 1974, took a wrong turning, then stopped the hire car to check my bearings. Then I looked towards the sea and thought: 'Wow! That is a view!' I had always planned to retire early and I was already looking for likely places to live. I later returned to the same place for a holiday and confirmed my opinion of what I still think is the best view in the Mediterranean, in Europe, in the Northern hemisphere…
>
> I was intrigued by the people, who are so laid back they are practically horizontal, like the Irish with added sunshine. They are always delighted to hear you have a problem, not out of malice or mischief but because they know how to cure it, or at least, have a brother-in-law or neighbour who can fix it, and they love being helpful. After a time, you may get promoted from 'friend' to 'family' and perhaps you can do your bit to help somebody else. And I now live exactly at the spot where I stopped the car in 1974.

As to why he enjoys living on Gozo, Revel adds:

> There are two English language newspapers here and three on a Sunday, which clearly signifies that English is the joint official language along with Maltese, although there are no local news broadcasts in English.
>
> English is spoken, in varying degrees of fluency, everywhere, because of a relationship that dates back to 1800 when Nelson's navy was invited to remove Napoleon's forces.
>
> The post office pillar boxes are still red, there are blue lamps outside police stations and many people of a certain age swear they remember the Queen living in Malta as a Navy wife. Although there are moves to make their own nationality more dominant, their friendship with the UK is sincere. They do drive atrociously but in so far as they pick a side, they drive on the left.
>
> The mostly free health service is excellent as most doctors and surgeons are English trained. Where there are charges it's about half the price of the UK. The main thing that appeals is the friendliness of the locals and the excellent climate. It's

baking here in August and these are the two aspects that English expats rate most highly.

Gozo, says Revel, used to be one of the best-kept secrets of the Med. It is half an hour away from Malta on the ferry, and where the Maltese themselves go at weekends and for their summer holidays.

It is cleaner and greener than Malta itself and extremely safe. Teenage girls confidently hitch lifts home at the same time as their grannies are setting out for early Mass. There has been one car theft in living memory and even there the miscreant was caught before he reached the ferry and thrown straight into jail for breaking the island's previously unblemished record. The Gozitan residents proudly boast that they never lock their front doors or cars, but since the car theft incident they sometimes add 'except at weekends when the Maltese come over on the ferry'. But that may be a joke.

There is a flat tax rate of 15 per cent, although to qualify for that rate incomers must have a minimum annual income or proven capital. Before Malta joined the EU, this amounted to an income of 10,000 Maltese lire or capital of 150,000 Maltese lire. As membership of the EU progresses, these rates may well change to put them in line with other EU countries.

The financial capital does not have to be brought into Malta, but can remain in the native country. Another good aspect of living in Malta, at least for retirees, is that inheritance tax, a major bugbear in the UK, was abolished in 1992. However, there is a 5 per cent transfer tax on real estate at the time of death. In the case of a spouse dying, this amount is levied on half the value of the property.

There are restrictions on the work an incomer is allowed to do, and no foreigner is allowed to engage in business unless this is first authorized by the Maltese Government. Malta has signed tax treaties with most countries in Western Europe, also Canada and Australia. These agreements enable Maltese residents to claim back tax from the country where the income originates, and obtain double taxation relief from Malta.

Pets can be imported under the usual restrictions regarding rabies and quarantine; details regarding certificates and vaccinations can be obtained from the Government Veterinary Services, The Abattoir, Marsa, tel: 00356 244236.

You do not need to take another driving test if importing your car to Malta, or buying one there, and driving is on the left. But don't take the Maserati, as the top speed limit is 40 mph.

Medical services are excellent, with most hospital specialists having obtained their postgraduate qualifications in the UK. There are also excellent schools, I am told, in both the state and independent systems. Fees at private schools, day and boarding, are greatly less than the £20,000 or so a year top UK boarding establishments charge, and the system of education is closely aligned to the British model. Pupils take GCSE and A levels which qualify them for entrance to Malta University or to British universities.

Because Malta is such a very popular holiday destination, there is a thriving rentals market. There are no restrictions on letting property to foreigners, and most estate agents have well-established letting departments. Those wishing to set up a rental business in Malta must obtain permission and check that they are actually allowed to do this as, in common with other small countries, you are not allowed to take business away from a native Maltese.

When you want to sell your property, you will be subject to capital gains tax unless this has been your main place of residence for the past three years. In general, Malta is a relaxed, peaceful, sunny, law-abiding little country with vastly lower taxation than in the UK.

Malta also makes sense from the point of view of pure investment, as new developments are now being sold off-plan. Since 2004, there has been a dramatic increase in the number of foreigners buying for investment, and this has caused property price rises to increase from 8 per cent a year to between 12 and 15 per cent a year.

Buying to let is also greatly on the increase, and here gross yields work out at between 4 and 5 per cent. Malta has good weather, year-round, and an attractive apartment can command at least a 60 per cent annual occupancy. Farmhouses in Gozo and the new harbourside apartments are particularly popular with renters.

Since 2004, the sole restriction remaining for EU nationals is that only one property can be bought for holiday purposes.

# Gibraltar

Gibraltar is a weird place. You access it by walking over a causeway on the southern tip of Spain and immediately enter a world like no other. In some ways, you feel you are entering a provincial British town, as the shops, currency, people and atmosphere all feel extremely familiar. To complete the provincial picture, there are many rather grim high-rise 1960s apartment blocks dotted around the place and spoiling the view.

Yet it's not quite like Harrogate or Bath, because on every street corner there stands a bad statue of a soldier, reminding the visitor of Gibraltar's overwhelmingly military history. Also, the entire rock has been tunnelled out for fortification purposes. Tours of these tunnels are available for visitors. Plus, the climate is Southern Mediterranean. So, it's a strange hybrid of a place.

Gibraltar remains a British Crown Colony, although it has had self-government for over 30 years. It is a tax and climatic haven, and in recent times has been targeted by property developers with the result that many luxury apartments, villas and complexes are now becoming available in the formerly rather dreary Gibraltarian interior.

The history of the Rock is entirely shaped by its strategic position; conquests have been attempted, and in some cases achieved, by many marauding hordes of the past. In its earliest history it was occupied by Romans, who coined the phrase *ne plus ultra* ('go beyond at your peril') to refer to those enemies who might dare to go beyond the Rock.

Later, the Rock was under Moorish occupation, and was reconquered by Spain in 1462. Gibraltar remained under Spanish occupation until the early 18th century, when Anglo-Dutch forces claimed it. This culminated in the famous, or notorious, Treaty of Utrecht in 1713, when Gibraltar was handed to the British 'for ever'.

During the 19th century, Gibraltar was heavily fortified, resulting in the phrase, 'as safe as the Rock of Gibraltar'. The Rock played a key role in anti-submarine campaigns during the First and Second World Wars, and was awarded self-government in 1969.

Logically, Gibraltar should belong to Spain, yet it remains a strange, anachronistic outpost of Empire. The Spanish have never quite given up their struggle for Gibraltar to become part of Spain, and yet, so far, it has not happened.

As Gibraltar remains a British colony, it is easy enough for British nationals to buy property on the Rock. Also, many British people living in southern Spain cross over the border to work for Gibraltarian companies. The advantages of Gibraltar – population around 30,000 – are its weather, its physical connection with Spain and its very British shops, currency and way of life.

In recent years, the property market in Gibraltar has been thriving, in spite of the ongoing political struggles between Britain, Spain and the native Gibraltarians. International companies are taking advantage of the tax incentives and buying properties on the Rock. Because available land is restricted, most of the new properties being built are apartments.

## Pros and cons of buying a property in Malta and Gibraltar

Pros:

▌ easy and cheap flights;

▌ a very 'British' feel about both;

▌ good weather;

▌ in Malta, large choice of properties – old, new, villas, apartments;

▌ not too 'foreign';

▌ easily obtained mortgages and finance;

▌ relaxed feel about both;

▌ sense of history about both.

Cons:

▌ none, really – if this is what you want.

# 11 Cape Verde

Cape Verde consists of 10 islands, each with its own distinctive features, and is situated 400 miles off the West Coast of Africa, so in a way it is a somewhat similar destination to the Canaries – but much more upmarket, as it is a newer entrant to the tourist and holiday homes market, and is trying to avoid the cheap developments which have spoilt much of the Canaries. The inhabited islands are Sal, Boa Vista, Sao Nicolau, Santo Antao, Sao Vicente, Maio, Santiago, Fogo and Brava. Santa Luzia, the 10th island, is a nature reserve and at the moment uninhabited.

The islands making up Cape Verde have a complicated history, although all now seems to be sorted out and there is now a stable, independent government which is focusing heavily on tourism and property investment. There are few other industries there.

Cape Verde was first seized by the Portuguese in 1462 when they arrived on Santiago and started to trade in slaves. This was very lucrative for a time but, when the slave trade ended, the islands severely declined in prosperity. There is no actual indigenous population, but the inhabitants, consisting of people of mainly mixed African and European descent, finally gained independence from Portugal in 1975 after a massive struggle.

Now, Sal is the main tourist island with 10,000 inhabitants. It very much has a Caribbean feel and is concentrating on property developments for investment and retirement purposes.

In 2005, London estate agent Paul Akwei decided to emigrate to Cape Verde and has established his own agency, Noscasa, there. Paul is very enthusiastic about the 10 Cape Verde islands, and says:

The big attraction is the weather, which is constant throughout the year, at around 24 degrees. It hardly ever rains and there are lots of restaurants here with no roof. And since the first direct flights became available in 2006, tourism and investment has grown very fast indeed. Because there is so little rainfall, all the water comes from desalination plants.

Each of the islands is different. Some have miles of white beaches whereas others are greener and lusher. The beachy islands have a lot of Italian influence and many Italian restaurants. Golf courses are being built and golf here is huge. So many people are obsessed, and Cape Verde is definitely catering for this obsession.

There are two main property types to choose from, the old colonial-style buildings which usually need total renovation, and the brand-new villas and apartments. Paul Akwei set up his estate agency because he foresaw Cape Verde becoming a big market for investors and retirees. He said:

When I first came here I fell in love with these beautiful islands and seized the opportunity to set up a business here.

We are five hours away from the UK by air and there are now many direct flights, which have greatly increased tourism and investor interest. As yet there are no cheap flights, and we are too far away for the weekend visitors, so we will never become like the Canaries.

So far as culture is concerned, we have theatres, art galleries, the annual Carnival and wonderful music festivals, so you need never be bored here. The Cape Verdians themselves are like the Brazilians, a mixture of black and white, although the new people moving in are mainly British. Before the British started coming, it was mostly Italians buying here, which is why there is so much Italian influence.

The government is doing its best to avoid cheap developments and there are good rules and regulations on new developments, although as the main industry is tourism, the government is put under a lot of pressure by developers, so we do have a few cheap developments. But we have a low-rise policy, so there will never be huge apartment blocks going up.

Cape Verde is being promoted as an ideal retirement destination as the climate, being bone-dry, is excellent for alleviating older-age and incurable conditions such as arthritis. Medical facilities are being built to cope with future need, as the retirement market grows.

The currency is pegged to the euro, and is a stable currency which never fluctuates, according to Paul Akwei. As tourism grows, rental yields are increasing and in 2008, are around 7 per cent. Prices are currently low and in 2008, new studio apartments in Boa Vista start at £30,000, although you can pay up to £250,000 or £300,000 for a villa in one of the popular tourist areas. As one Cape Verde enthusiast remarked, for the price of a deposit in Twickenham, you can have a whole beachfront apartment in Cape Verde!

Portuguese is the main language although English is widely spoken. The process of buying remains European, rather than English and, in common with other European countries, requires the services of a notary.

Mortgages are available either from Cape Verde or in sterling. The company MyMortgage Direct specializes in Cape Verde mortgages and works in partnership with the Noscasa agency. This broker, based in Surrey, has decided to concentrate on Cape Verde as they believe that this destination offers greater potential to Brits than either the established markets of France, Spain or Portugal, or the other emerging markets such as those in Central and Eastern Europe.

There are a number of mortgage options, such as releasing equity from your main home to arranging stage payments for off-plan developments. Mortgages can be financed by Cape Verde banks but have a higher rate of interest than UK mortgages. In any case, the maximum term is 35 years with an upper age limit of 75 years and the maximum loan-to-value is 85 per cent, so getting a mortgage on a Cape Verde property is pretty much the same as for any similar destination.

Cath Hearnden, director of MyMortgage Direct, says:

The advantages of buying in Cape Verde is that it is a brand-new market, but comes under Portuguese law so there is a well-established system of buying, and it is not going to be a risky purchase. There are no restrictions on how many properties incomers can buy or on taking money out of the country, as in some countries such as India and South Africa. Also, if you have investment properties there you can easily fly out to keep a check on them.

As yet, we don't know how the market will grow as Cape Verde is by no means fully developed but it has a lot of potential, and this will increase with the golf courses being built. There are as yet no bargain flights out there although you can get good deals in offpeak seasons such as school term-time. Cape Verde will not be able to join the EU as it is not part of Europe but although it cannot be a full member of the EU it was formerly a Portuguese colony, so the rules and regulations are very similar to those countries with full membership.

# North America

In recent years, there has been a terrific boom in buying second or holiday homes in North America, mainly Florida. But Canada has also started to attract a reasonable flow of British second-home buyers.

## United States

Although it's not all that uncommon for British people to own an apartment in New York, Florida remains the first love for UK second-homers, and for much the same reason as other hot places appeal: weather, weather, weather.

The town of Orlando, in Florida, has dozens of theme parks and is also the home of Disneyworld; as a result, Orlando has become the biggest tourist attraction in the world.

There is also the huge advantage for monoglots in that English is spoken in the United States and Canada; therefore there is (usually!) immediate comprehension, and less likelihood of being drowned in real-estate bureaucracy and documentation hard to understand unless you are already fluent in the language. In fact, the common language is a very potent reason why ever more English-speaking people are now picking North America – and overwhelmingly Florida – as their first choice for a second home.

Florida has a sub-tropical climate, which means it is warm, if not hot, all the year round. And although natural disasters such as twisters, hurricanes, lightning and torrential downpours can be a drawback at certain times of the year, as can the ever-present cockroaches, or roaches, Florida is gradually attracting ever more residents, both native and foreign.

Florida has much to recommend it for families with children. There are of course the many Disney attractions, plus any number of theme parks. There is a great deal of coast, and the intracoastal waterways also have their charm. There are many lakes, and though alligators lurk in most of them they can be easily spotted and avoided. There are also a great deal of sporting attractions. Further, residents maintain that the cost of living is low, and housing is cheap. That, of course, depends on which part of Florida you choose. The so-called Millionaire's Row on Miami Beach is anything but cheap, and of course many celebrities have made their homes in the multi-million-dollar art-deco pastel-coloured South Beach Miami homes. Coastal properties tend to be expensive, and as coastal areas are in any case limited most of the intense building programmes are taking place inland, where there is still any amount of undeveloped land.

The most obvious drawback of North America as a holiday-home destination for Europeans is the long-haul flights. Also, there is the expense of these flights, and the potential difficulty of getting flights exactly when you want them. Although good deals are sometimes available, it can also work out extremely expensive to fly to Florida, especially at short notice, and for families. Fares to Miami are particularly high most of the year, but can rise to a ridiculous peak during the summer months, school holidays and bank holidays. Airfares to Orlando and Fort Lauderdale tend to be cheaper, but at peak holiday times cheap deals may not be available anywhere.

Most of the property companies plugging new Florida homes make great play of their rental possibilities, as a way of affording a three- or four-bedroom, two-bathroom new home with its own swimming pool (a pool is an absolute must in Florida, either for letting out or for resale). Very few people will even consider buying or renting a Florida home without a pool, however small or shallow this pool might be. And even if they never use it!

Very many new housing developments are currently taking place in Florida, and buyers, both US and outsiders, are being eagerly courted by major construction companies.

But why choose faraway Florida, as opposed to nearby Spain or Portugal?

John Morrill, who now runs the UK branch of the World of Florida holiday sales and rentals business, was originally looking for a holiday home in Portugal. He says: 'When we first decided we would like a holiday home abroad, our first thought was Spain or Portugal. But then we went on a holiday to Portugal one February and it was bitterly cold and windy, which put me off.'

At the time, John was working for Bulmer's cider, and spent a year in the United States trying to interest US people in this peculiarly British beverage. Although based in Washington, DC (as opposed to the Big Apple, which might have seemed more appropriate), John discovered Florida whilst he was there, and fell in love with the United States generally:

> Whilst I was based in America, my family came out for holidays, and we all fell in love with it. The fact that we speak nearly the same language was a big plus, as you can get caught out if you don't know the language well, and are trying to do something major such as buy a property in another country.
>
> When in Florida I had a look at the properties on offer out there, and decided I would buy a new house. I bought the land, or the lot, not the *plot*, as you would say in UK English, as in American the term 'plot' means quite specifically a burial plot.
>
> The location I chose was New Port Richey on the coast and about 30 miles from Tampa. I wanted a location with easy access to the beach, and the nearest beach was literally five minutes away. Also, because of the grandchildren, I wanted easy access to the theme parks and Disney attractions. I also wanted to rent out the house when we were not using it.
>
> The other big advantage of the location for myself and my wife was that we are both golf freaks, and our house backs on to a magnificent golf course, a real dream. In fact, there are 30 wonderful golf courses in easy distance of our house.

The house they bought proved ideal in every way for their purposes, and John and his wife now spend six weeks at a time out there, usually from October to December: 'I play golf two or three times a week and I'm in shorts the whole time.'

What other inducements are there to buying a Florida house? 'For UK people, it's a fairly easy transaction, as the American system is similar to buying a new house in the UK. Because it's all reasonably familiar, buyers are not flummoxed or afraid of being taken for a ride, which can happen in Spain or Portugal, for instance.'

Florida, adds John, appeals to the British market because it follows the average Briton's mental picture of the ideal home: detached, with its own pool and double garage and, above all, plenty of space:

> For around £150,000 you get a house in its own grounds with huge rooms and a vast living room and kitchen.
>
> As between 80 to 90 per cent of UK buyers are also interested in the rental market, the attraction to holidaymakers is that the houses are immaculate, with all appliances and high-quality furniture and fittings already there. In fact, all these extras come as part of the deal, so there is none of that trawling round stores to find fridges, dishwashers and so on. US builders keep bang up to date and introduce new ideas as part of their marketing, so you are always getting a house which incorporates all the latest building ideas and improvements.
>
> Also, unlike say a Barrett or Wimpey development in the UK, or many developments in Spain or Portugal, all the houses are different from each other. There are at least six different designs to choose from, and the builders work hard to make all the homes look individual.

The main beauty of the houses, for UK buyers, is that, for what they are, they are extremely cheap. So, apart from the long flight times, which definitely put some people off, are there any drawbacks to making this type of investment?

Yes – and it is that the homes do not tend to appreciate in value. Because so many new ones are being built all the time, and the main attraction is of a brand-new home, resale values are relatively low. You may get your money back but should not expect to make a profit.

But there is the huge appeal of not having a foreign language and foreign ways to learn – the United States is highly familiar from films and sitcoms, even for those who have not previously been there. In Florida, the great draw is year-round sunshine – in fact Florida is known as 'the sunshine state' – and there is plenty of space, as well as potent attractions for children and sports fanatics.

Although nobody should bank on turning in a profit from rental income, the fact is that these new Florida homes, in the right locations, make very attractive rental propositions. 'Mainly, the rental market follows the school holidays,' says John Morrill:

Houses near Orlando will appeal mainly to families wanting to go to the Disney attractions and theme parks.

If you buy a place in Venice, Naples or Sarasota, their high season is our winter, and then you get all the snowbirds, as they are known, coming from Canada and North America, who want to rent for up to three months at a time.

The snowbirds are mainly elderly retired couples who like to spend their winters in the sun, and they negotiate different deals from the UK or US family holidaymakers. The big advantage of a snowbird booking is that they are there for a long time, during which there is hardly any wear and tear on the place.

Most US workers don't have huge holidays and so they rent for a week or two at most, but the snowbird market is different. They pay less rent but they are responsible for all the utilities, so it comes to much the same thing.

Do bear in mind that Florida is unique when it comes to the use to which a home is put. If you are buying a place to rent out, you must buy a home that is 'zoned' for rental. Although homes aimed at owner occupiers and those for rental are exactly the same as regards appearance, facilities and construction, you cannot rent out a home that is not zoned for vacation purposes.

For instance, in a development of 300 houses, 150 may be zoned for residential use and 150 for vacation use. In the residential areas, you are only allowed yearly rentals and the vacation homes cannot be used as main homes but only for short-term rentals of a week or two at a time.

Florida investment expert Kevin Fleury, of Conti Financial Services, advises: 'For new or risk-averse property investors, Florida has a lot to offer. I would always recommend buying on water as this tends to double in value every five years.'

He adds: 'If buying to rent out, look at the family market rather than single units and remember that Americans themselves often rent for a year before deciding where or what to buy.'

When considering purchasing a place in Florida, you have to consider what most appeals to you, and where you would like to be. The typical brand-new three-bedroom, two-bathroom new houses are aimed at family occupation. They are located near to family attractions and sports facilities. If you need rental income to make the place pay, you will have to choose a location that rents out easily. Anything 20 minutes or less from the Disney attractions of Orlando will be popular, as will properties near to beaches or watersports.

But be careful: not all areas in Florida are zoned for holiday letting, so before buying check that the area you're interested in permits this.

As long ago as 1979, Irene and Martin Goodman bought a brand-new four-bedroom holiday house in Coral Springs, near Fort Lauderdale, together with three other couples. The house, as is common practice in Florida, had to be different from all the other houses, and there were strict rules about how many trees they could have, what colours they could use and so on.

'We all put money in the kitty and shared expenses,' said Irene:

Funnily enough, we never clashed and were all there at different times. We were in a nice young town with no elderly people, and it was great for our children. But when our own two children grew up and didn't want to come on family holidays any more, it became too big and a bit of a liability.

After 12 years, we decided, along with the other owners, to sell it, partly as it wasn't being used so much any more and partly because the property taxes were going up so much that it was becoming expensive to maintain.

The consortium just about broke even when they sold, and did not make a profit. 'It's almost impossible to make a profit on resale,' says Irene:

because there is so much building going on all the time, and most people prefer the new, more modern houses. After 12 years, ours was a 'yesterday's home'.

> We found that having a place in America never worked out as a cheap holiday. By the time we had paid for four flights and built in seeing various attractions, it always worked out very expensive indeed.

Singles, sophisticated couples and those without children or families to worry about are likely to prefer Miami to the family-oriented houses. Veronica McHugh, originally from Ireland, who has lived in Miami since the mid-1980s, says:

> Miami does not seem to be the sort of place that traditional retirees or those with a young family would choose. We are definitely not sedate! Miami is an eclectic place with its young hip modelling and movie-making crowd, the Cuban contingent who have added so much to the prosperity of the city; there is a Haitian enclave and the next largest Jewish community outside Israel and New York.
>
> Miami is a very 'happening' place, and one of the premier news markets in the US. It's very beautiful, very alive, but does not seem to have the same appeal to Brits – well, older ones at least – as Boca Raton and West Palm Beach a little north of here.

If you go to a property fair in the UK or anywhere else in Europe, you will discover that all the US homes being expensively marketed are these new Florida developments. If you prefer to buy an apartment, say in Miami, you will have to go out and look for yourself, asking a realtor (estate agent) to show you one at a time.

In such cases, if you are new to the area and Miami seems bewildering, what should you look out for? Dwina Murphy-Gibb lives for a large part of the year on Miami Beach with her husband Robin (of the famous Bee Gees). Although Dwina and Robin live in a beautiful rock star's mansion there, they have also bought and sold other, smaller apartments in Miami since they first arrived in the city in 1984.

Dwina says:

> Most incomers buying in Miami want something close to the
> water, or with a water view. It's also important to get to know
> which areas are up and coming, and for that you really need to
> have a holiday here before making a decision.
>
> For instance, I bought a place on Morningside, in the Biscayne
> area of Miami, when there were no security gates. Then they put
> up security gates and the place immediately doubled in value.
> People are very worried about high crime rates in Miami.
>
> Land taxes in Miami are very high, so before signing anything
> ask what the property taxes are. They are based on the value of the
> property. For instance, at our home, we pay $70,000 a year just in
> property tax – the equivalent of British council tax. The local
> council come to revalue your home every five years or so, and put
> the tax up accordingly.
>
> When people can't pay their property taxes, you can even buy
> somebody's tax, and eventually own their house!

Dwina's overwhelming advice if buying in Miami, or indeed
anywhere in Florida, is: buy on water.

> It's got to be on water to make it here. It's also important to think
> about whether you want a south or a north view, whether you want
> sunrise or sunset, as you can't have both.
>
> Most apartments and houses now have air conditioning, and this
> is a total must. It's impossible to live in Florida without air condi-
> tioning. In apartments, it's best to have central air conditioning –
> where it comes from a central source rather than being installed
> individually in each room, as then you have those horrible boxes
> outside the windows. Any storage must also have AC, otherwise
> everything will be mildewed in no time as there is such high
> humidity here. Here we have a tropical climate with very dense
> humidity, and this should always be borne in mind.
>
> If buying into an apartment, you should also check whether it's
> been recently refurbished, or is about to be renovated at huge cost to
> the residents. Then, is there parking, and is this underground or

overground? Remember that if you are very close to the ocean, the salt water can ruin your car.

Ceiling fans are also essential, and should be in every room. Then there is the location. Is the house or apartment near the airport? Near to shops and facilities? Near to public transport? Nobody, but nobody, walks in Miami or, indeed, anywhere in the United States if they can possibly help it. In Florida, this is partly because of the heat, but also because US people have become unused to the idea of walking anywhere. When you see people out walking, they are either power-walking or resting from jogging: in other words, walking is considered exercise rather than a means of getting from A to B.

In general, if buying in Miami, it is better to go for an apartment, as it's not a good idea to leave a house unattended for any length of time, unless there are individual security gates, security personnel and also staff on hand, to make sure the place does not deteriorate too much in your absence. Remember, Florida is not only home to millions of tourists a year but also billions of termites, cockroaches and other creepy-crawlies associated with tropical climates.

In any case, it may be an idea to check whether a particular house or apartment has been treated for termites. Otherwise, you could find it's overrun with these undesirable insects when you return.

Tina Moore, former wife of the late England footballer Bobby Moore, reckons she has found 'a little bit of heaven' in Miami. She lives for several months of the year in a two-bed, two-bathroom apartment on the Venetian Causeway on Miami Beach. Her first-floor apartment is right on the bay, with fabulous views, and also very near the airport and the famous Lincoln Road shopping area.
Tina says:

I totally love Miami. I love its multicultural buzz, its beauty, its gorgeous weather and the fact that English is spoken. From my living room I can watch the dolphins and the pelicans, and the cruise liners coming into harbour. Miami is also miles cheaper than England, I would say 30 to 40 per cent cheaper, and the people are extremely friendly.

I have always loved America, as it's very accepting of everybody and there is no class system. I love Italy, but there is the language problem, and the weather is not as good as here. The only thing is, it's very difficult to get a Green Card to become a US resident. My place is designated a holiday home because I'm not allowed to live here all year round.

Originally I wanted to rent somewhere, but I came to look at this building and was totally knocked off my feet. The location is wonderful and everything you could want is here. The beach is less than 10 minutes away, there is a gym next door, and a bus service passes by at the front of the building. These apartments are absolutely wonderful – a little bit of heaven – and there is a special healing quality about them.

Other advantages to Miami, so far as Tina Moore is concerned, are that single people are completely accepted everywhere, and the Miamians love the British:

I feel younger and zippier here than I do in England. There is also the other enormous advantage that apartment blocks don't seem to suffer from the same running problems as in the UK. I live in an Edwardian mansion block in London, when I'm not in Miami, and it's full of legal, administrative, financial and other difficulties. That just doesn't happen here.

Anybody interested in buying an apartment in the United States is likely to be vetted closely by the residents' committee, or board of voluntary directors. They want to ensure that all newcomers fit in with the general ethos of the place, and are in a position to pay their service and maintenance charges. Sometimes, this vetting can be extremely gruelling, but it ensures that all residents are of the 'right' type and will not bring the building into disrepute or cause dissent and difficulty. So, expect to be interrogated when you are buying an apartment in the United States. If they don't want you, you won't be permitted to purchase.

As a UK resident you can buy a Miami apartment either for cash or on a mortgage. There are two types of apartments, designated as either co-ops or condominiums. With a co-op you are allocated a percentage share, and mortgage companies don't like them so much as condominiums, where you own a specific unit. As a general guideline, you have to put down a 30 per cent deposit to secure a co-op, but only 5 per cent for a condo, if going for a mortgage.

The way it works is that, if you intend to make an offer, you put down $1,000 deposit – whether or not that offer is accepted – which is put into an escrow account and untouched until the deal proceeds. If it falls through, for whatever reason, your money is refunded in full. This deposit is required to secure a valid contract and move the deal forward.

The next step would be to have an inspection, or survey. If buying on a mortgage, the mortgage lender would insist on an inspection; if paying cash, you may decide it is unnecessary. In any case, the buyer pays for the inspection.

Supposing the offer is accepted and the inspector gives the property a clean bill of health, you would then have to come up with 10 per cent of the purchase price, which would be held until the time of closing. Closure takes between three and six weeks, if there are no complications.

There will also be other costs. For the buyer, there is a so-called intangible tax, levied at 55 cents per $1,000 of the purchase price. This is a federal tax, similar to stamp duty, except that it is paid by the buyer. The seller also pays this tax, but at a higher rate.

There is also the title insurance policy, to ensure that the title is free from encumbrances and debts. If buying on a mortgage, this policy is compulsory; if paying cash, it's up to you. The policy costs, typically, around $1,500, and guarantees you the title, should it be subsequently challenged.

It's also necessary, as in the UK, to do a title search. On top of this there will be attorney's fees at, typically, $500.

With apartments, there will also be service and maintenance charges and, for any US property, yearly property taxes levied on the supposed value of the property.

When buying any apartment in the United States, whether in Miami, New York or another city, look very carefully at what you're buying. Many condos in the United States come complete with valet parking, live-in concierge, fully equipped gym and manicured gardens. It all sounds very nice, but don't forget that you as a resident will be paying for all this in your service and maintenance charges!

If you don't want all these extra services, don't buy into a building that has them. Also check that the accounts are in the black. In one high-end apartment block I visited in Miami, the management committee had overspent so much they were $1 million in debt. In apartment blocks, there is only one source of income: from *you*, the residents. Nowhere else.

If five men rush up to you to valet-park your car, be on your guard. All those men have to be paid! And paid out of *your* service charges.

If you are more interested in buying a brand-new Florida home, the process is very different. Most US companies selling new homes to foreigners, and even the home market, will offer hugely discounted inspection, or fly 'n' buy, trips to the site, where you are taken round the impressive showhome and given all the facts and figures. Whilst on the inspection trip you can choose your plot (or, rather, lot) and then sign up for a series of payments, the last one being made when the home is finished.

Rental companies will also have offices at the sites, so that the whole thing can be concluded there and then. When buying a Miami, or other town or city, apartment, you will have to do all the paperwork yourself, find your own lawyers and so on. Don't forget that in order to make a deal you will need to have a US bank account. It is also a good idea to discover how long you are allowed to stay in the country. If travelling on a visa waiver, you are only allowed 90 days at a time. The expiry date will be stamped on your passport at the time of arrival.

For Green Cards, you would need to contact the American Embassy to persuade them that you should be issued with one of these valuable documents. In general terms, you would have to be able to work or earn your own living there to qualify for a Green Card.

In the United States, the country that almost invented litigation, even the companies wanting to sell you a Florida home advise anybody interested to have a holiday in their chosen location first, at their own expense and without any sales pressure, to make sure they actually want to buy into this place.

They advise: choose the location; then make absolutely certain that this is what you want, and can afford, *before* going out on an inspection trip. By the time this trip is arranged, it should have come down to more or less a matter of choosing the style of home and the lot, not of trying to make up your mind as to whether this is what you really want.

## The process of buying

Whether you pay cash, or buy on a mortgage, the process of purchasing a new or resale home in the United States is extremely streamlined, as you would expect it to be, with little margin for error.

If buying new, as the majority of incomers do, you will first choose your future house and your lot. Estate agents, bankers and mortgage companies are all on site ready, so that you can close the deal there and then. If buying on a mortgage, you will be asked to send a down payment. Once this is received, the lot is bought and the construction begun.

With these new developments, houses are not built and then sold – they are pre-sold, and not started until they have already been bought. So you are not even buying off-plan – the house is built especially for you. Construction usually takes around four months, at which time the final payment will be made to the builder, either by you, if paying cash, or the mortgage company.

If paying cash, you would typically put down $1,000 on signing the contract, and then make payments at intervals of 25 per cent, with the balance due when the house is ready for occupation. Construction will not start until the first 25 per cent is received. The next tranche is due on completion of the slab, the following one on completion of the frame and the next on completion of the drywall.

Once the house is yours, you become liable to pay all utility bills, plus real-estate taxes. In Florida, these are calculated on the value of the home and paid in arrears. An average new-build home will attract an *ad valorem* tax of around $1,500 per year, or 1 per cent of the value of the property. This tax is reassessed every three years. There will also be insurance to pay, at around $150 a year.

## Taxation and immigration

Incomers are allowed to buy businesses in Florida, so long as they have at least $125,000 cash invested in the business, and the business is active. For these people, an E2 Treaty Investor Visa, valid for five years, can be obtained. This can be extended indefinitely. The cost of processing one of these visas works out at around $6,000. The American Embassy in London (website: www.usembassy.org.uk) can give details.

Pure investment into undeveloped real estate, for instance, is not allowed. In Florida (although other US states may be different) there is no state income tax as such, but you may be required to pay federal taxes. The highest rate of income tax in the US is currently 28 per cent, the lowest 15 per cent.

But anybody who receives income from renting property or by other means is required to file a tax return before 1 April each year. Tax relief is allowed on business expenses in a far more generous way than in the UK. If you intend to rent out your property, or earn a living by other means whilst in the United States, it is essential to obtain professional tax advice before making any irrevocable decisions. And, as with other countries, never try to be clever or buck the system. It just isn't worth it.

So far as immigration is concerned, it is easy enough to obtain a six-month visa if you own a holiday home. Proof of purchase will be required. Should you require a longer visa, this will take between two and four months to process, and an experienced immigration lawyer should be used. Once an application has been rejected, it may be difficult to obtain a visa at a later date.

As with other assets, capital gains tax is payable on your Florida home when you sell it. Note: as with purchases of second homes everywhere, it does not make financial sense to sell the property too quickly. In most countries, start-up costs are considerable, and you will almost certainly lose money, as well as having to pay maximum CGT, if you sell within a year or two.

Second or holiday homes should be regarded as medium- to long-term investments, and not opportunities to make a quick buck. If you are not resident in the UK, your gains on your US property will not be taxed in the UK, but in the United States.

Ever more UK people are interested in retiring permanently to Florida, but is this possible? At the time of writing, it is difficult to do, as permanent visas remain difficult to obtain, even for those who just want to relax in the sun for the rest of their lives.

Although there has been talk of a retirement visa, and legislation to effect this is 'in the pipeline', this has not yet become law. For most alien retirees, it is only possible to reside in Florida for six months at a time. Then you would have to leave, and return for another six months. You are only allowed to remain in Florida for six-month blocks at a time.

There are some exceptions, of course. If you are an immediate or close relative of a US citizen, you may be allowed to stay permanently. Otherwise, if you have a close relationship to an alien in possession of a Green Card (spouse or child), you may then be able to retire to Florida permanently.

Investor and priority worker visas are also available for those who can either invest a large sum of money in a US business or who have some special top-flight skill that may be unobtainable locally. Realistically, most retirees are not going to come into this bracket, although anybody with a substantial sum of money available to invest in the US has a good chance of being granted a permanent visa. More information about US visas and the restrictions currently in place is available from www.usembassy.org.uk, or from the Immigration and Naturalization Service website: www.ins.usdoj.gov.

Even though retirement visas are not currently available to aliens (although the indications are that they soon will be), a residential retirement complex known as The Villages, in Oxford, mid-Florida, is becoming highly popular with UK citizens. Their promotional material states that all UK retirees who own a home in The Villages must keep a UK base that they can call their 'main' home.

The Villages community is popular with retirees because it is known as an 'adult' community, meaning that all owners must be aged 55 or over. Children are not allowed, except on short visits, and all who reside in the complex must be aged at least 19. The rationale is that, all over Florida, there are many communities and developments aimed at families, and so here is one that is not.

The Villages complex contains golf courses, tennis courts, swimming pools, bridge clubs and other leisure activities suitable for this age group. There are deliberately no facilities for children.

And the homes themselves are aimed at the older market. For instance, most of them are bungalows, with one or two bedrooms. As with other Florida developments, if you are interested you must buy a lot and then watch your new home being constructed. Or you can buy a resale home.

Prices are from around £100,000 although they do go up to £250,000 or more. There are many restrictions on what you can do and how you can behave in The Villages but, according to the brochures, that's the way the residents like it, as it means nobody is allowed to upset the quiet, peaceful applecart there.

Because of the restrictions on residency for alien holiday home owners, renting in The Villages is allowed and even encouraged. As one might expect from a US development, everything from purchase to renting to immigration advice is available on-site. To find out more, contact: Beausdale House, Beausdale, Warwick CV35 7NZ.

The current restrictions on entry for retirees (or, indeed, any incomer wanting to live in Florida) mean that current conditions are not ideal, and the owners of The Villages are longing for the day when long-term renewable retirement visas become law. The fact is that many retired UK people who would like to live in Florida permanently, because of the sun and relaxed lifestyle, cannot easily afford to keep a bolthole in the UK; nor can they easily afford the flights to and fro.

There is some research to suggest that, once retirees are allowed to live permanently in Florida, the UK would be more or less totally emptied of its senior citizens! According to research by Mintel, around 54 per cent of British people would like to live abroad, in the sun. Teresa Dorsett, UK representative of The Villages, says:

> UK people love Florida because of the sun, the common language and because their health improves in the vastly better weather. Also, because US real-estate laws are based on and derived from English laws, there is not the same culture shock as when buying a place in Spain or France. Very many of our UK owners are people who've had a place in Spain and got fed up with it, so they are preferring to live somewhere that feels more British, but with guaranteed good weather.

Note: There are no reciprocal health care arrangements between the United States and the UK, so any 'adult' or older incomers would have to sort out their own health insurance, which could be expensive, especially for those with an existing health problem. Again, it's essential to take expert advice before making a decision to move as, if you are not in good health, hospital and medical care could soon drain away all your resources.

## Pure investment in Florida

Next to Spain, Florida has become the favourite location for pure investors. Because this sub-tropical state is so huge – about the size of Europe – and the appeal of Disney World seemingly inexhaustible, enormous building and development programmes are going on all the time. As in Spain, golf fanatics are well catered for and there are more than 60 high-quality golf courses in the Disney area alone.

As we have seen, golf is one of *the* most popular reasons for Britons buying abroad, as golf fanatics are so much better catered for in hot countries, where they can almost always rely on the weather not to let them down.

Those who talk up Florida as an investment Mecca point to its exceptional growth rate over the last few years, the continued high demand for properties both to buy and to rent in the Sunshine State, and the likelihood that present growth trends will continue, driven by huge and growing numbers of tourists and the continuing expansion of the Disney and other attractions.

Some experts point out that fewer than 20 per cent of Americans own a passport, and that it's not just foreigners who go on holiday in Florida – Americans do too.

At the time of writing, the exchange rate is favourable, although this could of course change. The mighty hurricanes that devastated much of Florida in 2004 have hardly dented its popularity, although much damage was inflicted on the areas affected. Floridians are well geared up for the possibility of hurricanes, twisters and tornadoes, and all buildings have to be hurricane-proofed, by law.

But beware! Before buying, enquire as to how far the property is hurricane-proofed, and what is covered by insurance. Here is a cautionary tale: a friend's house in Boca Raton was badly damaged by the 2004 hurricanes. He was in the UK at the time. On returning to Florida after the hurricanes, he called in his insurers who sent loss adjusters round. These people advised him to renovate the house to its previous high standard, which he did at a cost of $20,000, fully expecting the work to be covered by insurance. He then had to return to the UK – and eventually received a cheque from the insurers for only $600.

As usual, investing in Florida properties demands care, diligence, research and taking professional advice at every stage. Those properties likely to increase most in value are ones you can buy at a significant discount off-plan. In many cases, resale homes will go for less than the original price.

Florida is currently a highly popular destination for British tourists; the fact that English is spoken and the legal system is partly based on the UK model are undoubtedly major advantages.

The major drawback of Florida for British nationals who do not have a Green Card is that you are only allowed to stay there for six months at a time. For many years there has been talk of permanent visas being offered but at the time of writing this has not happened – nor has there even been much talk of it lately.

There are many attractive retirement villages in Florida where foreign nationals would like to spend their remaining days, as Florida has got the retirement business off to a fine art, but at the moment permanent retirement there is not a possibility. This is why, if you plan to live in Florida yourself for part of the year, it is important to choose somewhere that rents out easily when you are not able to be there yourself.

## California

Most of the marketing hype by developers of new properties in the world's most famous sunspots concentrates on the sporting opportunities – and Southern California is no exception. Less obvious than Florida, beach towns such as La Jolla, Newport and Santa Barbara are now being excitedly discovered by second-homers.

La Jolla, particularly, is famous for walking, yoga, lovely beaches and endless summers, as well as surfing, golf, tennis and windsurfing along this beautiful stretch of coastline.

## New England

New England in the autumn, or fall, is spectacular and the area is also highly sophisticated, containing Harvard University, Boston and Cambridge, and is starting to attract the foreign buyer – a different type, possibly, from the Florida buyer.

The area also has many ski resorts, and New England estate agents are now reporting a major increase in British buyers looking for second homes where they can ski in the winter and play golf in the summer (golf again!). Summer attractions also include hill walking and fishing. Agents say that most Brits decide to buy a holiday home in New England after enjoying a holiday in the region. Favourite areas include Killington in Vermont, the largest ski and snowboard resort in the Eastern USA, and the Sunday River ski resort.

The most popular areas are those within easy driving distance of Boston airport, where holiday homes can be had for between £100,000 and £190,000 for a three- or four-bedroom chalet-style home. Homes rent out well in both summer and winter, and rental income can usually cover about half the yearly running costs. Off-plan developments are also being offered to investors, both native and foreign.

# Canada

Why, you might wonder, should anybody want to purchase a second home in Canada? Before you dismiss the idea, here's what Professor John Bellamy, of Carleton University, has to say about Ottawa, to which he emigrated from England with his family in 1970: 'Ottawa has a nasty four-month winter, but the rest of the year it's terrific – long hot summers, vast stretches of water, parks, good roads, no slums, good pubs. My colleagues who travel a lot say it is the best place to live on the planet, with perhaps the exception of Adelaide, South Australia.'

One holiday-homer who would agree with this is magazine executive Jo Sandilands, who has bought a lakeside home in Canada with her husband David Briggs:

We had been going on holiday to Kawarthas, in north-east Toronto, where there is a series of lakes, every two or three years since my son Matthew was born in 1988. He would always want to go there if possible, so we went often and got to know and love the area. My son and husband are mad on all kinds of watersports anyway.

We tend to think of Canada as the acceptable face of America. Canadians do, in my view, have a sense of humour failure but apart from that it's a lovely place to be, especially in summer.

We were there one year staying with friends and it was a rainy day, so to pass the time we started flipping through local magazines, looking for places to buy. We contacted a local estate agent who showed us these log cabins. They were very cute, but extremely high maintenance and also extremely expensive. Log cabins are very sought-after these days.

Then we were shown a house right on the lake, with three bedrooms and a huge basement, a concrete structure built about 35 years ago. It cost around £70,000, and we were immediately interested, but David wanted to go back to the UK to think about it.

I stayed on, however, and bought it. It was a vastly better experience than buying in the UK, as once you've put in an offer that's accepted you can't be gazumped. As I was paying cash, I completed the deal in 10 days. The searches took three days, whereas in the UK they can take several weeks, and we could have easily got a mortgage.

I set up a Canadian bank account, and we instantly became part of the lakeside Canadian community. The community charges cost around £600 a year, and we have to pay local taxes as well.

Jo and her family now go there for six weeks every summer, and for two weeks at Christmas:

It's beautiful when it snows, but last year it didn't snow at all. In the summer, you can swim in really hot water, and in winter the lake is frozen solid. There are a lot of contrasts, and we like both seasons in their different ways.

Where we are in Canada is the back of beyond, and the crime rate is very low. I bought the house in September, then went back in October to find a builder, as the place needed a lot of work. I found a builder I liked, he got planning permission, we agreed the plans and I went back to the UK. The building work was done mainly by fax, and it worked out extremely well, even though the entire thing was an act of faith.

Whilst I was over there in the October I went on a huge shopping spree and bought everything – tiles, carpets, furniture and so on. It was all made easy because there was so little time, and I had to make decisions there and then. But it's all worked out.

Any drawbacks? 'Only the food, really. All that's available is fast-food American stuff, and the one decent restaurant is 45 minutes away. So mainly, we eat at home. The local supermarkets have everything, and the life we lead here is simple, by no means chic. It is totally water-based in summer.'

Jo herself admits that she hates all watersports, water-skiing, speedboats, everything connected with moving about on water. 'But it's perfect for teenagers and all children love it. We have a huge trampoline in the garden and friends to stay.'

From an investment point of view, Jo also reckons it's been a good buy. The improvements that she and David have made have added another £30,000 to the value of the place, and they have built a terrace now planted with shrubs and flowers:

We had to have Arctic plants, to survive the winter, and for that I had to employ a gardener as I knew nothing about this kind of planting. One year when I arrived the whole of one bank was full of lilies, which was lovely, and I didn't know they would be there.

If we hadn't already had friends there, Canada would definitely not have been at the top of my holiday home list, but as it is it's not a bad journey. We can leave our south-west London house at 8.30 in the morning, and be sitting in our lakeside house at 6.30 having a drink. It's long, but a do-able journey. Even so, to make it worth it, you have to be able to spend several weeks in the house at a time once you've made the effort to get there.

The other absolute essential for any second or holiday home in North America is a car. People do not travel anywhere on foot, even to the supermarket over the road, if they can possibly help it, and in many areas public transport is poor or non-existent. Also, since everybody is expected to own a car, life is geared up around it. Don't be tempted to buy in North America if you can't or don't drive, or hate driving. The United States and Canada are simply unmanageable without a car.

In the summer, the temperature in holiday areas of Canada would be up into the mid-80s with very little rain. The Ontario and Quebec areas form the Canadian 'shield', with many rock-surrounded lakes but not much beach. For beach front, you would have to go to Halifax and the Maritimes.

The lakes are pretty much pollution-free, and lakeside cottages are often the size of a substantial UK house. Many cottages, at least those designed as holiday or second homes, have been 'winterized', which means they can be used for skiing – mainly of the cross-country variety. Ski chalets are quite popular north of Montreal, where there is good downhill skiing.

Winter, summer and year-round cottages and apartments used mainly as second or holiday homes can be rented out when you are not there by the resort management organization. As with Florida purchases, many buyers of Canadian holiday cottages hope that rental income will help to pay off the mortgage. Crime rates in most parts of Canada are very low, and break-ins are rare.

As in Florida and also Spain and Portugal, golf is becoming increasingly popular in Canada, and golf apartments – or holiday apartments near to golf courses – are a burgeoning development.

Log cabins are an integral part of Canadian folklore, and luxury log cabins are now being built at a furious rate to satisfy the rental and second-home markets. Ski properties are also becoming increasingly popular, and many are being sold with a guaranteed 6 per cent rental return for the first two years. As ever, if you are interested in buying to let, make sure that the rental market is a real one, not an artificial one created by the developers.

In all, Canada is a relatively new investor destination, without the risks of buying in Eastern Europe or other emerging markets. Yet it is a sophisticated market at the same time.

Canada is extremely popular with British retirees, most of whom go to Vancouver Island, according to Nicola Way of Assignments Canada. Nicola is a Brit who emigrated to Canada in 1996 and now runs a website listing properties for sale. She also specializes in assisting UK buyers to purchase Canadian real estate.

Vancouver Island itself is the size of England, yet has 750,000 inhabitants and because it is surrounded by the Pacific Gulf Stream is not subject to the extremes of weather other Canadian citizens have to endure. Nicola says:

> In many ways it is very like old England with traditional teas being served at the Empress Hotel and red double-decker buses.
>
> House prices are much lower than in England, like for like. In December 2007, the average price for a three-bedroom house on Vancouver Island was around £170,000, with prices rising to around £250,000 in the capital, Victoria. So, for the price of a small one-bedroom flat in London, you could have a whole house in a climate where people can garden, golf and sail all year around, and speak English!

If you stay in Canada for six months or less each year, you are considered a non-resident. You are allowed to open a bank account and buy and sell property but if you want to live in the country for more than six months of the year, or permanently, you must apply for immigrant status.

## Pure investment in Canada

Very many Americans are now starting to buy second or holiday homes in Canada, and the most popular locations are cottages or log cabins on lakes, where there is a good chance of rental income during the summer. There is no reason for the British not to do the same, and indeed, the British have just started investing in Canadian properties, although as yet the market is not huge.

Canada is a massive country with a small population – only 30 million people in an area of 9.8 million square kilometres. Property experts say that prices vary greatly according to accessibility, and the further away from a major city, the cheaper the prices. Brand-new apartments are available from around £80,000, and selling off-plan, particularly with city condos, is becoming popular. Because so many new apartments are being built, prices are staying low – and are cheaper, like for like, than many European properties.

Many Canadian estate agents are already dealing directly with UK buyers, and this is probably the best way to go. After all, there should be no language problems.

Buying in Canada is reasonably straightforward as the process is well established. Be aware, though, that taxes will vary from state to state. Here are typical costs in 2007 for buying an off-plan property in French-speaking Quebec.

There is a non-refundable deposit of £2,000 payable on signing the reservation agreement, and a 25 per cent deposit on the purchase price must be paid within 14 days of returning to the UK. After this, stage payments become payable. Non-residents can apply for a mortgage of up to 75 per cent of the purchase price. Land transfer fees and notarial fees will also be payable, on a sliding scale depending on the price of the property.

There may also be a 7 per cent federal sales tax and 7.5 per cent Quebec provincial sales tax. This can be waived on occasion, so as always it is important to retain a lawyer fully conversant with Canadian real estate purchases. Canadian property experts also recommend that you retain a tax consultant as soon as the preliminary agreement is signed, so that the tax registrations can be completed accurately, as this can avoid payment of certain taxes twice.

It all sounds rather complicated, but remember that there should be no disputes over title or land as in some markets and, so long as all federal and state laws are complied with, no problem at all.

If buying a resale property, acceptance of an offer constitutes the contract. Once an offer is accepted, even verbally, the seller cannot accept another bid. Most purchases can be completed within two weeks, as opposed to the three months or more common in the UK.

Nicola Way, of Assignments Canada, explains the process:

When buying a house in Canada, an offer must be made in writing, and once you the buyer have signed the document it becomes legally binding. There is no gazumping in Canada and if you withdraw from the offer at this point you may lose your deposit and may be sued as well.

Everything that is included in the sale such as curtains and carpets must be written on the initial offer under 'chattels included'. Then the estate agent should insert two clauses stating that the offer will proceed subject to building inspection and that you the buyer are able to meet the financial obligations.

The offer is then presented to the seller, where further negotiations may take place. These may include changes in price, alterations to the chattels included and completion date. These changes are agreed to in writing by the seller, then presented to you the buyer and the resulting document, the Agreement of Purchase and Sale, is drawn up and the deposit paid.

If you are buying off-plan, you can sell on the contract before completion and currently many investors are doing this, selling on for a substantial profit before the building is completed and taking advantage of the booming housing market.

After you have bought, you will have to pay taxes and these are calculated according to whether the property is for use as a main residence, an active business or as a rental property. If used as a rental property, a 25 per cent non-resident tax must be paid on the gross rent, and if a property manager is used, this 25 per cent will, by law, be withheld at source and remitted directly to the Canada Revenue Agency (CRA). At the end of the tax year, 31 March, the property manager will issue an NR4 form which enables you to file a Canadian tax return. This allows you to claim expenses against the income and perhaps request a refund, as Canada has a double-taxation agreement with the UK.

In any case, before buying in Canada as an investor, you should contact a UK tax adviser conversant with the Canadian system, as otherwise you could lose out and pay much more tax than is legally necessary.

When you sell the property, you will be liable for taxes on any capital gain; Canadian tax rates are applied to 50 per cent of the gain and this amount will be automatically retained by the seller's lawyer until a clearance certificate is received from the Canada Revenue Agency. This normally takes around 6–8 weeks to arrive and if the certificate is not obtained, the buyer withholds between 25 and 50 per cent of the selling price. This money goes straight to the Revenue; it does not mean the buyer pays less.

Nicola adds:

Most provinces have no restrictions on UK ownership of real estate in Canada, although some areas limit that amount of property or land that a non-resident can purchase. In most cases, though, this applies only to large properties with land attached; small houses or apartments are not normally subject to these restrictions.

## Pros and cons of buying a property in the United States (Florida)

Pros:

- good weather and hot sunshine all year round;
- cheap price of new-build properties compared to the UK;
- many attractions, theme parks;
- beautiful scenery and landscape;
- good rental possibilities;
- smooth professional buying, renting and selling operation;
- you know what you're getting – little room for error;
- easy and cheap flights to Orlando and Tampa;
- English-speaking country;
- reasonably familiar culture and lifestyle.

Cons:

- little choice of property – although the houses have individual touches, they are all built to a similar overall design;
- property very expensive in some areas, such as Miami or Boca Raton – waterfront properties particularly expensive;
- no heritage or traditional culture;
- much of Florida is Disneyfied;
- probably have to rent out property to make it pay;
- eight-hour flights offputting to some;
- US way of life also offputting to some.

# 13 The Caribbean

Although the Caribbean islands have been a popular tourist and holiday magnet for very many years, the islands as a whole are now actively encouraging second-homers and expatriates to buy themselves a permanent stake in what many consider the most desirable tropical paradise on the whole planet.

As a result, many upmarket developments aimed at rich incomers are now being constructed on most of the islands, and the marketing thrust is beginning to rival that of Spain or Florida.

Tourism remains the major foreign exchange earner and for many visitors the Caribbean is an exotic and hedonistic experience. The main resource endowments are the natural ones of sea, sun and sand and as such, these islands have promoted leisure interests as their main attractions.

The Caribbean islands offer a huge cultural and ethnic mix, much art and music, many festivals, all sports, gambling, luxury hotels and leisure developments, fishing, golf and cruises. So long as you have the money to indulge your tastes, life in the Caribbean can be one long tropical holiday. Second and holiday homes in the Caribbean, often built these days in carefully landscaped gated developments with 24-hour security, are expressly designed to appeal to the idle rich.

The overwhelming attraction of the Caribbean islands to the second-homer has got to be the weather. Although situated in the tropics, the islands, being islands, are not unbearably hot and many consider the climate to be as near ideal as it is possible to get. There are rainy seasons, but it is never cold and a tropical downpour is usually followed by bright sun.

Natives consider the sea too cold for swimming when it is 78°F – a temperature the sea never ever reaches in the British Isles.

Many people who originated from the Caribbean and then emigrated to other countries, usually for work reasons, are now buying retirement homes there and the market for seasonal homes is becoming enormous. At the moment, the majority of purchasers are either retired or near-retired US citizens, or tax exiles, but there's nothing whatever to prevent anybody else who longs to laze in the sun for the rest of their days from buying a beautiful home on one of the 30 or so Caribbean islands.

The only considerations are that you have to be extremely solvent, and never to have had a criminal record.

Although each island has its own distinct appeal, there have been strenuous attempts since the early 1990s to form a united Caribbean community, so that inhabitants of the islands can coexist in harmony rather than being at loggerheads with each other, or trying to pull in different directions.

The aim has been to form a viable economic community, whilst enabling each island to retain its uniqueness. During the 1990s, there was much liberalization and deregulation, with the result that investing in the Caribbean is a much more attractive prospect than at any time in the past, when political unrest and unstable regimes could make life uncomfortable for expats, or put your money at risk.

Most of the islands offer a wide choice of luxury villas, condos, town houses, mountain farms and ocean-front apartments. Some also offer quaint 'chattel homes' dating from the time when much of the Caribbean's economy rested on imported slave labour.

It is also possible to buy an undeveloped plot of land to build your own house to your own design. As with buying a home in Florida, it is relatively easy to rent out your Caribbean hideaway to holidaymakers, as there is a thriving tourist industry in all of the islands, and also many rental companies who can organize the whole thing for you – at a fee, of course.

As each island retains autonomy each has its own legal system and, as such, slightly different method of purchasing and financing real estate. You would have to consult a specialist lawyer or estate agent if interested in buying into the Caribbean, as there is not one single system covering all of the islands. Here are a few examples.

# The British Virgin Islands

Before completing a deal on a house or plot of land, all overseas investors must possess a Non-Belongers Land Holding Licence. To obtain this licence, you would have to apply to the Government of the BVI. Your application must be supported by two character references, a police certificate of good standing (ie, you should not have a criminal record) and other supporting documentation such as bank statements, income tax returns and any existing mortgage details. You would have to satisfy the authorities that you had sufficient finance to purchase and pay for the property.

An overseas investor is free to let a property on a short-term basis as part of the licence application, when a trade licence would also be granted. This is usually a formality.

It is normal for a prospective purchaser to pay a 10 per cent deposit to the vendor's agent to be held in an escrow account before the signing of a purchase and sale agreement. The payment of a deposit does not constitute a legal obligation, but is to be taken as a clear indication that the purchaser is serious about the transaction. In the event of the purchase not taking place, any interest earned on the deposit is paid back to the purchaser.

If, however, the transaction proceeds to a contract stage, then interest goes to the vendor and the deposit becomes non-refundable.

Once there is agreement between the purchaser and the vendor, a legally binding purchase and sale agreement, drawn up by the vendor's attorney, is signed by both parties. This agreement usually contains a condition that completion of the deal is contingent on the purchaser obtaining the Non-Belongers Land Holding Licence. This licence costs around $300.

Once the licence has been obtained, then the final payment is made. It is not necessary for either the purchaser or the vendor to be in the BVI at any stage of the deal.

The legal system in the British Virgin Islands is based on a mixture of English common law and local legislation. Standard conveyance fees are 2 per cent of the first $50,000, and rise to 3 per cent for more expensive purchases.

Mortgages are available for all property purchases in the BVI, and indeed, most of the Caribbean, so long as the lenders are satisfied that repayments can be made. In general, mortgages are available for up to 80 per cent of the value of the property and are granted for terms of up to 20 years. It is also possible to obtain finance for buying a plot of undeveloped land.

Stamp duty in the BVI is levied at 8 per cent of the purchase price and an annual land tax is also payable. In addition, there is an annual tax levied at 1.5 per cent of the assessed rental value of the property. In practice, say Smith Gore Overseas, who specialize in property purchase in the BVI, taxes for an average two- or three-bedroom house will generally be under $500.

Anybody who wishes to work in the BVI will have to obtain a work permit. In most of the Caribbean, work permits will be issued only when it has been decided that the position cannot be adequately filled by a member of the native labour force.

As with most countries, non-belongers are allowed to stay in the BVI for six months at a time, although a certificate of residence may be granted to those who wish to reside there permanently.

Income tax is payable by all individuals who are resident in the BVI for tax purposes, and on any taxable income received as a non-resident; for instance, from renting out apartments.

## Barbados

The process of purchase for a non-national in Barbados, where there are many millionaires' and billionaires' homes, is somewhat different.

Although there are no restrictions on non-nationals buying real estate in Barbados, no financing is available. This means that all incomers must bring the entire purchase price with them, and this amount must be registered with the Central Bank of Barbados. Permission from this bank must also be obtained to buy property there. The official Government Tourist Board says that this is almost always a formality and that permission is rarely withheld.

Legal fees usually amount to 2 per cent of the purchase price and there is also a property transfer tax of 10 per cent, payable by the vendor.

Holiday homes in Barbados can easily be rented out, as there is high demand for most of the year. Golf is extremely popular, as it increasingly seems to be in every desirable second-home location.

Barbados is a small island with very strict development laws, although Barbados property is available to non-residents without restrictions. The property may be owned by you personally or through a company. Either way, you will have to pay tax on any rental income received, at between 15 and 25 per cent. If you rent out the property on a short-term basis, you will have to register for and pay VAT on the income received. This is usually 7.5 per cent. All Barbados properties are subject to annual land taxes (council tax) at varying rates, depending on the size and location of the property.

When you sell it, you may have to pay a property transfer tax of around 7.5 per cent, and stamp duty when you buy. There is no capital gains tax payable in Barbados.

---

*Top Tips*

1. Carry out as much research about the market as possible before you arrive and be clear as to why you want to buy. Will it be a second home, an investment, or both?

2. Employ the services of a reputable real estate agent, ideally with strong UK links, who will not only source the property but let and manage the property on your behalf after the sale should you so wish.

3. Buy in an offshore company name with your property as the sole asset. When you come to sell the company rather than the property, you will save yourself from a sizeable tax bill.

4. Employ the services of an experienced Barbadian attorney. UK solicitors cannot practise on the island. Some buyers employ a UK solicitor as well to provide further reassurance that all documentation is in order. Be aware that conveyancing will take far longer than you will have experienced in the UK.

Top Tips courtesy of Hamptons' Barbados office

# The Cayman Islands

When one hears what the Cayman Islands have to offer, it's a wonder why anybody would want to remain in the cold, windy, rainy UK where everybody is taxed up to the hilt and beyond.

The Cayman Islands are a well-known international tax haven and, as such, there are no property taxes, no income tax, no capital gains tax, no inheritance tax and no stealth taxes. There is no restriction on foreign ownership of property and, in fact, most real estates there actively encourage foreign investment. There's guaranteed good weather, year-round, as well. Crime rates are said to be low and the islands offer a luxurious lifestyle to those rich enough to be able to afford not to pay any tax.

Financial offshore services provide most of the islands' economy, out of which they do very nicely indeed, thank you.

The process of buying a property in the Caymans is supposed to be the simplest in the world. As one estate agent put it, 'the procedure is based on the American and Canadian system, with half the red tape of either'. The system of purchase is known as the Torrens, a mixture of Canadian and American real estate laws, and is widely used throughout the Caribbean.

As a British colony under internal self-rule, the Caymans are safe and the livin' is extremely easy. Very many of the current buyers are retirees, or people buying with a view to living there permanently on retirement. Mortgages are available, either from international or local banks, with typically a 25 per cent down payment being required, and a 10 to 15 year repayment schedule.

The only duty payable on the transaction is stamp duty, at between 7 and 9 per cent of the purchase price.

It is possible to purchase permanent residency in the Caymans for a one-off fee. You would also have to own property over a certain value to qualify for residency.

There is a thriving rental market and many purchasers finance their investment with rental income until they are ready to retire there permanently.

There are 533 banks on the Cayman Islands, making it one of the largest financial centres in the world after New York, Tokyo and London. Banking deposits in the Caymans amount to US $415 billion.

But the Caymans are not the only Caribbean tax haven; Bermuda is also blissfully tax free. So what other advantages do the Cayman Islands offer? First, there is an established economy, with well-developed ports, airfields, roads, utilities, medical and educational facilities. Telecommunications, essential in the modern world, are also good. There is also, apparently, an absence of racial tension, which is not the case in every part of the Caribbean.

All islands in the Caribbean, without exception, are very open to foreign investment and the Caribbean community is now doing all it can to encourage incomers, whether as transient tourists, seasonal stayers or permanent residents. If the romance of these tropical islands, with their often stormy and violent history, and the wonderful year-round climate appeals, then it's worth checking out what a plot of land, house or condo would cost, and how much you would need to be able to stay there permanently, given that you are unlikely to be allowed to earn a living.

Prices in the Dominican Republic range from, typically, $99,500 for a one-bed, one-bath luxury apartment, to $250,000 for a three-bed, two-bath apartment. Houses in the Caribbean cost on average from $250,000, although of course you can pay many millions for the luxury complex of your dreams. All real-estate agents marketing properties in the Caribbean stress the possibility of making the place pay for itself with rental income when owners are absent.

If, for whatever reason, you do not want, or cannot afford, actually to buy in the Caribbean, then it is possible to rent, year-round. There are a large variety of attractive properties available. When writer Graham Lord was on a television programme about David Niven, the subject of his best-selling biography, he was pictured outside his palm-fringed rented Caribbean home.

He rents a property on the island of Nevis, a tiny island 6 by 6 miles between Antigua and St Kitts, and says:

> Buying a house in Nevis is very expensive, and you have to pay a huge amount of tax on top. I love the Caribbean because of the beaches, the climate and the warm, relaxed way of life. In Nevis, the locals speak English immaculately – far better than the English do! I can have lunch on the beach in shorts in February and we have made lots of friends in Nevis. For us, renting makes sense although obviously we are taking a huge risk by not owning a property anywhere in the world.

Nowadays, most UK people imagine they have to buy somewhere if moving or living abroad, but this is not always necessary, and at least by renting you are not tying up a huge amount of capital, or paying interest on a loan.

As a writer, Graham does his research and interviews in Europe and the actual writing in Nevis, using the internet and Amazon. The medical facilities on Nevis are, Graham admits, 'pretty basic' and this requires him to be heavily insured for medical treatment, at a cost of over £2,000 a year. But the downsides of not owning property are, for Graham and Juliet, infinitely outweighed by the advantages of being fancy free and forever liberated from the cold and nasty conditions prevailing in the UK – as they see them, at least.

For those considering following in Graham Lord's footsteps, the Nevis website calls the island a 'lush tropical paradise', formerly a pearl of the British Caribbean. Nevis was 'the Queen of the Caribees' and became unimaginably wealthy from the sugar industry. On a historical note, it was on Nevis that Admiral Horatio Nelson wooed his wife-to-be Fanny Nesbit (before falling for the charms of Emma Hamilton, that was).

Nevis achieved independence in 1983 and is often known as the 'secret Caribbean'. The yearly average temperature is 79 degrees fahrenheit and rainfall is 55 inches a year. The northeast trade winds prevent it from becoming too hot and it really does sound a true paradise.

There are sites of historic interest on Nevis such as old plantation inns and fortresses.

# Margarita Island, Venezuela

This island is, in common with many Caribbean islands, a tax-free zone, although properties there are very expensive to buy. However, there is a cheaper way of investing in this island and that is to buy a share in an aparthotel.

These schemes are being heavily promoted in popular areas all round the world and are an update (and some say, great improvement) on the timeshare idea. Instead of buying an entire apartment or villa, you buy a stake in a hotel which gives you several weeks of free occupation, usually at off-peak times. In 2008, you could buy a share in an aparthotel such as the Marina Caribe, for £45,000, with a guaranteed 6 per cent of the purchase price in rent for the first 12 months. The scheme guarantees rent for 10 years, although it may not always be at this level.

If you are interested in buying into an aparthotel scheme, ask whether you will be liable for service and maintenance charges, as usually, these hotels are very high-end indeed, with swimming pools, golf courses, spas and other facilities which are expensive to maintain. Also, check whether you would be liable for community or council tax, and what will happen after the 10 years is up.

# Other Caribbean islands

There are 7,000 islands altogether in the region known as 'the Caribbean', so it is impossible to feature them all. Also, they vary in their tax, residency and investor requirements, so here is a general guide to the main aspects of buying into one of these exotic island paradises.

Many Caribbean islands now are highly regulated as to foreign purchases and investments, and you have to make sure that as a foreigner you are actually allowed to buy immoveable property, or real estate. You are not allowed to buy in Cuba, for instance, although many black-market deals take place, allegedly. But if you do buy outside the country's laws you may have the property confiscated.

However, Caribbean countries such as Jamaica, Barbados and Trinidad are actively encouraging foreign investment, and Caribbean property exhibitions are becoming popular in the UK. Usually these exhibitions have extremely lavish, beguiling presentations and promotional material, so be sure not to be too much swayed by beautiful pictures of palm-fringed isles, which can easily over-glamorize your view (they are intended to!) and make you temporarily forget the ongoing costs involved in owning a Caribbean property.

It is always important to check out currency fluctuations. Many Caribbean countries have linked their currency to the US dollar, but not all. Even so, most countries where the currency is not dollar-linked deal in US dollars anyway. One of the most important pieces of advice for the potential investor – and don't forget that places like Barbados, the Dominican Republic and St Lucia are currently being sold very hard indeed as investment hotspots – is to ensure that currency conversions do not adversely affect the profitability of the purchase.

Laws governing property ownership largely depend on which nations have at one time ruled a particular island or country. The UK once ruled huge amounts of the Caribbean, with the result that in countries such as Belize (formerly British Honduras) and Anguilla laws are based on the English system. In other countries there are strong similarities with the Netherlands or France, for instance. There is not a unified system of land or property purchase throughout the entire Caribbean region.

So, make sure that you know about all hidden costs – particularly ongoing ones – and complicated ownership laws. In the Dominican Republic, for instance, foreigners can purchase real estate in exactly the same way as natives, but the government has to hold a record. In this republic, tax is payable on 'luxury homes' but not basic homes or commercial property. So if your home is classified as luxury, there will be yet another tax to pay.

## Pros and cons of buying a property in the Caribbean

Pros:

- lovely weather most of year;
- never cold;
- very exotic locations;
- lots of opportunities to indulge a love of all kinds of sport;
- upmarket properties;
- if a tax haven, no taxes to pay;
- generally upmarket and luxurious lifestyle;
- good rental opportunities;
- easy to make journeys to other Caribbean islands;
- ideal for lovers of maritime activities.

Cons:

- unless a lover of sports, life can get boring;
- difficult to have a sense of purpose there;
- long, expensive flights from UK;
- in summer, hurricanes, twisters and torrential downpours with perpetual cloud blankets can inhibit outdoor activities;
- life is expensive on the islands;
- you need a lot of money to live the good life; hand in pocket most of the time tipping people.

# *14* **Emerging markets and other destinations**

The countries described so far in this book are those that have proved to be the most popular second-home locations for Britons and other Northern Europeans, who, increasingly, long for homes in countries that seem so much more lush, exotic and welcoming than their own.

But what about other places? It is certainly possible to go further afield than any of these countries, or to choose somewhere that, until very recently, would probably not have even entered into the realms of possibility.

Although the 'emerging markets' are lumped together in this chapter, they should not be regarded as exactly the same as each other. Some markets are very new indeed, while others are more established. Some, such as Bulgaria, have been very heavily hyped and marketed in recent years while others, such as Croatia, remain more secret and impenetrable. Geographically they may also be very different from each other, with greatly varying means of access. There are not always budget airlines available, and in some markets mortgages may not be available either.

Then they differ as to their attitude to tourism. It has become well established that property buying follows tourism, and this has been the case ever since Spain became popular with package holidaymakers in the 1960s. Tourism has also largely fuelled the popularity of buying in Florida. But where tourism is limited or not yet established, there is probably not a thriving holiday rentals market, and it might be difficult to make a holiday home pay for itself or prove a profitable investment.

One important aspect to consider is membership or otherwise of the EU for some of the emerging European destinations. Romania and Bulgaria joined the EU in January 2007, the 26th and 27th countries to join, and Croatia is expected to join in 2009. Turkey, which hoped to join in 2007, has been refused accession for the time being.

So how does EU membership impact on these new and growing markets? The most important aspect is greater economic prosperity through increased foreign investment, access to free trade among member states and access to financing projects through EU funding initiatives. Many of these new EU entrants also offer lower labour costs, thus encouraging large companies to relocate. This has happened in Poland, for instance, with razor company Gillette announcing plans to build its largest manufacturing facility there. Computer company Dell is planning something similar.

As a direct consequence, standards of living will improve and property prices will rise fast. Recent entrants to the EU are encouraging foreign investment into new property developments, and not just in the holiday resorts but in major cities as well. So far as tourism is concerned, EU membership not only gives the country concerned a much higher profile – many of us had hardly heard of Bulgaria and Romania until recently – but encourages foreign visitors. Of course, the countries have to have something to offer to tempt tourists. We are not all Dervla Murphys, seeking out inhospitable, inaccessible and remote places 'where no white man has been' for our holidays and travel plans.

Bulgaria, for instance, offers the wonders of the Black Sea, and developers have not been slow to spot this potential. Bulgaria also has wonderful areas suitable for skiing in winter. Croatia has a large amount of heritage buildings and the incomparable Adriatic coast. Climate is also a factor, so it is not just economic aspects that make a new country attractive to visitors.

In all, EU membership can only be a good thing for the positive development and economic growth of these emerging markets, especially as there is also emphasis on preserving the innate culture of the countries, before they were overtaken by Communist regimes, that is.

# Croatia

One such place is Croatia, now liberated from its former Communist yoke, and right next to Italy. Croatia has long had many holiday attractions, such as wonderful beaches and a welcoming climate, at least in summer. It was probably inevitable that, eventually, those who had enjoyed holidays there would consider the possibility of a second home in this interesting but often war-ravaged country.

As yet, there is no established infrastructure for buying properties in Croatia, but so far they are relatively cheap and, as a distinct advantage for some, the place is not yet full of Brits or other incomers. There is no large-scale development going on to attract vast numbers of second-homers, nor are there, as yet, very many estate agents. This may change when Croatia joins the EU in 2009. It's mainly a matter of looking in local newspapers to find advertisements placed by private individuals wishing to sell. Since the fall of Communism, estate agents have begun to spring up, but they are a relatively new profession and so far largely unregulated.

Maria Bennett, a Croatian property expert who bought a two-bedroom flat in a former medieval convent in Dubrovnik for £25,000, says: 'To begin with, the estate agent tried to sell me his aunt's property and pay the money into a foreign bank account. But once I had a lawyer on board, he was fine, and showed me genuine properties.'

Problems came when Bennett wanted to renovate her newly bought property: 'Workmen would multiply the price by two or three times. I spent 18 months looking for workmen, and that was with Croatian friends to help me.'

According to all accounts, Croatia, as a new recruit in the tourism and second-homes market, is determined not to go the same way as France, Spain and much of Italy, with concrete ribbon developments along the Mediterranean. The Minister of Tourism has announced that he will develop tourism without resorting to ruining the country's coastline.

Before buying in Croatia, incomers must obtain permission to buy from the Croatian government, although this is usually a relatively simple process. Buyers who are used to the sophisticated marketing methods of French, Spanish and Italian estate agents have to realize, though, that as yet the Croatian market is relatively unestablished and fairly chaotic.

In 2008, there are two distinct ways to buy a Croatian property: either as an individual, or as a company. If you are able to pay cash there are no problems but if you have to borrow, you will have to set up a Croatian-registered company. There is also a system known as operative leasing, where you buy, in effect, a lease on the property. Whichever way you buy, the system is complicated and it is essential to secure the services of an English-speaking lawyer.

The transaction has to be witnessed and signed in front of the notary public, who charges around 1.5 per cent of the purchase price. There will also be a 5 per cent stamp duty-type tax on the property. These systems will probably become simpler and more streamlined when Croatia joins the EU in either 2009 or 2010.

At the time of writing, there are many new apartments being built in the popular tourist areas of Croatia, which between them attract 250,000 tourists a year. A new two-bed apartment would typically cost around £85,000 in 2008. Ryanair and easyJet now fly to Pula and Rijeka, and other low-cost flights are available to Dubrovnik and Split. As we know from other places, property prices and tourism generally rise in accordance with the ease of getting to a place.

Maria Bennett, who has decided to specialize in Croatian properties, has properties on her books from around £30,000 to £400,000, and also entire islands priced at up to £1.3 million. The best step, as with buying in other places, is to take a holiday in Croatia and suss out available properties and prices.

The language problems are shrinking, say buyers, as ever more younger Croatians now speak English, and also know German and Italian. Bennett believes it's necessary to have a Croatian friend with you when trying to close a deal on a property there.

Crime rates – always a cause of concern when buying into foreign lands – are considered to be low in Croatia, and it's possible, say property owners there, to walk through the streets of Dubrovnik in perfect safety at two or three in the morning – always assuming one wants to do this, of course.

Croatia has already become a focus for second-homers among Germans and East Europeans, who tend to choose the coastal areas. Coastal properties cost between £50,000 and £100,000 and, of course, the Yugoslavian coastline has for many years been a popular holiday destination. In fact, it looks as though Croatia is set to become as popular as somewhere like Cyprus in the coming years, and the attractions are rather similar, with the exception that the place is (so far at least) not full of second-home Brits.

Croatia's economy is rapidly becoming more stable and, since 2006, the buy-to-let market has started to take off. Previously, most foreign owners just kept their property for themselves, and many would-be investors were put off by having to obtain a rental licence if they wanted to let their property. There are rumours that Zagreb offers the opportunity for long-term lets but at the time of writing this market is untried and untested. You would have to be brave at this stage to risk it.

Mostly, Croatia offers heritage buildings either in need of restoration or already restored. And prices are rising rapidly; since 2003 they have gone up by 20 per cent a year. While it is still possible to buy cheap properties, a three-bedroom restored stone house with land and sea views in Dubrovnik can easily cost £300,000. If you are prepared to do the restoration yourself, properties can be picked up very cheaply.

## The new Europeans

Apart from those already mentioned, the 'new Europeans' are Estonia, Lithuania, Latvia, the Czech Republic, Slovenia, Poland, Slovakia and Hungary, which joined the EU in 2004. Bulgaria and Romania joined in 2007. Only four years into EU membership for most of them (at the time of writing) these Eastern European countries have come under the investor microscope and speculators have visited them to see whether or not there are rich pickings on offer, now or in the near future, for the brave or adventurous purchaser. We will look at them briefly one by one.

## Bulgaria

Bulgaria has easily become the most hyped, the most promoted and the most talked-about of the 'new Europeans'. Very many developers have descended upon this country, and there are now specialist Bulgarian exhibitions taking place and cut-price inspection trips are being offered. If it all sounds very much like the up-and-coming Spain, this is underlined by the fact that almost every newspaper property supplement you open will now contain an article or update on Bulgaria, mainly because developers have been falling over themselves to offer free trips to property journalists. In fact, Bulgaria is fast becoming a property-abroad cliché.

But it's by no means over. In fact, in some ways, Bulgaria has only just begun. Its GDP growth since it was freed from Communism has been one of the highest in Eastern Europe, and developments have been going up everywhere, long before the EU accession happened. Since accession, the country is likely to become an ever faster-growing hotspot.

One might ask: why? Well, one answer is that Bulgaria has so much to offer. Its natural resources are stunning, with wonderful beaches, mountains and natural spas, and there is also plenty of room and scope for growth and development. Tourism is on the up, and most popular of all is the Black Sea coast, which is fantastic for summer holidays. Bulgaria also has a very fast-growing ski industry, and its ski resorts are being developed very quickly, with property at a fraction of the price of a ski chalet in Switzerland or France, for instance. The ski resorts of Bansko, Borovetz and Pamporavo have started to attract investors, with Bansko being the most favoured.

Golf courses, always a sign of upmarket investment, are being developed in the highly popular Sunny Beach and Golden Sands resorts. There are also spa resorts such as Velingrad, Albenia and also Kyustendil, famous for its mineral waters since Roman times.

One major disadvantage is that there are not, in 2008, any low-cost airlines operating to Bulgaria, but that may change in time.

The country's capital, Sofia, is rapidly developing into a modern European city, with new-build apartments aimed at the burgeoning buy-to-let market. Bulgarian property experts advise investors not to go too cheaply – in 2007 you could still get a studio apartment for £15,000, with some properties being offered for as little as £5,000 – but to buy a property in a complex that has good facilities such as restaurants, swimming pools and bars, all the things that tourists and visitors demand you would have to spend much more.

Although Bulgaria, which is a big country, has many natural attractions, people have been put off buying there because of what they imagine are insuperable complications. It is still the case, in 2008, that you can buy buildings but not land. Foreigners are allowed to acquire title to buildings or part of buildings – such as apartments – and the right to construct a building on land belonging to somebody else. You are, though, allowed to form your own Bulgarian-registered company and buy the land in the name of that company. To do this, you would have to first find a Bulgarian solicitor who speaks English and who can set up the company for you. Alternatively, there are now property companies operating in Bulgaria that can do it all for you. As the country is harmonized into the EU, the process of buying will become ever easier.

In 2008, there are many conflicting views about whether it is a good idea to buy – or at least invest – in Bulgaria. In February 2008, a report in the *Financial Times* stated that British buyers had disappeared from the ski resort of Bankso as prices started to fall fast. The famous US 'credit crunch' has adversely affected Bulgaria's still-fragile economy, according to the global credit rating agency Fitch.

However, all these things are subject to constant fluctuation and by the time this book is published – as opposed to being written – the situation could have radically changed. But the fact remains that there is always a risk when buying into these newer destinations which have not yet fully found their feet in a market economy.

Around 40,000 Britons have so far taken the plunge to buy in Bulgaria, as well as many Russians and Greeks, who are snapping up the still-cheap properties. So far as mortgages go, it is possible to borrow up to 75 per cent of the purchase price and the maximum term is 25 years.

Christo Iliev, chief executive of the development company Bulgarian Land Development, explains how it all began for him.

> I started the company in 1989 when all the land was owned by the government. When the Communist regime ended, this land was given back to the original owners, or the children or grandchildren of those owners. This meant that the whole of Bulgaria was parcelled up into tiny pieces of land, and we started buying from owners piece by piece. If you buy land, you have to be local, and know the people who own it.
>
> During the Communist regime, every country in the Soviet Union had its own specialization and Bulgaria was popular as a resort, so it already had a tradition of service, which was not common generally in Communism. It's easy to see why as apart from having the twin attractions of sun and snow, Bulgaria is the same distance from Moscow, Stockholm, Berlin and London, so easy to get to from several capitals.
>
> It remains the cheapest resort in Europe, and you can in 2008 get a fully furnished two-bed apartment for £50,000, with a sea view. Bulgaria is also small, so there will never be huge numbers of properties or areas to choose from.

The first foreigners to buy in Bulgaria after communism, says Christo, were the intrepid English, who initially arrived in 2000.

> In those days, the only properties available were old houses in villages which needed major renovation, and these people bought either holiday homes or came to live there; they were not what we would now call pure investors.
>
> Now, though, around 70 per cent of British and Irish people who buy in Bulgaria do so as an investment, although 70 per cent of Russians are still buying for themselves.

There are several kinds of tourist market in Bulgaria, says Christo: summer visitors, skiers, golf enthusiasts and those in search of spas.

> All of these expanding markets are making the tourist season longer, meaning that investors can buy with confidence. The

most expensive properties are those right on or near golf courses, but another option for investors is to buy in cities, where year-round rents can be commanded and the properties are easier to resell. There are also now many vineyards in Bulgaria, and these have their potent attraction as well.

In the past, the biggest problem for many tourists was actually getting to Bulgaria, but since October 2007, easyJet has been flying to Sofia. There are three main political parties active in the country, and Bulgaria has the lowest income tax in Europe, currently set at 10 per cent.

It seems that Bulgaria can only grow as an investor destination but any foreigner wanting to buy into the country must go with a developer who has a good and long track record of building successful developments on land which has been properly bought from its original owners.

If buying off-plan or new-build, you must check that the developer has all the necessary permissions in place and is an experienced developer. It can be risky to buy from a new developer in a new country. Several developers are now offering rental guarantee schemes but, as always, you have to ensure that there is a genuine market after the guarantee period ends. When buying old properties, it is vital to check the validity of the title, as these often got lost or destroyed during the Communist era.

As to making a quick profit from your Bulgarian purchase, don't expect prices to rise straight away. The massive building programme going on currently in the country means that supply is likely to exceed demand for some time. Regard it as a long-term investment. Also, never try to evade the local tax system, as the penalties are severe. Bulgarians aren't daft!

If I were interested in buying in Bulgaria I would first contact all the main developers now operating in the country, get their brochures, look carefully at their websites and compare, compare, compare, before making a purchase decision.

## *A retirement haven*

In 2006, only around 800 British people were actually resident in Bulgaria, although property prices have been rising 25–30 per cent a year. There are signs, though, that Bulgaria is becoming a new retirement haven for adventurous British people who feel that France, Italy and Spain have become too built up and commercialized.

One such couple, Yvonne and Stephen Kent, bought a newly built two-bedroom, three-bathroom house in Kosharitsa for £34,000 in 2003 and reckon that, three years later, the property had tripled in value. In their village, they say, there are already five other retired British couples, and they are learning Bulgarian, which they maintain is one of the hardest languages in the world to learn, particularly when you are no longer young.

The cost of living is low, and this is a potent attraction, particularly for those no longer earning. A bottle of wine costs around £1 and beer only 20p. Groceries and utilities are cheap compared with the UK, and there are plenty of fresh vegetables available at local markets, all sold for practically nothing – and even nothing, at the end of the day, when the market stallholders are packing up to go home.

At the moment, around 1,000 Britons are buying in Bulgaria each year, but most are investors and holiday-home owners rather than retirees. One piece of advice for those considering Bulgaria as a retirement destination, is to choose a city or village, as the popular tourist spots become ghost towns from October onwards, when the temperature gets distinctly cooler. The new ski resorts are set in beautiful scenery and there is also a possibility for retirement homes.

## Romania

If Bulgaria is set to become the new Spain, then Romania is set to become the new Bulgaria. Its accession to the EU in 2007 means that many changes are in place that will benefit both tourists and property investors. Chief among these are plans for new airports and new roads. As with many Eastern European countries, it has not been possible to buy land directly in Romania, except by establishment of a Romanian-based company. This will all change in 2012, when direct freehold ownership of land by foreigners will become possible. The euro will also become Romania's currency.

At the moment, according to Romanian property experts, the amount of red tape required to buy a property is incredible. For this reason, it is essential to buy through an established Romanian property company and to retain the services of an English-speaking Romanian lawyer – if such can be found. Also, as many homes were forcibly seized during the Ceausescu era, it is essential to establish title on older properties and ensure that these homes are not likely to be claimed by former inhabitants or owners.

In 2008, it is still possible to buy a house in the country requiring extensive renovation for around £5,000. The choice of properties in Romania consists of resale homes, old and newish, off-plan and new-build, although the Romanian government has passed laws to limit the amount of speculative building projects.

Bucharest is two hours away from London by air, and the once-mysterious area of Transylvania, reputed home of Dracula and the apparent setting for many Hammer horror films, is now being developed as a distinctly non-horrific ski resort. Bucharest is attracting foreign businesses, with Boeing, BMW, PricewaterhouseCoopers and Hewlett-Packard all now with a presence in the capital.

Another potent attraction is the low cost of living, although this will inevitably rise with EU harmonization. Presently something of an uncharted territory, Romania looks interesting for both investors and second-homers. In 2008, prices start at £35,000 for a new studio apartment and £55,000 for a two-bed apartment.

## Estonia

Estonia has some fabulous renovations in the old part of the capital, Tallinn, but apparently the new-builds are in greater demand. Around half of the new properties now go to foreigners, some of whom are business people who need a permanent base in the city, and others are people buying to let.

British people are already buying up properties in Estonia, where you pay 26 per cent tax on a second home bought as an investment property. A one- or two-bed apartment in Tallinn costs around £50,000 and you can pay up to £150,000 for a smart renovated apartment in the highly sought-after medieval old town.

Estonia is not, though, Spain or Florida, temperature-wise. It can be below freezing from mid-December to late February.

Estonia is set to adopt the euro in 2011, and this should have a positive impact on property values. According to a survey by the Royal Institution of Chartered Surveyors (RICS), Estonia saw more capital appreciation in 2006 than any other European country, and foreign business, particularly from countries like Sweden, Finland and the United States, investing in the country. There is a booming tourist industry, with foreign tourism having increased 40 per cent since 2004. Wages are increasing, and interest rates are low, around 3.3 per cent. EasyJet has arrived and mortgages have become available for foreign buyers.

According to Estonian investment expert Darren Goodson, Estonia is set to become the Hong Kong of Eastern Europe. It seems ever more that these countries, for so long cut off from the rest of the world by the yoke of Communism and the Iron Curtain, are set to explode on the world stage as never before.

But Darren Goodson also reminds us that Estonia is not all about making money from property. The capital Tallinn is a beautiful city and its Old Town is one of the oldest still standing in Europe. For the moment, though, there is not much development or investment outside of Tallinn.

## Lithuania

This is the largest of the Baltic States and, by all accounts, an investor's dream. The capital, Vilnius, is a vibrant cultural centre where property prices are now rising fast.

The old town and city centre are the most popular areas for investors and prices for flats are rising by 15 to 20 per cent per annum. There are now no restrictions on what foreign buyers can purchase.

It is worth bearing in mind that new properties in Lithuania are often sold without interiors such as kitchens or bathrooms, so need work by you before they become habitable. Mortgages are available and you can borrow up to 90 per cent of the purchase price. Lithuania, like France, operates on a notary system, and you would typically have to pay this person 1 per cent of the purchase price.

In 2008, the average price for a family home was £120,000 and outside the city, £56,000.

## Latvia

Latvia's most sought-after properties, at least by foreign buyers, are in the old town area of Riga. Prices are increasing rapidly, apparently because Russians are becoming serious investors; city centre prices grew by 20 per cent in 2004.

At the moment, around 15 per cent of sales are to foreign buyers, with Britons making up only 15 per cent of these. There are no restrictions now on what foreigners may buy, but the estate agent profession has not really got going and you will have to research areas on your own. There are also, in all these new European countries, language problems and maybe alphabet problems as well. Make sure you understand what it's all about!

At the time of writing, a two-bed apartment in Latvia costs around £50,000 and a three-bed house, around £100,000. Local banks are willing to lend money to investors and on property there is a stamp duty of 2 per cent. There is also an annual real estate tax of 1.5 per cent of the property's value.

## Czech Republic

In the Czech Republic, Prague has been established for a long time as a major tourist city and very many Britons have already bought apartments there. Prague remains the main property hotspot, with all other places lagging a long way behind.

Membership of the EU in 2004 has already had a major effect on property ownership by foreigners. Before that date, foreign buyers had to form a company in order to buy property. Now, though, individuals can buy, but have to apply for a residency permit. For this, a lawyer conversant with local laws is necessary.

Taxes in the Czech Republic remain low, but there is a 3 per cent transfer tax payable when you buy a property. As yet, prices are not wildly appreciating, but this may change.

Alan Goss, a property and finance consultant and former mining engineer, decided to invest in Brno, the second-largest city in the Czech Republic and the judicial centre, after intensive research into all the Eastern European markets.

He said: 'I felt the Czech Republic was stable compared to many Central European countries. In addition the rate of literacy was good, and in spite of the language problems, it didn't feel as "foreign" as some places and the currency is stable as well.

'As I also have a Czech girlfriend, the language problem could be easily overcome, and I took her with me to meetings as she could translate for me. I then had to decide which type of property to go for, and after getting to know just what was available, I felt that First Republic apartments built in the interwar years, with their good solid construction and good proportions, offered the best investment prospects. The apartments are well planned and aesthetically pleasing.'

Alan Goss was looking for apartments he could rent to native Czechs rather than holidaymakers, and his first purchase was a three-bedroom apartment costing £46,000, which gives him a 9 per cent gross yield.

The buying process, he adds, is very different to that in the UK. 'They are definitely at least 10 years behind and have as yet no recognized profession of estate agents. The whole property business is very new, and you have to start off by spotting a property you fancy and then asking if it might be for sale. You have to remember that during the Communist years nobody ever swapped property, so there is no recent history of buying and selling homes. The apartment I bought went into private ownership in 2000.'

You can get a Czech mortgage, and establishing title – often a problem with emerging countries – is not difficult here because the land title is held in a central registry, which is open for the buyer to consult. All properties, whether apartments or houses, are held freehold and there is no such thing as leasehold. 'But,' warns Alan, 'you have to be sure the seller understands everything as it is easy to get mistaken translations when there is no exact equivalent of terms.'

Since the Czech Republic joined the EU in 2004, there has been a double-taxation exemption, so buyers do not have to pay property taxes twice. British buyers are extremely welcome, as it is assumed they are all vastly rich and can pay high prices and, according to Alan Goss, they have the added cachet of being considered 'sophisticated foreigners'. Alan Goss also says that even if you accidentally pay over the odds, property is still cheap compared to the UK and you are still likely to get a bargain. You will definitely need an English-speaking lawyer, and also need to use the Czech language, as English is not much spoken.

Alan Goss is also looking to invest, both for himself and on behalf of others, in Slovakia and Poland. He believes that the best property investment possibilities lie in Eastern European countries, rather than more established markets, especially as many people still fear to tread there.

Also, the emerging markets still have a long way to go. There are many ways of investing, and one should not always just think of buying in order to rent to holidaymakers, or with the holiday or tourist trade in mind. Alan Goss is doing something different by renting to natives, for the long term, rather than just looking at short-term holiday lets.

It is absolutely essential to secure the services of a Czech-speaking (or understanding!) lawyer as not only will the important documentation be written in Czech but you will also need somebody on your side to protect your interests. As Alan Goss pointed out, 'rich investors' from abroad are often seen as easy game. Also, in many areas estate agents are not regulated or licensed although, having said that, by all accounts Prague now has a number of excellent estate agents who can handle every aspect of the buying process.

Some buyers find it easier to set up a limited liability company to cover Czech property purchases although this will incur ongoing fees as well as annual accounts to file and corporate taxes to pay if you are renting the property out.

In any case, around 8 per cent of the purchase price should be allocated for fees and services, and there will be ongoing costs such as annual property taxes to pay, as well.

## Slovenia

Slovenia is a tiny country of less than 2 million inhabitants and is already a popular tourist destination with good beaches, a Mediterranean climate and skiing in winter. There are as yet very few Slovenian estate agents and, it is said, reliable information on properties for sale can be hard to obtain. For these reasons, very few Britons have taken the plunge and bought property, but Slovenia (capital Ljubljana) is a beautiful country, and those prepared to take a risk could eventually reap a significant profit.

As ever, with any successful investment, those in first make the greatest gains.

Heather Mills, the former wife of Sir Paul McCartney, has a bolthole in Slovenia where she escapes when things get too much. Slovenia is a completely clean, well-ordered country and on a visit there in 2007, I did not see one speck of litter anywhere. There are many beautiful, upmarket hotels and the countryside is rather like Austria or Switzerland. Slovenia is very much a country of extreme sports, so if this is your interest, that will be the place for you.

English is very widely spoken and taught in all schools. The alphabet is also now the same as ours – a useful reform brought in by President Tito, I was told – although the visitor may wonder whether there are rather too many 'l's in the language.

So far as properties are concerned, there is not as yet much new building going on, but most of the existing properties are in extremely good condition and there are few Communist-type apartment blocks. The most popular properties for foreigners to buy are the 'Heidi'-type chalets.

Readers of this popular children's book may remember how, as a child, Heidi lived in a summer chalet in the mountains with her reclusive grandfather. In those days, farmers used to take their cattle up into the mountains, and stay there with them all summer, then go down in the winter, except that Heidi's granddad refused to do this and stubbornly stayed in his mountainside chalet all year round. Nowadays, these quaint little chalets have all been turned into holiday homes, while keeping much of their traditional flavour.

There are, at the time of writing, no mortgages available for buying in Slovenia so you would have to finance your own purchase fully. Buying in Slovenia, for foreigners at least, used to be a long-drawn-out and complicated process taking up to a year, but since the country joined the EU in 2007, with its new legislation opening up the country to foreign buyers, this has become vastly simplified, with no restrictions, and need only take a few weeks.

You would need a Slovenian bank account to cover standing orders for utilities, property taxes and other ongoing costs. Tourism is by far the fastest-growing industry, so Slovenia is certainly one to watch, and low-cost airlines are already flying direct from Stansted. If you go from Gatwick you will have to change in either France or Germany.

## Poland

As with most of the former Soviet countries, the greatest property price increases have so far been in the capital, in this case Warsaw, where residential prices rose by 25 per cent in 2003.

In 2008, the Polish economy appears strong and the 'hotspots' include Warsaw, Cracow and Gdansk, where demand is uniformly high. As in Lithuania, new apartments are often sold without interiors and many may not even have flooring.

Mortgages are readily available for foreign investors, and £1.4 billion was given in home loans in Poland in 2003. Foreigners can freely buy and sell, and apartments range in price from £50,000 to £100,000. There are not many estate agents in the country, but

Ober-Haus is one company that has many branches in Eastern Europe, plus a good reputation.

In Warsaw, around 10,000 new apartments are now being built each year, but demand still greatly outstrips supply, as many Poles are moving to the capital and investors also now have a beady eye on Warsaw apartments. Real estate agents Ober-Haus say that the biggest demand in all Polish cities is for newly built flats, and these are now being sold off-plan.

But – unlike the Czech Republic – it appears that there is not a ready rental market in Warsaw or other major cities, and investors are advised not to rely on rental income to repay a bank loan or mortgage. Foreign currency mortgages, particularly those in Swiss francs, are increasingly popular.

As well as Warsaw, foreign buyers are starting to discover Cracow, the cultural capital of Poland, for investment purposes. Situated two hours' drive from Warsaw, Cracow has become the financial services centre for companies such as PricewaterhouseCoopers, BP and Tesco, which are sending their high-flyers on relocation packages to this ancient city.

In the past, it has not been possible for financial whiz kids to find the kind of apartments or houses that suited their lifestyle or pocket, but upscale apartments are now being developed, often out of existing medieval buildings. Prices for apartments being renovated in the city's Grand Square hover at £1 million, so they are not cheap, but some property developers are certain that there is a big potential market to be tapped for the wealthy British (or Polish) investor.

Violinist Nigel Kennedy lived in Cracow for several years, so it's not just business people who are being attracted to the place, and cheap flights are now attracting ever more tourists to the city. Many property experts are seeing Cracow as the new Prague – before this city became the favourite destination for riotous stag parties, that is.

Currency in Poland is still in zlotys, which can confuse some investors – the country is expected to change to the euro in 2010 – and as ever, it is important to know how the costs stack up. There will be an agent's fee of around 3 per cent; stamp duty of 2 per cent, lawyer's fees of 1 per cent and between £3,500 and £6,000 to register the property.

Once the property has been owned by the same person for five years, there is no capital gains tax to pay by foreign investors, although advice should be taken on this before buying, as the situation is not totally clear-cut, especially as the Polish authorities always assume that property bought by a foreigner is for the purposes of being rented out rather than being lived in as a home.

Mortgages of up to 80 per cent are available for foreign buyers and property prices are rising fast in Cracow, as more ancient buildings are being restored, often to a very high spec.

It is unlikely that a UK bank will be able to arrange a mortgage on a Polish property, but you can release equity in your main home to pay cash. Alternatively, specialist credit companies will be able to arrange a Polish mortgage, although this service can be expensive, as it is complicated. Obviously a lot of number-crunching is needed as, although properties may seem cheap compared with UK homes, for instance, the cost of borrowing can be high.

As with all once-Communist countries, it is vital to be able to establish title, particularly when buying a Communist-era property. Several potential buyers have asked whether a relative or descendant of a Jewish Holocaust survivor might claim that the property was seized during the Second World War. Although this is very unlikely, and is becoming ever more unlikely with time, there is a faint possibility that it could happen, so the question needs to be asked. If it did occur, the chances are that the government would pay compensation to the claimant, although there are still some properties that are considered not to be 'clean', which means you would not be protected by the law if they were claimed.

Because of the complicated and often traumatic history of Poland, it is important to look at the history of transactions of older buildings, particularly in the case of apartments where there is only one registry number but several separate units within the building. These apartments are designated 'community owned' and are cheaper than others, but there may be problems with untangling what is your bit when you come to sell. They are best avoided by foreign investors.

Many older properties in Poland are in dire need of renovation and, although Polish workers have a good reputation, buyers would probably be better off choosing a property being renovated by established developers. Polish workers have a less positive reputation for charging foreigners much higher rates than when they are building for natives.

However, many developers in Cracow, for instance, are now buying up long-neglected, dilapidated buildings and selling them off-plan before work starts. Many of these are architect-designed and will be wonderful when finished.

So far as taxes are concerned, Poland has a double-taxation treaty with the UK, which means you will not be taxed twice on any tax you pay in Poland. It is advisable to open a Polish bank account once you have bought your property.

The Polish economy is growing fast but its successively weak governments since the fall of Communism have been racked by corruption scandals.

As with many Eastern European markets, familiarity with the language is a must, and Polish is not a language much spoken by outsiders. Therefore, a bilingual interpreter is essential when you buy, especially in Cracow, where prices already tend to be very high.

## Slovakia

Slovakia is a sliver of a country, and one of the poorer new EU countries, yet it has some of the loveliest scenery and landscapes in Europe.

In 2008, this country remains high risk for foreign property investors, due to its fragile economy. Wages are low and unlikely to rise, which means property prices are unlikely to rise significantly, either. This country is only just starting to think about foreign investment, and has a long way to go. As with many Eastern European countries, there are very few estate agents.

Slovakia has been called one of the rising stars of Eastern Europe. But then, don't they all enjoy this reputation? Most have experienced phenomenal growth since joining the EU and, in Slovakia, there has been direct investment from the United States and this has encouraged developers to start building new complexes. Only about 13,000 new properties are being constructed annually, so there is plenty of demand to meet the restricted supply.

Since Slovakia's accession to the EU, the Slovakian government has been encouraging foreign property investment by waiving stamp duty, so this, combined with the very low prices, makes investment attractive. Two-bedroom apartments are available from £29,000, and many developers are offering a 7 per cent guaranteed rental yield for two years. As ever, you need to be sure there will be a strong rental demand after the end of the guarantee period. Older-style properties are also popular, as are well-maintained pre-war blocks.

The capital, Bratislava, is very similar to Prague in appearance and both are on the River Danube. The fact that the country is next to Austria means that commuting to Vienna is easily on the cards.

## Hungary

Again, the capital, Budapest, is the hotspot, with District V the most sought after. There are lots of coffee houses, good value restaurants and high culture available. Hungary has a reputation of being – so far – the most successful of the former Eastern bloc countries in terms of attracting foreign investment, and many international estate agents now have branches there.

The majority of property sales are of flats and many are extremely spacious, not to say grandiose. It may be difficult to obtain a mortgage in Hungary, but as apartments in the capital go for around £70,000, cash buyers are being attracted. Overseas buyers must apply to the local authority for permission to buy, and it may be necessary to set up a Hungarian company. Again, reliable legal advice is essential.

All the expert predictions are that *now* – that is, 2008 – is the time to buy, before the long-expected boom takes off. According to reports, investors are already looking at Budapest with a beady eye, and in 2003 around 1,000 properties in Budapest went to foreign buyers. Most of these purchases were new apartments, but there may also be scope for buying older properties in need of work.

To sum up, these Eastern European countries, which joined the EU in 2004 and 2007, offer exciting, if somewhat risky, opportunities to the foreign buyer. These emerging markets need watching closely, as they could represent not only attractive investments, but also offer the exotic excitement of owning a place in a country relatively unspoilt and undiscovered.

# Finland and Lapland

When the first edition of this book came out, nobody in their right minds would have considered investing in those regions consisting mainly of frozen waste, Finland and Lapland. However, things have changed and now the buy-to-let investor is being heavily targeted in these areas which most of us only seem to think about once a year, when Santa Claus gets on his sleigh behind his reindeer.

Although there are still more reindeer than people, the Lapp government is starting to invest in the tourist industry, aiming mainly at the ever-growing ski market. You can ski for six months of the year in Finland, should you want to and the property company abovethearctic has properties in three resorts in Lapland – Yllas, Levi and Ruka.

Foreigners can also now invest in traditional Lapp tepees in the Snow Village, where there is a hotel built entirely of ice. The hotel stays in place all winter and then gradually melts in the summer. The tepees are not that cheap – around £100,000 for a one-bedder complete with sauna and whirlpool – but they are newly built, and owners can rent them out to tour operators. Ryanair now flies to Tampere, near the capital, Helsinki, and the special 'Santa' flights are increasing in popularity each year.

More than 4 million tourists visit Finland every year and enthusiasts say that although there is almost 24-hour darkness in winter, by contrast, in summer it never gets dark at all. It is also supposed to be quite warm in summer but mainly, you would have to enjoy snow and snow-type activities to get much out of the country. It is the case, though, that snow is increasing in popularity all the time, not just for skiers, but also for cruises. Cruises to Alaska and Antarctica are becoming the most popular of all and there is no doubt that desolate regions of snow can be dramatic to glimpse – at least from a safe, warm distance.

# Turkey

Turkey has already entered the imaginations of foreign buyers, and there have been several television programmes featuring Britons who have bought second homes in Turkey.

Some people feel that Turkey is not really a 'proper' European country and should not be allowed to join the EU. Because of this, Turkey as an investment or second-home proposition is very much still up in the air. Currently there is not a good or reliable local legal system and no mortgage or legal infrastructure in the country. Estate agents have only been established for a few years, have not yet become a proper profession, and few have any experience of dealing with foreign buyers.

Turkey has only really been on the property scene for foreign buyers since 2003, but is attracting investors because of its beautiful coastline, large size and wonderful beaches.

The Bodrum peninsula is the main hotspot and already contains prestigious and expensive properties, largely because it has one of the best climates in Europe (if you consider Turkey part of Europe). It is also glamorous and sophisticated. Yet you can buy a two-bed apartment within walking distance of Bodrum for under £50,000. Aficionados maintain that modern Turkish architecture is not only breathtakingly attractive, but the construction is of high calibre as well.

The main reason for Turkey's entrance onto the international property scene is its EU aspirations, and prices could rise by as much as 50 per cent if Turkey manages to join. However, at the time of writing, this is very uncertain and the subject of heated controversy. There is also much space for expansion and the recent deregulation of airways means it has become possible to fly into the country easily from all over Europe.

Turkey is being talked up as the new Spain, but the legal and administrative systems remain frail, and there is much 'illegal' property around. So – as yet, Turkey remains a high-risk area to buy property. But if you have around £50,000 or so to play with, you *could* make a killing in a few years.

Very many speculators, developers and property companies are advertising Turkish properties, aimed at investors. But, as a money-making venture, buying Turkish property remains a high-risk venture. Most investors are banking on EU membership, but to the author at least, this looks like playing for very high stakes.

## Investment opportunities in Turkey

At the time of writing, around 9,500 British people are resident in Turkey and around 65,000 have homes there. In recent years property prices have been rising 30–40 per cent a year. A two-bedroom apartment on the West Coast costs around £65,000 in 2008, but prices are likely to rise fast, which is one reason why many potential investors are keeping a beady eye on Turkey with its undoubtedly very beautiful landscapes, coastline, little villages and, also, modern developments.

The property market, though, remains largely unregulated and those who have already bought warn that there is a lot of red tape involved in buying a property and in particular, in establishing title. Yet potential investors can be beguiled by glossy brochures and high-powered marketing.

If considering investing in Turkey, you should make sure you use an agency that is a member of FOPDAC – the Federation of Overseas Property Developer's Agents and Consultants. This is important with all foreign transactions, as FOPDAC members have to abide by a code of practice, but it is even more essential when dealing with emerging markets.

You must also make sure you do not do direct deals with owners to save money, and also that you plan to hold the property for a minimum of four years, as after that time there is no capital gains tax to pay. At the time of writing, mortgages are not available in Turkey, so you would have to borrow in the UK, and most experts advise using a good currency broker, as you will almost always get a better rate than from the bank. Again, use a FOPDAC member.

The best property investments probably lie in areas where new roads and airports are being built and, as ever, sports facilities. There is quite a good rental market for holiday properties, and the season lasts from April to October. If buying an apartment, make sure you understand the type of tenure; most flats operate on the US condominium system.

Mortgages are available at rates from around 5.9 per cent in sterling or euros only and an extra 0.6 per cent is levied if the property is rented out. At the moment, only Turkish nationals can obtain Turkish mortgages. You can borrow up to 80 per cent of the valuation of the property, but only for certain areas such as the Turkish Riviera and Istanbul. You cannot normally borrow money on an off-plan development until after completion and the property has been legally registered in your name. Rental income in Turkey is taxed at 20–25 per cent, and community fees for apartments average £20–£50 a month. There is currently no capital gains tax levied on properties owned for more than four years.

All foreign buyers must be vetted by the Turkish military to ensure they are clear to buy the property. Although usually something of a formality, this process still takes about 8–10 weeks and only after clearance can a purchase proceed. Most buyers say that a bilingual lawyer is essential, as in common with many emerging markets not all titles in Turkey are automatically guaranteed.

# Morocco

Morocco still sounds impossibly exotic to some of us, but it is fast becoming a property investor market as well, thanks partly to budget airline Ryanair having signed a deal with the Moroccan government. The North African country has a long-established and possibly partly mythical reputation as the haunt of émigré artists and writers wishing to escape the restrictive laws and practices of their own country, but hard-nosed investors are finally starting to sniff around as well.

Certain Western outsiders, such as Paul Bowles and William Burroughs, have lived in Morocco, so there is a slight tradition of Westerners having homes there, and it certainly became popular with flower-power children in the hippy era, although the investor market is new.

The Moroccan government is keen to encourage tourism and overcome the somewhat negative aspects of the country, such as tourists being put off by being continually hassled by over-insistent vendors in the markets and on the beaches, and with some success. Tourism grew 18 per cent in 2007. Marrakesh, as the one Moroccan place most people have heard of, is not surprisingly the most popular place for investors, but new developments are starting to go up along the less well-known coast, and a huge range of new developments is being planned, aimed mainly at investors and the buy-to-let market. There is strong rental demand year-round, and the second-home interest is growing fast as well.

Morocco is also trying hard to position itself as a top ski destination. Oukaimeden in the Atlas Mountains is already an established ski area, but there are plans to turn it into Africa's only dedicated ski and golf resort (golf again!).

# Brazil

Brazil, in common with many other countries featured in this book, is working hard to give itself a new, improved image, with the result that foreign investment in property is proceeding apace. The most popular areas are of course Rio de Janeiro, famous for its carnival and multi-ethnic society, and Ipanerna and Leblon.

The Brazilian government is pouring money into the state of Bahia, where you can buy a ready-furnished apartment for £30,000. Many new apartments, in common with those in other investor countries, come with a guaranteed rental for a couple of years.

In order to buy in Brazil, you have to obtain a personal identification number before you can set up a bank account, and there is a fee for this, but most developers will have all the necessary documentation to hand.

Property contracts are written in both Portuguese and English, to make things easier, and the contract represents a binding guarantee of the full title. There is not, though, the inherent problem with title in Brazil that happens in some other emerging markets.

Brazil attracts 5 million tourists a year and is said to have a sound, stable economic structure. As ever when new tourist destinations are being developed, many golf courses are being built. Its economy is set to grow and, already, it is an attractive country for adventurous Brits although the 11- to 12-hour flights can be off-putting.

Because the buying system is based on Portuguese law, the services of a notary are required. Financial experts warn that mortgages in Brazil aimed at international investors attract interest rates of up to 35 per cent, so any finance needed should be raised in the UK.

# Uruguay

Uruguay, with its wide sandy beaches and old colonial towns, is also starting to attract international property investment. It is not perhaps the first choice of many, but luxury new developments are going up or being planned, all with the usual complement, now de rigueur, of sports facilities, bars, gyms and clubs.

So far as buying property goes, incomers have exactly the same rights as Uruguayan nationals, and there are no restrictions on transferring capital in or out of the country. An added attraction is that there is no income tax or capital gains tax for individuals, only businesses. Uruguay is Spanish-speaking and has a population of around 3.5 million, half of whom live in the capital, Montevideo. It is the second-smallest country in South America and has traditionally been better off than many other South American countries. Its main sport is football but, as tourism expands, so does the inevitable sport of golf.

For many UK people, this country was put on the map by novelist Martin Amis, who lived there for several years with his Uruguayan second wife, Isabel Fonseca. As yet, though, Uruguay is not really a tourist destination for Europeans and the investor potential is at the moment limited. With these faraway places, it is essential to go there, see what it is like and get a very strong feel about the place before buying, and never to be seduced by off-plan opportunities advertised online.

# Panama

Most of us in the UK would probably never have considered buying or investing in Panama until we saw pictures of the supposedly missing canoeist John Darwin and his wife Anne, smiling in their holiday home there. Then Panama was put on the buying abroad map.

The stranger-than-fiction story is that after being declared dead by a coroner when he supposedly drowned in a canoe accident, Darwin presented himself at a police station five years later saying: 'I think I am a missing person.' Reporters traced Anne Darwin to Panama after she was located there through a Google search. They showed her recent pictures of herself and the very much alive John at their faraway holiday home. Anne's reaction was to comment: 'Those pictures say it all, don't they?'

Later facing serious charges of obtaining money by deception, and remanded in custody in their home town of Hartlepool, this strange pair at least alerted the rest of us to the possibilities of ordinary people buying in Panama. The international property company escapes2.com says that Panama enjoys a low cost of living coupled with a booming economy and as such, is fast becoming an attractive investment and retirement destination. Many new apartments are being built and some companies are now offering fly'n'buy trips out there for potential investors and retirees. John and Anne Darwin had intended to retire quietly there after salting away large sums of money in Panama bank accounts from the sale of their UK properties, and their story certainly kept the whole world entertained towards the end of 2007.

# South Africa

South Africa, also a place of intense political torment for very many years, is beginning to emerge as an upmarket second home location. From the UK, it takes around 11 hours to get to Cape Town, and the climate and scenery are rather like those of Spain. In fact, South African-born Michele Sadler, who with her husband

# Fairmont
## HERITAGE PLACE
### *Zimbali*
#### SOUTH AFRICA

# A PLACE WHERE YOU BELONG

www.fairmontzimbali.com

Exclusive Private Residence Club - **Ownership from R750,000 (approx. £54,000)**

As an investor in the **Fairmont Heritage Place, Zimbali** - South Africa's Premier Private Residence Club - you will enjoy the pleasures of owning a spectacular vacation property in one of the world's finest resorts, the internationally acclaimed **Zimbali Coastal Resort**, without the many concerns and burdens of maintaining a traditional second home. Enjoy preferred access and privileges that include reciprocal rights at many of Fairmont's legendary hotels and resorts around the world.

**To invest in the Fairmont Heritage Place, Zimbali contact:**
Tel: +27 32 538 1205  Cell: +27 79 494 1527
Email: sales@fairmontzimbali.com  sales@zimbali.co.za

HOTELS & RESORTS
www.ifahotelsresorts.com

ZIMBALI
COASTAL RESORT
www.zimbali.co.za

# Fairmont
## HERITAGE PLACE
### Zimbali
#### SOUTH AFRICA

**ZIMBALI**
COASTAL RESORT

**Along the magnificent** Dolphin Coast of South Africa's Kwa Zulu Natal province, lies the undisputed "jewel in the crown" of the east coast of Africa – Zimbali Coastal Resort. Zimbali is a spectacularly beautiful destination and an example of the most environmentally sensitive residential and resort development in South Africa.

IFA Hotels & Resorts (IFA HR) is a global hotel, resort and real estate development company listed on the Kuwait and Johannesburg stock exchanges. IFA HR is committed to its investments in South Africa and recently announced that Fairmont Hotels & Resorts will manage its new resort in Zimbali. Fairmont Hotels & Resorts is a leading global luxury hotel management company with over a century

include 11 Signature beachfront Villas, 56 designer Apartments, 6 Hillside Villas, and 21 Golf Chalets and the Fairmont Heritage Place, Zimbali – South Africa's most exclusive private residence club.

Fairmont Heritage Place, Zimbali presents the astute investor with the opportunity of owning a magnificent holiday home without the downside of maintaining a second property. It also offers owners a range of outstanding services and amenities designed to make the experience of each visit incomparably enjoyable. Personal services include doormen who greet you by name, concierges that attend to your every need and chefs, masseurs, child minders and housekeepers – all delivering a memorable

*18th Fairway of Zimbali Golf Course*

*Fairmont Heritage Place, Zimbali Villa*

of experience in the hospitality industry. Fairmont's portfolio includes 56 distinctive hotels, including landmarks The Fairmont Banff Springs, The Fairmont San Francisco and New York's The Plaza.

The Fairmont Zimbali Hotel & Resort will offer the ultimate in luxury accommodation to hotel guests and residents alike. The world class five-star 157-suite Fairmont Zimbali Hotel will include conference facilities, a Willow Stream Spa, beach club, restaurants, wellness centre, and the new Gary Player signature golf course – the second championship course for Zimbali.

In addition, the Fairmont development will

level of service.

The Fairmont Heritage Place, Zimbali consists of 18 residences ranging in size from a generous 316 sqm two bedroom townhouse to a grand 566 sqm four bedroom villa. Both options have palatial terraces and private pools, stunning open living spaces, and expansive outdoor areas. Gourmet kitchens are state-of-the-art and feature oversized granite-topped breakfast bars, separating them from the generous living areas. Custom-built cabinetry, year-round complimentary storage space and branded stainless steel appliances offer privacy, functionality and style.

Every home is beautifully appointed and furnished. Attention has been lavished on the smallest of details. Fine artwork, exotic rugs, handmade fabrics, fabulous lighting, indulgent bed linen and magical outdoor spaces all contribute to creating a very special environment. Colour palettes of rich earth tones unite the homes with the African landscape.

Each one is a haven of luxury and perfection. Pricing is from R750,000 (approx €75,000) for a 1/13th share in a 2 bedroom unit, and R1,3000,000 (approx €130,000) for a 1/13th share in a 4 bedroom villa.

Every owner is entitled to an annual minimum of 21 pre-booked days at their Private Residence Club in Fairmont Heritage Place, Zimbali. In addition, extra days referred to as "Heritage Time" are available on an ad hoc basis during the year. Whether planning well in advance or indulging in spontaneous travel, the Club will go out of its way to ensure that owners are accommodated.

With the spectacular Indian Ocean as a backdrop to the range of excellent facilities, every day at Fairmont Heritage Place, Zimbali is an opportunity to play to the fullest. For tranquil pursuits, one can take a languid stroll along the pristine golden Zimbali beach or indulge in the Willow Stream Spa. Golf is integral to the premium lifestyle, with the keen golfer accommodated by the Tom Weiskopf-designed championship course rated as one of South Africa's finest golfing experiences. Currently under development is a 18-hole, par 72, Gary Player Signature Golf Course, modern Club House and a Gary Player Golf Academy with state-of-the-art driving range.

A world of luxury, fine hospitality and special privilege awaits owners of the Fairmont Heritage Place, Zimbali. Reciprocal use of other Fairmont Heritage Place communities, Fairmont and Raffles Hotels & Resorts in some of the world's most desirable destinations as well as discounts at all Fairmont Hotels & Resorts worldwide are included. Automatic entry into the ultra-exclusive, invitation only Fairmont President's Circle is an added benefit to be enjoyed. Fairmont Zimbali hotel amenity use privileges and value-added services such as transportation, personal shopping and professional childcare are provided.

Fairmont Heritage Place, Zimbali is a rare combination of elegance and sophistication within a naturally beautiful setting, making it a desirable destination where cherished memories and made and shared. Featuring a limited selection of exquisite residences with dazzling views of the Indian Ocean and lush surrounding landscape, together with a choice of excellent five-star facilities and amenities, there is every reason to visit often and enjoy a place you can call your own.

**Forever.**

Fairmont Zimbali Site

has bought a holiday home in Spain, said that she would choose South Africa like a shot if she felt it was safe and secure.

Most second or holiday homes offered in South Africa are extremely smart, very expensive and situated in their own gates or secure compounds. South Africa offers low interest rates, low inflation and, as such, is attracting an increasing amount of foreign property investors.

Although nobody is pretending that South Africa has a stable political regime, there are a number of reasons to consider a holiday home there. And heading all those reasons is our old friend, the weather.

As we have seen, just about everywhere in the northern hemisphere is cold in winter, and even sunny places such as southern Spain and Greece have their cold, inhospitable couple of months. South Africa, of course, has its summer when Europe has its winter, so by going so far south it's possible to escape the European winter altogether.

Because of the continuing political instability, most foreign buyers in South Africa are looking for secure multi-unit complexes. The country is popular because it represents value for money and an 'affordable, idyllic' lifestyle, according to the marketing spiel.

But you have to be sure that South Africa is what you want. Popular with the British because of the language and the longitude, the country also has some downsides. Two friends recently visited Cape Town with a view to buying a winter home there. This is their report:

The country is very beautiful indeed and extremely cheap. The restaurants offer wonderful food at very cheap prices indeed. There is a lot of development going on and house prices are cheap. You can get a nice flat for £40,000–£50,000 and a house with a pool for £100,000. There are lots of French, German and Dutch people with second homes there as well as English people.

Those are the upsides. Here, as we saw them, are the downsides. There are electrified fences everywhere keeping undesirables out. Everything seems to shut down at 5 pm and it does not feel safe to walk. You have to get taxis everywhere. The sea is too cold to swim in because it's the Atlantic Ocean. At least, it's too cold for those looking for warm sea in their holiday home.

Also, as yet flights are very expensive. There are no budget airlines operating to South Africa. From the UK, you are looking at a 12-hour flight and, although you don't exactly get jetlag because you remain in the same time zone, a long flight is a long flight.

Racism and segregation are immediately apparent to the foreigner, although those living there permanently probably wouldn't notice it. Also, there are a lot of shanty towns which are very large and totally poverty-stricken. It's a difficult one to hack – with many pros and cons.

However, Mike and Eileen Duffy, who import beauty products, have owned a house in Cape Town since 1997 and reckon it's the best thing they've ever done. Their one-storey house cost just £35,000 and Mike, who has a serious heart condition, spends five to six months there every year. Eileen says:

We'd been going to South Africa on business for many years anyway, and already loved the country. The climate is far better than in the UK and the country generally is less stressful – so long as you choose your area carefully. I would not be interested in Johannesburg or Durban, but Cape Town is lovely, sort of old English, and very safe and secure as well.

I don't have any reservations about the regime, but Mike and I feel that, if there is a coup and we lose our property, well, that's like losing some of your pension. It's a risk we are prepared to take.

The process of buying was, says Eileen, very simple and painless:

We bought a plot, as you do in Florida, and bought the house from the guy who built it. So far as we were concerned, it had every-thing we wanted for a holiday home. It was very easy to set up a bank account, very easy to buy the house and, as all the transactions were in English, there wasn't that nasty feeling there's something going on you don't understand.

Living is much cheaper than in the UK so the money we spend on flights is offset by the lower cost of living. Mike and I never really thought about buying a holiday home anywhere else, and that was partly because of our business.

In the beauty trade, our quietest times are Christmas and the New Year, so if we want to take a holiday at that time we have to go far afield to get the weather. So part of the reason for choosing South Africa was the way our professional lives work.

And although the flight is long, because it's in the same longitude you don't get jetlag. I always fly at night, taking the 9 pm flight; then I arrive at my destination at 9 the next morning. I'm tired but, because I don't have jetlag, I can cope the following day.

I now travel business-class because, as a frequent flyer, I clock up voyager miles and can upgrade an economy ticket.

Any drawbacks?

The only downside that we've come across so far is that, as British people, we can't get South African credit cards. All your finance has to come from the UK. But that has an upside as well, in that you're not tempted to spend as much money.

South Africa is a very beautiful country with many smart districts, and a typical Cape Town residence with sea views, five bedrooms, swimming pool and multi-car garage costs around £500,000. Vast town houses are available from around £300,000 and old manor houses from about £400,000. One of the most popular styles for incomers is the Dutch thatch.

In the past, most people who bought properties in South Africa were those with historical or family links to the country, but now it's being discovered as a place in its own right to buy a dream home. The currency is the rand; the exchange rate is about 0.727 UK pounds to the South African rand (ZAR), although of course subject to constant change.

The east coast is semi-tropical, rather like Florida, and can be humid in summer, again like Florida. Temperatures in both winter and summer are high, although it can get cold at night. There is little rain for most of the year.

So far as residency is concerned, EU citizens may stay for up to six months at a time, so long as they can support themselves and have a return ticket. Anybody who wishes to stay for a longer time has to acquire a residency permit, and an employment permit if intending to work there. This applies to self-employment as well as employment. But if property has already been bought in the country, its value will count towards your residency qualifications.

Income tax is payable only on income produced in South Africa, such as rental income. There is a top rate of 45 per cent. Private health insurance is advised, although state hospitals have a good reputation.

All types of property are available for incomers, from coastal properties to grand mansions and game lodges. All money brought into the country must go through the South African Reserve Bank, although you may take any money made on property resale out of the country. Buying a property generally takes about 10 weeks, start to finish, and it's possible to get mortgages for up to 50 per cent of the property's value. Estate agent fees come to around 5 to 7 per cent, and there is also a transfer tax payable by the buyer. This is similar to the 'intangible tax' levied on US properties.

South Africa would probably appeal to the kind of people who like the idea of Spain, but have been put off by the vast amount of cheap housing and ugly hotels along the coast. So far, South Africa has not been spoilt in this way, and now this looks unlikely. It remains, like Italy, an upmarket destination and, if you avoid Johannesburg, crime rates are no higher than in the UK – at least according to what this author has been told by estate agents marketing South African properties.

It is possible to get permanent residency in South Africa if certain conditions are met. For a retired person permit, which is what the majority of incomers would most probably require, you have to be able to prove a minimum monthly pension of £1,711 from the country of origin, or have a net worth of £1 million. Retirement visas are normally for four years, after which time they can be renewed.

# Australia

Because of its great distance from the UK – an arduous 20-hour flight – Australia may not be an obvious choice for a holiday home. However, increasing numbers of UK citizens are retiring there, moving there or buying investment properties there. The reasons are many – Australia is a vast country with never-ending opportunities to explore, there are thriving and exciting towns and cities, much culture and although the country was originally colonized by the British, there is now a multicultural feel about it.

There are huge numbers of Chinese in Australia and particularly in Sydney. Their ancestors were initially attracted by the gold rush in Victorian times and many of them are now fifth- and sixth-generation. They are fully integrated but preserve many of their customs and festivals, such as observing the Chinese New Year and there is an exciting Chinatown, vastly more vibrant and lively than the London Soho equivalent. There are also many Indians, Vietnamese and of course the indigenous inhabitants, the Aboriginals. And if you like sport, well, Australia is definitely the country for you as they are obsessed with it, particularly cricket and rugby, although in common with the rest of the world, golf is growing fast.

There is a rapidly growing 'prestige' market in Australia, where high-priced, high-end properties are bought mainly by expatriates. Many of these are in Sydney, which is much, much smaller than London, yet has a huge array of cultural activities, museums, art galleries, theatres and of course the world-famous Sydney opera house and something London certainly doesn't have – the famous Bondi Beach. The climate is vastly better than in the UK and although the cost of living is cheaper, the standard is at least as high. Sydney has everything, really, but because it cannot be substantially extended, house prices are rising fast.

Waterfront properties are in most demand in Sydney, and elsewhere, new residential apartments are being converted from old

# Australia Welcomes Your Investment

The Australian Property Market is considered one of the most stable in the world. Many years of steady population growth and a diversity of styles and locations has seen Australia develop a strong and stable property market that adequately meets the needs of the Australian based and foreign investor alike.

It is common for international investors to consider Australia as an option to include in their property portfolios due to its consistent growth, stable market and high standard of construction.

Australia does impose a buying restrictions on Foreign Nationals that do not have approved Permanent Resident Visa status. The restriction acts to limit the property purchased to new property.

According to Steve Douglas, Chairman of aussieproperty.com, this is done as a protection mechanism and to ensure maximum financial benefit to the Australian economy as a whole.

"By directing Foreign purchasers to new property, substantial jobs and activity is created as well as ensuring a steady increase in the accommodation pool" Mr Douglas said, "it also protects the local property market from excessive price competition on established housing, as most foreign investors would easily be able to out bid an Australian based buyer, not least because they will no doubt have the benefit of rental collection, making the acquisition easily affordable."

Under the Foreign Investment Review Board guidelines, approval must be sought by any person, other than Australian Citizens or Permanent Residence Visa holders, when they intend to acquire a residential property. Provided that the property is recently constructed and no one has previously lived in it, then the approval is almost automatic and issued very promptly.

Under these rules, Foreign Nationals can acquire land provided that they commence construction of a dwelling within 12 months, apartments, newly completed houses, townhouses, villas or any other style of newly constructed dwelling.

Holding land without commencing construction is not permitted.

Importantly, when any property is acquired with the intention to develop or improve it, either for resale or to keep, then this is permitted provided a commitment to spend an additional amount of at least half of the original property price is undertaken.

Commercial or Rural property do not have the same restrictions, so any one can freely acquire interests in these type of properties.

These regulations have been highly successful in ensuring the Australian Market has maintained affordable and sustainable levels of growth over the long period.

It has also greatly benefited the standards of the construction industry as the consistency have allowed the development of many trade skills and educational  programs that ensures only highly skilled and regulated tradesman work in the construction industry.

The directing of foreign investment capital towards new construction, has been a major contributor in the high quality of Australian property.

The Australian government has also ensured that the regulations supporting investment in Australia strongly protect the foreign investor.

The legal system ensures Freehold title to the owner, finance is readily available for up to 80% of the purchase price and there are many special tax incentives available to property investors that can ensure that no tax would be payable on their investment with proper planning.

Aussieproperty.com is a specialised Australian property website that focuses on the education and support of foreign based investors, intended migrants and Australian expatriates and was recently launched to satisfy the increasing demand for information on Australian property investment, and is free to access.

"The site is essential for anyone considering investing in Australia, we have developed special financial tools that easily explain the process from a financial and taxation aspect, as well as many valuable reports and statistics on all the various issues of acquiring property in Australia whilst abroad." Mr Douglas added.

For investors looking for premium built quality, in a stable and strong long term growth market, then Australia is certainly worthy of investigation.

# AUSTRALIAN TAXATION SYSTEM
# LURES PROPERTY INVESTORS

It seems that the Australian Property Market has many reasons for investors to look towards Australian shores.

Stable economy, steady interest rates, low entry price and global value for money all encourage people to look at Australian Property as a true investment option.

Surprisingly, another major influence is the Australian Taxation System.

According to Steve Douglas of Australasian Taxation Services Pty Ltd, most foreign investors should be able to have a tax free investment if they use sensible and legitimate tax planning techniques.

These normally focus around the benefit of using bank loans to assist in the acquisition of the property, and an array of favourable tax incentives offered by the Australian Government.

Interest expense on borrowed money used to purchase income producing property is allowed as a full deduction each year against any rental income. This can reduce or eliminate any potential income tax that may have been payable had the property been acquired for cash consideration.

Due to its preferential status by lenders, it is surprisingly easy to arrange a loan to support your purchase of up to 80% of the purchase price, for terms up to 30 years regardless of the age of the borrower.

Under Australian Taxation Laws, every expense incurred as a landlord can also offset any Income Tax, or in some cases the future Capital Gains Tax. This also includes travel expenses associated with the inspection of your property.

In addition, The Australian Government allows substantial depreciation allowances on the construction cost of the property and the internal fittings.

When combining the interest, ownership costs and tax incentives, it is normal for no Income Tax to be due and a surplus of tax credits available to carry forward indefinitely and offset future income or capital gains.

Once a property has been owned by an individual for more than 12 months, only half of any Capital Gains are subject to tax. As this can then be reduced by any tax credits from previous years it is very easy for foreign based investors using prudent debt levels, to ensure that no Capital Gains Tax will arise on the eventual sale of the property.

As such many investors can look forward to a tax free investment in their Australian Property.

Mr Douglas stresses the need to assess your particular circumstances, plan sensibly and ensure you can keep within prudent debt levels, in order to achieve the best results.

"The important aspect is to choose your property carefully so you can maximise your return whilst enjoying the many tax benefits available to you." Mr Douglas states. "For full clarification, we have a unique financial model and is available free on line on our website at **aussieproperty.com** called the 'Property Tax Estimator' which fully details all the taxation, finance and investment implications of Australian property ownership."

warehouses or industrial buildings. Melbourne, Brisbane and Perth are also popular with prestige clients. Apartments in the major cities are becoming extremely popular with downsizers and empty-nesters who are looking for water views, high ceilings, security and entertainment facilities within an estate, managed environment rather than a hard-to-maintain separate house with a garden.

Most of the marketing thrust aimed at the foreign investor is in new or off-plan apartments, because these are the only ones such people are allowed to buy. With many new developments, a maximum of 50 per cent of the units can legally be sold to foreign investors. It is also possible for investors without Australian citizenship or permanent residency to buy 'bare land' for building, but this is a complicated strategy and not recommended for the novice.

For those interested in pure investing, Australian properties in the major cities are more affordable than in similar-size cities in the UK, and in all urban areas there is a thriving rental market. This consists of the inevitable students, young professionals, older people downsizing and those who are renting while they make up their minds about what to buy – in other words, the tenant profile is exactly the same as in the UK rental market. And don't forget that the Australians invented the controversial tenancy deposit scheme, now law in the UK as well!

Some new developments are sold with guaranteed rentals for a time and in Sydney, at least, there is an acute shortage of high-end apartments available for rent. So, buying to let in Australia could certainly make good sense.

But as always, it is recommended that you not only pay your chosen area a visit but walk around and get to know it well. Anything can look good on the internet, but you need to know what the surrounding areas are like, what the public transport is like and whether there are any noisy pubs or clubs round about.

So far as the buying process goes, this is not only different from the UK but also varies from state to state. In general terms, though, contracts are exchanged almost immediately on acceptance of an offer, and often within a few days. When this happens you as the buyer are committed. The completion of the sale usually takes another six weeks; again, it happens far quicker than in the UK.

However, the business of buying in Australia can be complicated in other ways, as usually any foreign investor, even on a small scale, has to seek prior approval through the Foreign Investment Review Board. Foreign nationals who hold permanent visas are allowed to buy residential property; otherwise you would have to put in a formal application. The idea is to maintain the affordability and availability of housing for Australian residents.

These restrictions may not apply if you are interested in buying a holiday home in what is known as an 'integrated tourism resort', as these are exempt from the stringent foreign investment qualifications.

Timeshares are regarded as an investment in residential property, and normally a visitor would not be allowed to spend more than four weeks in a year in the timeshare apartment.

The rules for taxation are pretty much the same as for other countries: if you remain more than six months in the year in Australia, you become liable for Australian income tax.

General information on visas, residency and investing in Australian real estate is available on the Australian High Commission's website: www.australia.org.uk.

Holiday and second homes are big business in Australia, although as yet the numbers of UK nationals owning property in Australia are small, and virtually confined to celebrities such as Michael Parkinson, of chat show fame, or others whose work takes them to Australia anyway.

It is not easy to acquire an Australian property at long distance. You would have to earmark your chosen area, visit the place and then take advice from Australian real-estate agents and lawyers, as the rules are complicated and also quite restrictive. It is true to say, however, that holidays to Australia are becoming big business, and inevitably the purchase of holiday homes by foreign nationals is set to grow.

Towards the end of 2002, writers Derek and Julia Parker decided to emigrate to Sydney. Although they are authors of many best-selling books on astrology, they didn't rely on looking into a crystal ball or read their horoscopes to discover their ideal destination, but put in plenty of hard research before taking the plunge.

In the event, they found the whole process far more difficult than they had anticipated. Derek says:

> Julia and I had been coming to Australia for the past 15 years, and loved everything about the country – the physical aspects, the climate, the people. For several years, we'd talked idly about the possibility of moving; then eventually Julia said: 'Look, if we don't do something about it we'll be like those three boring sisters never getting to Moscow!' We already knew the major Australian cities quite well, but for us Sydney was the only possibility. Perth is heavenly but there's nothing much to do there; Adelaide is sweet and relatively tiny; Melbourne is handsome and stately; but we've always been very much into theatre and music, so it wasn't really very difficult to decide on Sydney.

Derek and Julia first went out in March 2002 to have a serious look at the place, and view possible properties. They rented an apartment in Woollomoloo for a month, doing the shopping, finding out about the supermarkets, going to the theatre and driving around. Their idea was that, if they took an apartment rather than staying in a hotel, they would get a clearer idea of what it might be like actually to live in Sydney. Whilst there, they spent a lot of time looking around the city and driving round the suburbs to see where they might be happy to settle.

> Our month out there [says Derek] decided us that we would really like to be there, permanently. So we went back in June with the firm intention of finding a house. We had already put in an application for a visa, but we did not have the visa in our hands. In retrospect, this was a severe mistake. You are advised not to even start house hunting until you have the visa in your hands, and now we wish we had waited because we nearly lost A $100,000 by ignoring this advice. We found a house we liked, a 1907 Federation house in Mosman, a suburb on the North Shore. Thanks to a

favourable exchange rate, the money we got on our smallish flat in West Kensington, London almost paid for the four-bed house with large lounge and two patios. It cost A $1.3 million, which is not nearly as much as it sounds – about £475,000 in sterling. However, it was more than we meant to pay and we had to get a small top-up mortgage. That was not difficult to get and will be largely paid for with the rent from a cottage near Cambridge which we are keeping as a UK bolthole.

The visas, says Derek, were something else:

They were not difficult to get, but the actual process was tedious and expensive. We had the choice of an investment visa – very expensive indeed as it demands a large investment of funds and would have left us with very little capital – or a retirement visa. This is granted on the basis that one has sufficient funds to live on without working, and also means you have to take out very expensive medical insurance, as the state Medicare is not available to expatriate emigrants.

The main requirement of the retirement visa is that one has to undertake not to work. This presented us with some problems as obviously we intend to go on writing books, and we reckoned that the kind of books we write would hardly take work away from an Australian. But the agents working on our behalf told us that the retirement visa was granted only on the understanding that one would not work, full stop. In the end, we took the matter to a leading immigration lawyer who ruled in our favour. The upshot is that we can go on writing for UK publishers, but we must not earn money in Australia.

As Australia House in London will no longer help potential immigrants to obtain a visa, we had to use a specialized emigration agent, based for some reason in New Zealand. We had to send details of all our possessions, income, medical records and so on. The whole process took over a year and every month brought a new and quite heavy bill.

The total cost came to more than A $3,000. Finally a visa was conditionally granted subject to a medical examination, on a four-year renewable basis. This meant we could stay until 2006, when we had to reapply. The granting of a renewed visa was not guaranteed, but we managed it. Although astrology did not play much of a part in our decision, we used what is known as relocation astrology, which indicated we would both be happy here. However, Julia did correctly predict the date when the visas would be granted, and the date when our furniture and effects arrived.

Derek decided to import his new UK car, which was a relatively simple matter; however, he had to take another driving test – 50 years after passing the first one!

Any surprises?

Not really. Theatre and music compare very well with the UK and, although in Sydney you rarely get the big star names, we have seen Warren Mitchell in a revival of John Mortimer's *Dock Brief*, and Nicole Kidman in Ibsen. The best thing is that we can afford the tickets: good seats at the theatre are between £9 and £11, and stalls at the opera are around £30. You can get a good restaurant meal for around £5 each.

Every day, we become ever more convinced we have done the right thing. Our dog is now with us after being in quarantine, and he loves it too. Every morning I take him on a wonderful walk, and of course the weather is divine.

The people are extremely friendly, the supermarkets excellent and we have a little village of shops in the next street. You can get Prince Charles' biscuits and real marmalade.

Derek says that he and Julia plan to return to the UK from time to time to visit friends:

The loss of close friends is really the only downside of emigrating – but I now can't think of anything that would tempt us back permanently. The only thing we start to wonder about at our age is what will happen when one of us falls off the twig. Would the

> other want to stay in Australia permanently? But that's something
> we can't worry about too much at present. It's one reason, though,
> if you are older, why it's not a bad idea to keep a toehold in the UK.

There are two ways of emigrating to Australia without encountering all the fuss that Derek and Julia Parker experienced. One is to marry an Australian – for some, maybe, a rather drastic step. In this case, the authorities have to be convinced the relationship is genuine and not a marriage of convenience simply to gain entry to the country. Evidence must be in the form of joint bank accounts or other shared financial interests, and the relationship should have lasted for at least a year.

The other method, if you are not ready to retire, is to apply as a skilled professional. Here, a points system operates whereby you are awarded points according to type of skills, previous job experience, qualifications and so on. In this case, you may have to wait up to 18 months for a visa, as demand for Australian visas is so strong. Jobs in demand include: nursing, teaching, building trade workers, engineers and accountants.

In any case, as with Derek and Julia Parker, medical and police records will be closely scrutinized, and any drink-driving offences, for instance, will be taken extremely seriously. Charges for processing visas range from £500 to £2,000.

At the moment, no British bank will lend money to buy property in Australia although it should be easy enough to secure a mortgage from an Australian bank.

If you are an overseas buyer, you have a number of choices when it comes to financing your Australian property. You can pay cash (of course – as ever, anywhere); you can raise finance at home, usually by releasing equity in your main home; you can use an overseas mortgage lender or secure an overseas mortgage with an international mortgage provider; or you can if you like use local financing from a developer in Australia. This last option will only apply if you are buying off-plan, or 'off the plan' as they say down under.

As with buying into any foreign country, you would have to be aware of possible currency fluctuations and all extra costs such as service and maintenance charges on apartments, local taxes, utilities and other running costs. If buying on a mortgage, overseas purchasers will have to produce very detailed accounts and bank statements to ensure that they can afford to keep up the payments.

In 2007, there were many repossessions on Australian properties, where owners could not afford to keep up payments, but there is no record that this has happened to a foreign buyer.

Note: all visa arrangements for Australia apply equally to New Zealand, except that you do not need a visa to just visit New Zealand.

# New Zealand

New Zealand is a lot like Britain, with added space, a better climate and vastly lower health care costs. Some people consider the country the nearest to a paradise on earth, and it is now being enthusiastically discovered by Britons in search of second homes, holiday homes and somewhere nice to retire.

Britons are able to purchase most types of property, but to buy something in an intensely desirable area such as an island or beachfront home, you would need to obtain permission from New Zealand's Overseas Investment Commission.

The country has no stamp duty or capital gains tax, unless you are trading in property as a profession. There is also no such thing as gazumping, and the average time taken to complete a sale is three to four weeks, compared with the three to four months in England.

Mortgages and loans are readily available from New Zealand banks, and you are also allowed to rent out your property, should you wish to.

There is no stamp duty, inheritance tax or capital gains tax, although there are constant rumours that this last tax will one day be introduced.

If you want a new-build home, you will have to go to a city centre, but outside of urban areas there is no such thing as a purpose-built development and you would have to work individually with a developer to design your new home. It is far easier to buy a resale home, although most are sold at auction these days.

Excellent capital growth combined with low taxation levels means that New Zealand is reasonably safe for investment, and there are plenty of rental opportunities, with many management companies that can oversee the whole thing for you. If buying to let, it is probably better to buy a city-centre house or apartment rather than a holiday home, as there is significant year-round demand for rentals from migrants.

Auckland, the biggest city, has enjoyed a lot of investment in recent years, with the entire waterfront being regenerated. Most New Zealand property experts recommend Auckland for its buzzy atmosphere, wonderful waterfront views, bars, cafés and restaurants.

Wellington, the world's most southern capital city, has seen phenomenal growth in house prices in recent years, and Queenstown, the home of the bungee jump, offers many other, less adrenalin-inducing sporting activities as well.

It is difficult to get permission to settle permanently in New Zealand to work as you have to prove conclusively that you are not taking a job away from a native New Zealander and that you are offering a high-level skill not otherwise available.

Alan and Jenny Knight, originally from the UK, have been living on Waiheke Island, off Auckland, North Island, since 1998. In order to be allowed to settle, they first had to satisfy the authorities that they had enough points in their favour to be welcomed as immigrants, and this took a few years. Alan works as a brewer and Jenny as an executive at Qantas airlines, in Auckland. They have also founded a small theatre company on the island, on the cusp of being amateur and professional, so have become thoroughly integrated Kiwis.

Their life seems enviable in the extreme. Waiheke Island, reached by an hourly ferry from Auckland, has about 8,000 inhabitants, although many of them are Kiwis or Australians with second or holiday homes on the island. Alan and Jenny live in a wooden house which they never, ever lock, and which looks out onto a wooded hillside. Alan says: 'Everything regenerates very quickly here and if you plant a tree, it grows in no time. The climate is very kind and there is an amazing ability of all things to grow.'

Property prices on Waiheke island have shot up sharply in recent years as it is so desirable, and it has turned into a millionaire's paradise. Alan drove me round the island on my visit there and I noticed there were many properties for sale. When I expressed interest in a property on the market for NZ $900,000, Alan said that he was sure I would be allowed in as a resident if I could afford to buy such a property outright. Others have said the same: you can get into NZ if you have enough money! But then, that's probably the same story everywhere.

Waiheke Island has lots of contemporary dwellings with lovely sea views and the island itself is very wooded. The island is full of little wineries and breweries, and Alan said that most of these businesses are carried out for fun rather than money. Alan brews real ale on the island.

In common with Waiheke Island, most of the properties on the market in New Zealand are new or newish and almost all are timber-frame. There are no nasty towns, no slum areas and very many properties are set in idyllic surroundings, in both the North and South islands. The country is spotlessly clean, with not a crisp packet or lager can anywhere around, and everything is at a high standard. There is every kind of scenery you could wish for, from rainforests to beech forests to glaciers, mountains, rolling hills and wooded glades although on the West coast it can certainly rain.

Everywhere I went I saw development land for sale, and this is advertised in ordinary estate agents' along with the already built properties. Here, you would buy your chunk of land on which to build your own house.

New Zealand is also very much the country of sheltered housing, or assisted living. In all of the towns, these 'age-executive' developments were being built or advertised, and this is a thriving and fast-growing market.

As with Australia, New Zealand is too far away from the UK to make it sensible (probably) to have a holiday home there, and as a non-resident, you would be allowed to stay in the country for no more than six months at a time, and would not be allowed to work unless you had a work permit. There is a big holiday rental market as tourism is a major industry in the country, but year-round or long-term rentals would only be possible in the major towns.

However, there are many property investors in New Zealand and this type of investment is encouraged. It is also increasingly an off-plan country, with many such developments aimed at the investor. I also noticed on my visit there newspaper ads for get-rich-quick property seminars, so with all this, buying in New Zealand would feel very familiar.

Although so far away, New Zealand does not feel at all strange to the British visitor, probably because the Queen's head is on the currency, they drive on the left and they speak English. The culture, apart from the Maori elements, feels very British as well, with an extreme (some might say) emphasis on sport. There are also very many golf courses.

The population of New Zealand is mainly expatriate British people, now third- or fourth-generation, and Australians who prefer the place to their own country. And then of course there are the Maoris, not quite native New Zealanders but who settled there many centuries ago. For many years the Maoris, like the Aboriginals in Australia, were treated as second-class citizens but now they are becoming educated and are integrating with the rest of the 4 million population – as well as becoming militant and suing other New Zealanders for infringement of their property and land rights. The country looks very prosperous indeed, and all the sheep, cows and goats are in beautiful condition.

New Zealand is very proud of its heroes and heroines and famous New Zealanders include the authors Katherine Mansfield, Ngaio Marsh and Janet Frame, the film maker Jane Campion, singers Dame Kiri Te Kanawa and Hayley Westenra and of course, their all-time hero, Everest climber Sir Edmund Hillary, who was given a state funeral in Auckland in January 2008. New Zealand also has a long-term woman prime minister, Helen Clark.

All in all, New Zealand is modern, relaxed, casual, clean and prosperous and with probably the world's finest range of scenery and landscape. The country also puts an extremely high value on education, and there are very many fine schools and universities there.

# Dubai

In November 2003, a party of property journalists went out on an all-expenses paid trip to a new holiday and second-home development in Dubai. As a result, several weeks later there were highly enthusiastic reports about how wonderful Dubai is as a second-home destination, and how it is fast becoming the new Caribbean. Around 250,000 new homes are currently being built in Dubai, all aimed at the foreign buyer. John Arlidge, reporting for the *Sunday Times*, wrote:

Dubai is – literally – building itself a future. It is transforming itself into a hypermodern, Western-style tourist destination – a cross between Miami, Hong Kong and Barbados. What it does not have – islands, grass, rivers – it simply invents. No state, no fascist dictator, no Bond villain has ever tried to pull off something so extravagant.

But one man has. The Dubai property extravaganza is the vision of one man, Crown Prince Sheikh Mohammed Al-Maktoun, working in partnership with the less exotically-named British estate agents FPD Savills.

It's a good story, and Arlidge goes on, 'throw in a three-mile long marina, neat Florida-style suburbs, a dozen golf courses, two race courses, a couple of equestrian ranches, a Formula One circuit, a snow – yes, snow – dome with ski lifts, two airports, two ports and six-lane motorways'. The country needs 500,000 foreign investors to make this enormous development pay, and is spending huge amounts on PR and celebrity gimmicks to attract the right type of investor. One such gimmick was to offer David

Beckham and other England footballers luxury apartments for nothing – or at highly discounted rates, depending on which account you believe. Now everybody else is expected to follow suit; the difference being that ordinary punters are expected to pay.

In some ways, the publicity people will have an uphill struggle to persuade investors to part with large sums of their cash. The country is seven hours away from London, it is much less well established than other holiday markets, and the United Arab Emirates, of which Dubai is a part, has a serious image problem anyway.

Rightly or wrongly, Westerners imagine that alcohol is not allowed, that women have to wear veils and cannot drive cars, and that you are likely to be thrown in prison for 20 years at best, or publicly executed, at worst, for a minor offence. Dubai is not quite so restricted or illiberal in this sense as some other parts of the Middle East but it is still a Muslim enclave, with at least traces of Sharia law remaining which may prove irksome to hedonistic Westerners.

For instance, Ramadan, the month of fasting, applies to everybody resident in the country, and foreigners, in common with locals, should not be seen eating or drinking during daylight hours. Hotels and restaurants catering for foreigners are open, but tactfully screened off. As for topping up your tan, women are not allowed to go topless, although journalist Anne Cuthbertson, of the *Sunday Telegraph*, spotted some female Russian tourists sunbathing in G-strings, concluding that bottomlessness is not equally banned.

Although Dubai is not as extremist as some of its near neighbours, there is a definite political risk to the place. The whole of the Middle East is volatile, and buying property there is not exactly the same experience as purchasing in France, where at least all aspects are known. There is also, as yet, no modern culture as such although numerous sports facilities are being constructed.

The weather is unbearably hot in June, July and August, and in truth there is nothing much to do. If you are not a sports fanatic, Dubai may not appeal. As yet, shopping is limited and in any case, goods are expensive, apart from petrol for your car, which is cheaper than water. The place is also an artificial enclave, although the same could be said of many parts of Florida and the Caribbean, in that they are playboy areas rather than 'real' places.

But what all these artificial paradises offer is sun, dry heat and lack of rain or persistent drizzle. The water in naturally arid Dubai comes from vast desalination plants.

In 2008, Dubai is somewhere between construction and completion. There is a wonderful seven-star hotel, reputed to be the most luxurious in the world, and the finished part of Dubai already looks gorgeous.

The country has some indigenous population, but the bulk of the residents are expatriate workers – nearly a million of them – who have been attracted by the generous taxation and sunshine provision. Although many developments are aimed specifically at expatriate workers, Dubai is also working hard to attract tourists, which in turn gives rise to a rental market. And although astronomical returns on property of up to 50 per cent annual increase have been bandied around, the more conservative estimates give a relatively modest 10 per cent per annum increase in value so far.

And as with all new developments, some are better than others. But Dubai still has a long way to go, so from a pure investment point of view it would be hard to lose out. There is currently no capital gains tax levied in the emirate, another huge advantage.

Another factor is that so many properties are now going up that nobody can predict whether Dubai will represent a good investment, either for purchase or as buy-to-lets. As yet, prices are low, but will the properties have a resale value? Nobody knows. Also, there may be risks for the foreign investor, simply because the concept of foreigners owning land in Dubai is brand new, and as yet not truly tried and tested. Visas could be another issue, as normally in Dubai they only last for two months. Residency is a possibility, but usually only if you work there. There is also, or may be, a question of different inheritance laws, and Sharia laws may well override those of the UK or Europe. Under existing Sharia laws, a wife cannot inherit property (there you go – a stumbling-block already) so a clever bicultural lawyer is needed.

There is little or no tax, always a great incentive. HSBC and Barclays are offering mortgages on properties in Dubai.

As Dubai enthusiastically and expensively develops its tourist and second-home industry, many questions remain. Will it become increasingly Western, or will vestiges of its Muslim heritage remain? The more fundamental the regime, the less likely it is to attract foreign investment on the scale envisaged.

All in all, Dubai remains a bit of a leap into the unknown, with its uneasy compromise between Eastern and Western laws and customs, but it has to be said that the properties themselves are beautiful, constructed to a high standard, and apparently good value. Apartments cost from about £160,000 and in most apartment blocks the gyms and sports facilities come at no extra cost. Before very long, Dubai may well be a serious rival to the much more distant (from Europe) Caribbean.

Dubai's advantage is that it is seriously up and coming as a newly created tourist, leisure and property paradise. The oil is likely to run out within 30 years, and the government is pouring money into the development of Dubai as a modern, attractive international centre. Predictions are that it will become a world conference and international business centre.

It is possible to obtain mortgages on Dubai properties but experts warn that the set-up costs are higher than for a UK mortgage. Again, legal advice is needed before you take the plunge, as there may be an exchange rate risk. The United Arab Emirates' unit of currency, the dirham, is dollar-linked, which makes it a relatively known factor so far as investors are concerned, but there may be currency traps for the unwary. Know what you are getting into before buying off-plan in Dubai.

There are currently people of around 150 different nationalities living and working in Dubai, so it already has an international flavour. In fact, although it sounds a new place to most of us, the British have been heavily involved in Dubai since the 18th century, with the East India Company.

Dubai is growing fast and is poised midway, culturally and geographically, between East and West. The official language is Arabic but English is widely spoken and understood.

There are now many tower blocks and villas under construction and the aim is to build a leisure and property haven on sand. However, for the time being, a question mark hangs over the eventual profitability of Dubai property, owing to its system of Sharia law and the legal ban on females purchasing and inheriting real estate. As, these days, at least 50 per cent of buyers and investors in foreign property are female, this ban could adversely affect the profitability of investments.

# Thailand

Phuket was a well-known and highly popular destination for holidaymakers and, increasingly, for second-home buyers – until the tsunami hit on Boxing Day 2004, after which the market for both tourists and potential buyers ground to an almost complete standstill.

Although Phuket contains many very upmarket and stylish developments, the area – long before the tsunami – was also swamped with low-cost, low-quality holiday apartments. Not only that, but some of these suspiciously cheap developments often involved disputes over land ownership, which could mean the value of the investment being completely wiped out when the land was eventually claimed by somebody other than the supposed owner. High-pressure sales techniques are in action at the lower end as well, particularly where apartments are priced at £20,000 or less.

However, apartments on or close to the sea could soon rise significantly in value, as following the tsunami, the Thai government is considering banning new homes within 200 metres of Phuket's high water mark. The government points out that although tsunamis only hit, on average, once every 400 years, people have been badly frightened and now expect some kind of protection. It is also the case that future large-scale developments will have to undergo rigorous environmental studies before being granted planning permission. The Thai government is keen to learn from Spain's example of over-development – as, indeed, are many countries new to the second-home market.

Potential investors looking for more exotic and faraway property investments than the obvious, are asking themselves, now that Thailand has well and truly broken into the overseas property market: will it become the new Spain, at least as far as popularity goes? The answer is that, however well developed, well regulated and well designed the developments, Thailand still remains a long-haul destination for UK people. Also, it gets dark at 6 pm every night without fail. Darkness descends all of a sudden and there is no such thing as dusk.

So far as rules and regulations are concerned, foreign nationals are allowed to own property but not buy land. Apartments are held leasehold, and most leases are for 30 years only, with an option to renew after that time. Men marrying a Thai bride can buy and own property, but only in her name, and presumably, vice-versa, but for some reason there does not seem to be such a ready market in Thai husbands as in Thai brides. Be that as it may, it is important to bear in mind that in much of Thailand, however popular it is becoming with property investors, strict building regulations apply.

The majority of properties are being sold off-plan in Thailand. There have been concerns that in some cases the land on which the development will be built has not been bought and is not owned by the developer, so if you are interested in buying off-plan at what seems like an absurdly cheap price make sure the land has been officially transferred. There are different grades of land in Thailand and as it is a rather mysterious country with a very different culture, religion and attitude to the West (in spite of everybody being familiar with *The King and I* – a film that is permanently banned in Thailand, although pirate versions are widely available there) ensure that you understand every aspect of the buying process and stage payments.

The best way to do this is not to make stage payments until you have a 100 per cent guarantee that the land has been legally transferred from the official owners to the developer and so can be in turn transferred to you, the buyer.

# China

Many foreign investors have flocked to buy in China, particularly Shanghai, although the buying process is complex. There are, though, differing reports about whether or not the Chinese government wants to attract overseas investment into property. Some reports say that, yes, the government is enthusiastic, although others state that foreign property development is being restricted. The opportunities for both capital appreciation and rental growth have already attracted big companies such as Citicorp and Morgan Stanley to invest hundreds of millions of US dollars in Chinese residential and commercial property, but new legislation is restricting the amount of speculative investment to prevent a property crash. It is likely that foreign investors will face further restrictions and, as there are plenty of other destinations to choose from, China is probably best avoided as too much of an unknown quantity for the small or amateur property investor.

# India

India is, however, a different proposition, with huge developments now going on in this late-booming country, many at attractive prices for second-homers and investors. Hamptons International, for instance, is marketing The Views, Mohali Hills, in Chandigarh, a development of two- and three-bedroom apartments and four-bedroom two-storey houses. Chandigarh is the capital of Punjab and Haryana, and an area undergoing huge regeneration. Prices start at £46,000 for a two-bedroom apartment, although Hamptons warns that all prices are subject to currency exchange and may change without notice. This applies to all new-build properties in India.

Goa is another area where huge new developments are being constructed. Although India is becoming increasingly open to international investment, especially as regards property, as yet it is not an ideal country for the individual or amateur investor as you are not allowed to take out of India more money than you have brought in, which could make it difficult to realize a profit on real estate. It remains much easier for buyers of Indian descent to purchase property than others, and at least one Indian property website comments than no Western country would dare have such racially discriminatory laws.

In any case, buyers must have prior approval from the Reserve Bank of India to buy, and approval is normally available on substantial investments over US$10 million, purchases in Special

Economic Zones, purchases on serviced plots and houses on short leases of five years or less.

It is likely that these constraints will one day be lifted, but for the moment this country is probably best avoided, at least by the amateur investor, that is, unless you can prove you are of Indian origin if domiciled outside the country.

Nick Booker, whose property company, In2Perspective, began by finding cheap council housing for clients to buy-to-let, has now decided to concentrate on property in India, and has forsaken the UK.

Why? Nick, who has joined forces with Assetz India, a new company now looking at ways for foreigners to invest in this vast and still mysterious country, said:

India's economy is growing fast and it will be bigger than the UK's in 10 years time. IT, textiles, electronics, are all major growth areas. Japan is now investing in India and 50 per cent of the CEOs of Silicon Valley are now Indian. The population is growing, particularly among the educated, and there will be a need for new properties of all kinds. Technology is now becoming available to outlying villages as they only have to wire up and computer costs are coming down fast.

I am looking now at opportunities for outsiders to invest in property in India, to buy off-plan or to rent out.

At the moment, Nick admits, India is not an open market but there are various ways that foreigners can buy property, even so.

One way is to take a rolling lease from the owner, but the drawback to that is that there is no legal recourse if the owner wants it back. Foreigners can invest in real estate construction although they are not allowed to buy an existing building. Or, you can invest in a property fund if you have a minimum of £250,000 to spare.

Foreigners can also invest in aparthotels, where they buy a hotel room. This is probably the safest way to invest at the moment, and we are in the process of building a chain of hotels across India. They will be ordinary hotels, not at the highest end, but comfortable, well-serviced hotels for tourists and travellers.

So, I asked Nick, why are there restrictive laws on foreigners buying?

The main reason is that the government is worried about foreign investment coming and going and not benefiting India at all. If foreigners invest, make money and then take it out of the country, this means they are just using the country as a cash cow and it is what India is most keen to prevent. There is a major fear of currency flight, although I believe that eventually the rupee will take over from the dollar as the world's primary currency. Everybody has too much dollar debt, and India is the world's most populous country.

Nick himself is allowed to invest in India as one of his ancestors lived in India permanently, so he can claim family residency. However, most foreigners would not be able to do this. But he is convinced that India is the country of the future, and the one to watch.

# Conclusion

Wherever you decide to buy, you should not forget the art of negotiating. Although people tend to be nervous of negotiating in foreign countries and in foreign languages, it's important not to be so overawed, or so much in love with the property that you forget to employ the negotiating skills that would automatically be used when buying a property in the home country.

What you want to achieve is a win–win situation, and buying a foreign property should not become a battle of wills. If it does, this will sour the deal and may cause lasting resentment, which would adversely affect future enjoyment of the dream home.

When considering a property abroad, you should ask yourself the same important questions that you would when parting with very large sums of money to buy somewhere in the home country. First of all, when you see a property that you would like and believe you can afford, make a list of the issues that are a priority for you and identify which ones you may be willing to concede to the seller. For instance, would you expect the property to include kitchen appliances, carpets, curtains and furniture? Would you be prepared to pay extra for any of these, or walk away from the deal if the seller insists they are not included?

If interested in the property, it's in order to make an offer but not to insult the seller by making a ridiculously low offer. Once the seller is enraged by a low offer, he or she will probably counter-offer with something equally ridiculous, and there is no basis for negotiation.

Does the place need extensive repairs or renovation? If so, the seller might be willing to lower the price, once you have had a surveyor's report. But don't go round the place picking off peeling paint or knocking against walls, and then shaking your head. For the seller, the property is a prized and valuable possession; if you undervalue it, you're not being canny, but stupid.

The key to successful negotiation, advise estate agents, is to see the transaction from the seller's point of view and ask yourself what you would do in that position. Your credibility will also be greatly enhanced by putting down as much money as you possibly can, as a deposit. Money does talk, and the more money you are able to put down the more points you will be able to score.

Also remember that when buying and selling property it's a matter of give and take. It's rare that both parties get exactly what they want, and so there should always be some room to manoeuvre. Decide which issues are the most important to you, and take it from there, rather than arguing over light bulbs, Venetian blinds or whether a dishwasher is to stay or go.

## Points to consider if buying mainly for investment

In the past, the vast majority of people bought properties in other countries to improve their lifestyle, rather than as an investment. Although most buyers naturally hoped their purchase would increase, rather than decrease in value, profit was by no means the primary motive.

This is still the case for most buyers, but as we have seen, ever more people are buying properties abroad they will never use for themselves, and may never even see. What should such buyers bear in mind?

First of all, it is important to remember that property investment is emphatically something to take seriously, rather than to be dabbled in. The sums of money are too high, and the potential risks too great, to invest in an amateurish way. Nor is property investment a quick fix. It takes time for the investment to show a profit. In fact, all wise property investors take a long-term view, which enables them to ride out a weak market as well as benefit from a strong one.

Here are 10 top tips.

---

*Top Tips*

1. Research the country of your choice thoroughly, as to climate, transport links, infrastructure, political stability, economy, currency, tourism, and facilities on offer to holidaymakers. How long does it take to get there from the UK? What is the flying time, frequency of flights, and proximity to airports? Do budget airlines go there?

2. Research the very specific location of your choice. Are you looking for somewhere inland, on the coast, in a new, gated, development, next to golf courses and other sports, on a marina, secluded, urban or countryside?

3. Make sure you understand the entire buying process, start to finish, in your chosen country. It could differ significantly from practice in the UK. Ask yourself why you want the property. Is it for holidays, a second home, retirement or investment? Are you considering emigrating?

4. Be guided by knowledge, not emotion. Although gut reaction is always important, make sure you understand all the costs involved, not just with buying, but maintaining the place as well.

5. Conduct a thorough survey on the property or, if buying off-plan, the development. Make sure your wonderful sea view will not be obliterated by newer developments nearer the sea.

6. Make sure you employ a good, independent lawyer, rather than one hired by the developers.

7. Sort out all your finances – mortgage, cost of buying and maintaining the property, transport and ongoing running costs, before making an offer. The purchase price is only the start. There is also the fact that property, unlike stocks and shares, may not be so easy to liquidize. A villa or apartment could take a year or more to sell; until you have a firm buyer, it stays on the market.

8. Make sure you investigate all the mortgage options, including releasing equity in your own home. There is 'good debt' and 'bad debt': make sure you understand the difference. 'Good debt' is, for instance, a low-interest mortgage taken out with

a reputable mortgage provider, which is covered by the rental income on the place. 'Bad debt' is borrowing on high-interest credit cards, for example, when you have no idea how you will repay the loan, or taking out a high-interest loan to pay the initial cash deposit. Know that you have some way of paying back any loan you decide to take out.

9. Make sure you draw up a local will as soon as you complete on the purchase – and that you understand all capital gains and inheritance tax implications on the foreign property.

10. Insure the property for its intended use – for instance, if you plan to rent it out. There have been many stories of people buying abroad whose home has been broken into during their absence, or whose tenants have caused considerable damage, only to discover they were not insured for their absence, or for renting out the place.

In addition, jet-to-let expert Dominic Farrell believes that when all is said and done, successful investing in other countries comes down to two major aspects which are:

▌ thoroughly research your chosen country;

▌ always factor in every single cost, both upfront and ongoing.

And most of all, says Farrell, never, ever buy somewhere you cannot really afford in the vain hope that somehow, you will come out on top when the music stops.

## Last word from the author

Having studied and researched the practicalities of buying a property abroad and spoken to many people who have already taken the plunge, which country or place would the author pick?

All things considered, my favourite place to buy an apartment is Miami. These are the reasons: Miami is an exciting city, possessing all the advantages of city life such as opera, theatre, film, social functions, restaurants, cafés, exciting shops. It is multi-cultural and multiracial but, at the same time, it is not so large or daunting as somewhere like New York, where the pace is highly frenetic and the weather extremely bitter in winter. Miami is a manageable city, sizewise, yet it is sophisticated and vibrant.

Then it has a wonderful climate for most of the year. Much of Miami is on water and, for my money, a waterfront apartment is essential. It is also, although modern (Miami did not exist 100 years ago), very beautiful. Even the high-rise buildings have their charm.

There is an international airport, with direct cheap flights available (so long as you book well in advance), plus the nearby airports of Orlando and Fort Lauderdale. It's also possible to fly to Miami via a gateway city in the United States.

Then, I would have something to do there, which is also important. I already have many friends in Miami, so there is the beginning of a social circle. It's possible for me to work in the United States, as the language problem hardly exists, so I would not just be sitting around gossiping and filling in endless aeons of time.

I would choose an apartment rather than a house for security and safety reasons, as I would not be there all the time. Houses deteriorate rapidly in the owner's absence and, if termites or roaches invade when you're not there, they could have taken the place over by the time you return. Most apartments in the United States are run extremely well by the voluntary management committees, so you would feel confident about leaving the place for a month or two at a time.

There is a strong rental market in Miami, especially if the apartment is on, or overlooks, water, so at least some of the running costs could be covered by rental income.

I love France, but for me the climate is not good enough year-round. I also adore Italy, but would not want to undertake massive, long-term renovation. Holidays there will suffice. I also like Spain and Portugal but, again, the climate is not reliable enough all the year round. Greece and Cyprus are possibilities, but with any European country there remains the problem of what I would find to do with myself after a couple of weeks or so of relaxing and sunbathing.

So, Miami it has to be. Buying a home in another country is an intensely life-enhancing experience, so long as you choose the place that's right and that resonates with you.

There are many variables, and ever more as the years go by, as more countries open themselves up to tourism and foreign investment, and welcome incomers, either permanently or for part of the year.

Financial journalist Maria Scott, formerly of the *Observer*, who recently emigrated with her partner to New Zealand (she was born and brought up in NZ, so automatically qualified for residency), believes that before you ever put in an offer on a place in another country you need to take careful stock of your finances. She says that, even after many years writing about personal finance, she still spent many hours over her calculator agonizing over every aspect of the cost.

After she and her partner bought a house in Christchurch, they decided to rent it out for a year to cover costs while selling up in the UK. The finances were delicately balanced anyway – and then their New Zealand tenant stopped paying rent. She won the case after taking it to a tribunal but then wondered whether the aggravation of renting is worth it, especially from such a long distance.

Of course, unless you are a pure investor just wanting to put your money somewhere it will wonderfully increase, buying a place in another country is not only about finance. But even when buying or living a dream, finances have to be firmly in place before any of the more exciting life-changing or irrevocable decisions are made.

The place you eventually choose will depend on your personality, inclinations, linguistic abilities, pocket, passions, hobbies and interests, and preferred lifestyle. With so many countries to choose from, there is now something for everybody who has ever dreamt of a second home in the sun, or even in the snow or ice.

It's just a matter of ensuring that you make the right choice for you. I hope this book will help to make the choice clearer.

# Resources

## Books

Barrow, Colin (2005) *The Complete Guide to Buying Property in Portugal*, Kogan Page, London

Blake, Fanny (2001) *A Place in the Sun: Buying your dream home abroad*, Channel Four Books, London

Brame, Genevieve (2008) *Chez Vous en France: Living and Working in France*, 4th edn, Kogan Page, London

Bray, Roger and Raitz, Vladimir (2001) *Flight to the Sun: The story of the holiday revolution*, Continuum, London

Clarke, Stephen (2004) *A Year in the Merde*, Bantam Press, London

Davey, Charles (2006) *The Complete Guide to Buying Property in France*, 3rd edn, Kogan Page, London

Davey, Charles (2004) *The Complete Guide to Buying Property in Spain*, Kogan Page, London

Davey, Charles (2004) *The Complete Guide to Living and Working in Spain*, Kogan Page, London

Farrell, Dominic (2006) *The Jet-to-Let Bible*, Lawpack, London.

Hawes, Annie (2001) *Extra Virgin: Amongst the olive groves of Liguria*, Penguin, London

McMahon, Barbara (2004) *The Complete Guide to Buying Property in Italy*, Kogan Page, London

Mayle, Peter (1989) *A Year in Provence*, Hamish Hamilton, London

Mayle, Peter (1991) *Toujours Provence*, Hamish Hamilton, London

St Aubin de Terán, Lisa (1995) *A Valley in Italy*, Penguin, London

Searl, David (2003) *You and the Law in Spain*, 14th edn, Aldington Books, Ashford, Kent (sales@aldingtonbooks.co.uk)

Smith, Stephen and Parkinson, Charles, *Letting French Property Successfully*, Pannell Kerr Foster (Guernsey) Ltd, PO Box 296, St Peter Port, Guernsey GY1 4NA (tel: 01481 727927)

Stewart, Chris (1999) *Driving Over Lemons*, Sort Of Books, London
Stewart, Chris (2002) *A Parrot in the Pepper Tree*, Sort Of Books, London
Unsworth, Barry (1997) *After Hannibal*, Penguin, London

# Magazines

*French Property News* (monthly)
www.french-property-news.com also gives information on exhibitions held regularly in the UK. For more information on exhibitions and seminars, contact Dick Shrader on: 020 8543 3113.

*Homes Overseas* (monthly)
www.homesoverseas.co.uk

*International Homes* (frequency of publication not stated)
www.internationalhomes.com

*Italy* (bimonthly)
www.italymag.co.uk

*Living France* (monthly)
www.livingfrance.com; subscription enquiries: 01283 742971.
Also gives information on seminars about buying French property.

Other general titles promoting France and French property include: *France*, *Everything France* (bimonthly) and *Bonjour*.

*Private Villas* (monthly)
www.privatevillas.co.uk
A magazine aimed at property owners abroad who wish to rent out their homes. For more details call 020 8329 0121.

*Property Investor News* (monthly)
info@property-investor-news.com

*Spain* (monthly)
www.spainmagazine.info

# Exhibitions

Homes Overseas Exhibitions (information line: 020 7939 9852).
International Property Show
  Details: 01245 358 877
  Website: www.homesoverseas.co.uk/Exhibitions
The Property Investor Show (annual; London)
  Information: www.propertyinvestor.co.uk
  www.homesgofast.com
Global Property Group
  Website: www.thegpg.com
A Place in the Sun exhibitions
  Website: www.aplaceinthesunlive.com
The Second Home International Expo is held twice a year in Utrecht,
  Holland. Information from: www.secondhome.nl
Seminars about buying abroad: information from International
  Law Partnership Ltd, The Vaults, Holborn Hall, 193–197 High
  Holborn, London WC1V 7BD
  Tel: 020 7061 6700
  e-mail: info@LawOverseas.com
  Website: www.LawOverseas.com
Abels Moving Services
  Wimbledon Avenue
  Brandon
  Sussex IP27 ON2
  Tel: 01842 816 600
  e-mail: enquiries@abels.com
  Website: www.abels.com
Federation of International Moving Companies
  Website: www.fidi.com

# Video

An extremely useful and clearly presented video, *Sun, Sea and
Small Print*, has been produced by the College of Law to guide
potential buyers through the complications of buying property in

Spain. Presented by solicitor Bernadette Whitters, the video deals with the following subjects: finding and financing the property; dealing with Spanish estate agents; buying off-plan and financing; surveyors and valuers; hidden costs; function of the notary public; searches and enquiries; registration of title; hidden costs; disposing of the property; capital gains tax, property and other taxes; inheritance laws.

Although aimed at the legal profession, the video is easy to follow by the layperson, and, although expensive in itself, could save a lot of money as it guides the buyer through the difficult ramifications of the Spanish tax system for residents and non-residents, plus giving helpful hints on avoiding capital gains tax, which in some cases can go up to 80 per cent of the gain.

The video, which is accompanied by full explanatory notes, costs £210 plus VAT and is available from Legal Network Television Ltd, 2 Bream's Buildings, London EC4 1PJ (Tel: 020 7611 7400; website: www.college-of-law.co.uk).

Note: the information in this video is relevant only to buying *Spanish* properties.

# Useful information

Information on pensions:
The Pension Service International Pension Centre (tel: 0191 218 7777) gives information on state pensions for those living abroad.

Pensions abroad:
http://direct.gov.uk/en/BritonsLivingAbroad/BeforeYouGo/DG_4000018

The International Property Law Centre
The Max Gold Partnership
Suffolk House
21 Silver Street
Hull HU1 1JG
Tel: 0870 800 4506
www.internationalpropertylaw.com

Information on private health care:
www.siphealth.com

Information on SIPPs, REITS and other property funds:
Keith Boniface
Tel: 01494 601022
e-mail: keith.boniface@tebcltd.co.uk
www.sipps2006.co.uk

Currency brokers:
CurrenciesDirect
www.currenciesdirect.com

4X Currency
www.4xc.com
(you can check live currency exchange rates and deal online)

Conti Financial Services
Mortgages available in about 30 countries
Tel: 0800 970 0985
e-mail: enquiries@mortgagesoverseas.com
www.mortgagesoverseas.com

Money Corp
www.moneycorp.com

Foreign Currency Direct
www.currencies.co.uk

Currencies4less
www.currencies4less.co.uk

SGM-FX
www.sgm-fx.com

ECU Group PLC
www.ecugroup.com

HIFX
www.hifx.co.uk

MCM
www.multicurrencymortgages.com

Mortgages:
www.mortgagesoverseas.com

Accountancy advice:
Wilkins Kennedy
Chartered Accountants
(Overseas buy-to-let club)
Tel: 01702 348 646

Information on pets abroad:
Animal Airlines
Tel: 0870 833 8020

DSI International
Retirement and Leisure Homes Abroad
info@drstange.com

General websites:
www.fopdac.com
Official website of the Federation of Overseas Property Developers.
You can download factsheets for each country.

www.fnworldwide.com
Gives information on the practicalities of relocation, including transportation costs.

www.bewarethesharks.com
Property abroad investment courses.

Financing for overseas investments:
www.fuelinvest.com

# France

French legal advisers:
FRALEX
Tel: 020 7323 0103
Pgaudin@fralex1.freeserve.co.uk

Bilingual service:
www.perigord-property.com

Hamptons International (offices in Nice)
168 Brompton Road
London SW3 1HW
Tel: 020 7589 8844
e-mail: international@hamptons-int.com
www.hamptons-int.com

*French Property News*
www.french-property-news.com

New-build properties:
A Place in France
Tel: 023 9283 2949
www.aplaceinfrance.com

Francophiles Ltd (mainly period properties)
Barker Chambers
Barker Road
Maidstone
Kent ME16 8SF
Tel: 01622 688165
e-mail: Fphiles@aol.com
www.francophiles.com

Simmonds en France
PO Box 1737
Fordingbridge SP6 3NQ
e-mail: simmonds@enfrance.co.uk
www.enfrance.co.uk

Paris Property Options (for Paris apartments)
19 Warrior Gardens
St Leonards-on-Sea
E Sussex TN37 6EB
Tel: 01424 717281

www.bbc.co.uk/homes/property
Guide to buying in Europe. See French section.

www.buyfrenchproperty.com
List of properties for sale, plus links to removals, finance, banking,
mortgages and legal advice.

www.french-property.com
Information on the financial side of buying French property.

www.hirf.co.uk
Properties for sale in France, plus information on removals,
mortgages and legal advice.

www.holidayhome.co.uk
Properties for sale.

General information on French property:
VEF
Tel: 020 7515 8660
www.vefuk.com

For Alpine properties and ski resorts:
Alpine Apartments Agency
Tel: 01544 388234
www.frenchalpinechalets.com

Erna Low
Tel: 020 7590 1624
www.ernalowproperty.co.uk

Leaseback properties:
info@french-real-estate.com

Maison Individuelle
Tel: 01707 376255

Investors in Property
Tel: 020 8905 5511
www.investorsinproperty.com

Overseas Homesearch
Tel: 0870 240 3258
www.overseashomesearch.co.uk

Premier Resorts
Tel: 020 8904 9806

Assetz France (information on investments)
Tel: 0161 456 5000
www.assetz.co.uk/France

General information on overseas property:
www.timesonline.co.uk/overseasproperty

James Properties France
www.jamespropertiesfrance.com

Latitudes
Tel: 020 8951 5133
www.latitudes.co.uk

Courses on running a *gîte:*
e-mail: TimdWilliams@wanadoo.fra

Information on *gîte:*
Gite-gers.com

Ownersdirect.co.uk

Cheznous.com

Holidaybank.com

French leaseback properties:
www.pierreetvacancesimmobilier.com

Golf resort:
www.premierleroc.co.uk

Ski resorts:
www.alpint.net

Mortgage broker:
Tel: +33 231 536 202
www.capfi.com

General properties in France:
www.Propertyfranceonline.co.uk

Specialist bilingual solicitor:
Barbara Heslop
Fox Hayes LLP
118 North Street
Leeds
West Yorkshire LS2 7AN
Tel: 0113 383 8447
e-mail: frenchlaw@foxhayes.co.uk
www.foxhayes.co.uk

# Spain

Hamptons International (offices in Marbella and Calahonda)
168 Brompton Road
London SW3 1HW
Tel: 020 7589 8844
e-mail: international@hamptons-int.com
www.hamptons-int.com

Prestige Villas
The Spanish Property Centre
1 The Smithy
Church Road
Rainford
St Helens WA11 8HD
Tel: 01744 886258
www.spainonshow.com

Atlas International
Atlas House
Station Road
Dorking
Surrey RH4 1EB
Tel: 01306 879899

World Class Homes
14a High Street
Wheathampstead
Herts AL4 8AA
Freephone: 0800 731 4713
www.worldclasshomes.co.uk
www.one-stopspain.com

Websites:
www.buy-spanish.co.uk

www.chelsea-homes.co.uk

www.barclays.co.uk

www.IberianInternational.com

www.ProfileSpain.com

www.andaluciandreamhomes.com

www.propertysalespain.co.uk

www.spanishventure.co.uk

www.kyero.com

www.vivaestates.com
Freephone: 0800 093 8838

newskys.co.uk

www.paradorproperties.com
Properties in many Spanish locations, including specialist retirement homes.

www.murciapuchades.com
Mainly properties on the Costa Blanca.

The *Interealty Property Gazette* lists properties all over Spain, the Balearics and the Canaries.
Contact: inform@interealtynet.com
www.interealtygazette.com

The Canaries:
Lanzarote: www.lanzarote.com

www.cesarmanrique.com

Tenerife:
info@Horizonpropertygroup.com

www.homesinfuerteventura.com

www.p41.co.uk/international-canary-islands

The Property Finders
www.thepropertyfinders.com
Tel: 01908 218753

Spanish Freehold Property Centre
Tel: 0800 783 9637

Tenerife Property Shop
Tel: 0871 871 6131
www.tenerifepropertyshop.com

For prices in Spain
www.kyero.com

# Portugal

Hamptons International (offices in Lagos, Western Algarve)
168 Brompton Road
London SW3 1HW
Tel: 020 7589 8844
e-mail: international@hamptons-int.com
www.hamptons-int.com

World Class Homes
14A High Street
Wheathampstead
Herts AL4 8AA
Freephone: 0800 908 984
e-mail: info@worldclasshomes.co.uk
www.worldclasshomes.co.uk

Property Search Portugal
Tel: 0800 052 3948
e-mail: psportugal@aol.com
www.propertysearchportugal.com

www.garveigh.com
Guide to buying, plus information on finance, building, insurance
and so on.

www.holiday-villa-portugal.com
Property and legal advice and information.

www.bipportugal.pt
Information for buyers, including advice on property taxes.

www.estatealgarve.com

www.centralportugalproperties.com

www.lapis-lazuli.co.uk
Tel: 0035 239 455 773

Portuguese Embassy UK
11 Belgrave Square
London SW1X 3HR
Tel: 0870 005 6970
www.portugal.embassyhomepage.com

www.thisistravel.co.uk
Comprehensive information on Portugal.

Golf developments:
Vilamoura@intercim.pt

Vila Sol Developments:
Tel: 0800 962 147

Jones Homes Portugal
www.joneshomesportugal.com
Portugal Property Guide
Tel: 01833 353333
www.headlands.co.uk

Solicitors:
Lita Gale
Portugal-only specialists: 45 Gower Street, London WC1W 6NA
Tel: 020 7580 2066
www.litagale.com

Madeira:
Blue Lavada Estates
Tel: 00 351 968 626 139
www.property-in-madeira.com

Palheiro Real Estate
Tel: 00 351 291 794 015
www.palheiroestate.com

UK Sales Agents for Madeira:
Tel: 0122 765011
www.selectresorts.co.uk

Portuguese Tourist Board
Tel: 0845 355 1212
www.visitportugal.com

# Italy

www.italian-network.it
Information on Italian properties for sale.

www.casatravella.com
Specializes in information on buying property in Italy.

www.informer.it
Survival guide to living in Italy.

www.dolcevita.com
Guide to Italian life: fashion, food, wine and events.

Tuscany and Sardinia:
127 High Road
Leavensden
Herts WS25 7AP
Tel: 01923 893764
www.casealsole.com
www.larchitrave.it

Homes in Tuscany:
L'Architrave
Tel: +39 0187 472068
info@larchitrave.com

Umbria:
Italian Property Network
Tel: +44 (0) 1425655 654
www.europropertynet.com

Venice
403 Parkway House
Sheen Lane
London SW14 8LS
Tel: 020 8878 1130
www.venice-sales.com

Information on Italian village renovation:
Gruppo Norman
Tel: 0039 02 777 1101
www.grupponorman.com

Knight Frank
www.knightfrank.com

Colletta di Castelbianco
www.collettadicastelbianco.com
Sales enquiries:
www.savills.co.uk

Home from Home Overseas
Tel: 01323 470308
www.homefromhomeoverseas.co.uk

www.gladinodivo.com

www.castleofcampiglia.com

# Switzerland

www.alpineswitzerland.com

www.hartmannsingleton.com

# Greece

Cybarco
Cybarco House
Dollis Mews
Dollis Park
London N3 1HH
Tel: 020 8371 9700
e-mail: achilleas.l@uk.cybarco.com

www.oconnorproperties.gr

www.apropertyingreece.com

Information on Rhodes:
www.rre.gr

Information on Corfu:
begeorge@cornwall-country.com

Steve@placesinthesun.co.uk

www.aegean-blue.com

www.hellenic-homes.com

www.allgreece4u.co.uk

www.greeceforyou.co.uk

www.newcenturyhomes.gr

www.adstudio.gr

www.apropertyingreece.com

Crete:
www.europa-crete.com

www.creteproperty.co.uk

www.halcyon-properties.co.uk

Crete Property Consultants
Tel: 020 7328 1829
www.crete-properties.co.uk

Cretan Traditional Homes
Tel: 01763 849 309
www.cretantraditionalhomes.com

www.certain-homes.co.uk

www.cretehomefinders.eu

www.phoenix-villas.com

## Southern Cyprus

Cybarco
Cybarco House
Dollis Mews
Dollis Park
London N3 1HH
Tel: 020 8371 9700
www.cybarco.com

Cyprus Property Services
Mercia House
3 Brickhill Close
Blunham
Bedfordshire MK44 3NF
Tel: 01767 641564
e-mail: gaubery@lineone.net
www.paphosproperty.com

Cyprus Property Direct Limited
Tel: 01387 270777
www.cypruspropertydirect.com/overseas

Living-Cyprus.Com
www.living-cyprus.com

Aristo Developers
Tel: +357 26 811 600
e-mail: market@aristodevelopers.com
www.aristodevelopers.com

Paphos Homes
www.paphos-homes.com

Real estate agent and surveyors:
Antonis Loizou and Associates
Aloizou@logos.cy.net

Law office:
Stelios Stylianides & Co
Ch_stylianides@hotmail.com

Cyprus Tourism Board
www.cyprustourism.org

Cyprus Homes
Tel: 01904 746909
www.cyprus-homes.net

Investincyprus.com
Tel: 0151 482 5526

Kanika Developments
www.kanikadevelopments.com

www.CyprusEastCoast.com

www.thegrovesparesort.com

Legal advice:
www.cypruspropertylawyer.com

# Northern Cyprus

Unwin Estate Agents
www.unwinestates.com

Cyprus Bay Properties
Tel: 01889 561740
www.cyprusbay.co.uk

Landmark Estate Agency
0090 392 815 1481
www.landmark-northcyprus.com

Savyon Village
Tel: 0800 088 7966
www.cyprus-invest.co.uk

# Malta and Gibraltar

Useful Maltese property websites:
www.propertymaltadirect.com/

www.propertylinemalta.com/

www.mol.net.mt/property/

www.realestate.escapeartist.com/Properties/Malta

www.riainvestments.com.me/

www.ired.com/europe/malta.htm

www.franksalt.com.mt/ppforeignmalta.html

Frank Salt Real Estate
Tel: 020 7935 5333

Useful Gibraltar property websites:
www.realestate.escapeartist.com/Properties/Gibraltar

www.gbrltr.com/

Taylor Woodrow, now constructing luxury apartments on Gibraltar,
can be contacted at: www.taywood.gi/

*The Gibraltar Magazine*
Guide Line Promotions, Ltd
Inossi House
Irish Town
Suite 6377
Box 651
Gibraltar
e-mail: gibmag@gibnet.gi
Useful general information about Gibraltar, plus political updates.

## Cape Verde

www.mymortgagedirect.com

www.noscasacv.com

Sambala Developments
Tel: 01608 813160
www.sambaladevelopments.com

Cape Verde Property
Tel: 01735 859233
www.capeverdeproperty.co.uk

## United States

The World of Florida
St Ethelbert House
Ryelands Street
Hereford HR4 0LA
Tel: 01432 265599
e-mail: homes@worldofflorida.co.uk
www.worldofflorida.co.uk

American First Realty
Tel: 020 7624 8700
e-mail: Bob@a-f-realty.com
www.a-f-realty.com

The Superior Real Estate Group Ltd
The Aztec Centre
Aztec West
Bristol BS32 4TD
Tel: 01454 203450
www.4avilla.com

www.eliteresidences.com

www.floridacountryside.com

The Villages, Beausale House, Beausale, Warwick CV35 7NZ
Tel: 01926 484578
('Age-exclusive' developments for over-55s)

Coldwell Banker Team Realty
www.ColdwellBankerTeamRealty.com

Orlando Holiday Homes
www.ohhorlando.com

Also: The Superior Real Estate Group Ltd, Moat Farm Barn,
Farlands, Pucklechurch, Bristol BS16 9PN
Tel: 08707 555 585

Clearsky Developments
Tel: 01749 518825
www.clearsky.co.uk

New England
www.century21.com

www.mahoosucrealty.com
New England homes being sold off-plan.

www.mountainrealestatevt.com

Florida Gold Homes
Tel: 001 941 474 0555

International Property Link
Tel: 0800 955 555

Madison Metro West
Tel: 001 407 445 1771
www.MadisonMetroWest.com

California:
The most comprehensive website is: www.HomeGain.com, which contains information on condominiums, town homes, vacation homes, new homes, foreclosures(!), mortgages, legal advice and properties in all Californian counties.

Also:
www.californiarealestate.com

www.vacationrentals.com/vacation-rentals/California.html

# Canada

Positive Realty Investments
Tel: 001 888 864 6818
www.sellcanadianproperty.com

Humber Valley Resort
Details: Chesterton 0800 783 6783
www.chesterton.co.uk

AHC Developments Ltd
www.pinnacle-ridge.com

Remax House of Real Estate
www.remax.ca

Canadian Estate
www.canadian-estate.com

Premier Resorts
www.premierresorts.co.uk

Northland Properties
Tel: 01427 754485
www.canadian-land.co.uk

www.AssignmentsCanada.com

For advice on emigrating:
www.EmigratingExpert.com

# The Caribbean

Hamptons International (offices in Barbados)
168 Brompton Road
London SW3 1HW
Tel: 020 7589 8844
e-mail: international@hamptons-int.com
www.hamptons-int.com

Caribbean Property List
PO Box 816 Fort Myers
Florida 33902
USA

Resort Consultants, Ltd
PO Box 577
South Wellfleet
MA 02663
USA

This company also publishes the *Caribbean Report*, a regular magazine detailing properties, places and events of interest, property news, political information and island updates. It costs $89 an issue.

For the British Virgin Islands:
Smiths Gore Overseas Ltd
Britannic Hall
PO Box 135
Road Town
Tortola
British Virgin Islands
e-mail: info@smithsgore.com

For properties in Mustique:
www.knightfrank.com

For properties in Tobago:
www.abrahamrealty.com

For properties in Barbados:
The Lakes Development
Tel: 0800 389 0084
www.thelakescaribbean.com

www.MarinaCaribe.com
www.investin.co.uk
www.St-Vincent-Real-Estate.co.uk
www.TheCrane.com/real_estate
www.instantpropertyinvestor.com

# Brazil

Someplace Else
91 Munster Road
London SW6 5RF
Tel: 020 7731 2200
www.someplaceelse.co.uk

www.JacumaBeachResort.com

www.DreamHomesww.com/Brazil

## Morocco

www.moroccanproperty.eu

Saffron Villas
Tel: 01635 253121
e-mail: info@saffronvillas.com
www.saffronvillas.com

Moroccan Embassy
www.morocco.embassyhomepage.com
Tel: 020 7581 5001

## South Africa

Cluttons
Tel: (UK) 020 7403 3669; (South Africa) +27 21 425 8989
e-mail: Cluttons@africa.com

FPDSavills
Tel: 020 7824 9077
www.fpdsavills.co.uk

Pam Golding International
www.pamgolding.co.za

Sotheby's International Realty
Tel: (UK) 020 7598 1600
www.sothebysrealty.com

Capsol for Cape Town properties
Tel: 00 27 214 611 083

South African Property Overseas Marketing Association (SAPOMA)
Tel: 00 27 31 573 1966
e-mail: mark@elan.co.za
www.sapoma.co.za

Cape of Good Hope:
Aida
www.aida.co.za

Marina Residential (Cape Town)
www.waterfrontmarina.com

Property Partners
e-mail: mail@property-partners.co.za

Property Finders International
www.newskys.co.uk

AGS Properties
www.agsproperties.com

Rawson Properties
www.rawson.co.za

Era Real Estate
www.era.co.za

richard@oceanprojects.co.za

# Turkey

Gascoignes International
Tel: 01483 756633
www.gasgoignesinternational.com

Nicholas Homes
Tel: 0870 240 9028
www.nicholas-homes.com

The Turkish Property Centre
Tel: 0191 214 5533
www.theturkishpropertycentre.co.uk

Ibak Homes
www.ibakhomes.co.uk

www.turkeyapartment.com

European Villa Solutions
(advice and information on Turkey)
Tel: 01223 514241

Aqua Vista
Tel: 01580 850170
www.aquavistaproperty.com

ASEM Construction Dev Ltd
Tel: 0800 169 4647
www.turkey4life.com

Derin and Derin
Tel: 0090 256 614 80 52
www.derinanderin.com

Gascoignes International
Tel: 01483 756633
www.gascoignesinternational.com

Holiday Homes in Turkey
Tel: 01788 542073
www.holidayhomesinturkey.com

RG Estates
Tel: 0845 2577010
www.rgestates.co.uk

www.bestbodrumvillas.com

# Croatia

Information on Croatian properties:
Croatian Embassy
Tel: 020 7387 1790

Homes in Croatia
Tel: 020 7502 1371
www.homesincroatia.com

Your Property Partner in Croatia
www.croatiansun.com

Gascoignes International
www.gascoignesinternational.com

www.sunshineestates.net

www.visit-croatia.co.uk

www.croatiablue.com

wwww.croatiaholidayandhome.co.uk

www.winkworth.co.uk/croatia

www.croatianvillasforsale.co.uk

www.winkworth.co.uk/international-developments

# Bulgaria

Balkan Holiday Homes Ltd
www.balkanholidayhomes.co.uk

Bulgaria Investments Ltd
Tel: 020 8900 0562
www.bulgarproperty.com

Orpheus International (ski villas)
Tel: 0800 083 507
www.orpheusinternational.com

www.project-rhodopipearl.com

Properties in Bulgaria
www.propertiesinbulgaria.com

Address Real Estate
www.addressworldwide.co.uk

Avatar International
Tel: 020 8434 3752
www.avatar-international.com

www.BulgarianLiving.com

Eurosilex
2 Heath Street
London NW3 6TE
Tel: 0871 990 3525
www.eurosilex.com

www.experiencebg.co.uk

Advice on buying in Bulgaria: Bulgaria4U Ltd Services
e-mail: info@bulgaria4u.biz
www.bulgaria4u.biz

www.Q4Properties.com

Select Property Overseas
Tel: 0845 430 1404
www.selectpropertyoverseas.com

Quinaries Real Estate Agency
www.quinaries.com

Jigsaw Properties
Tel: 01344 884433
www.jigsawproperties.com

Perfect Homes Ltd
Tel: 020 7228 7427
www.bgbalkanestate.com

Bulgarian Land Development plc
www.bld.bg

www.yooBulgaria.com

## Lithuania

Baltic Experts of Realty
www.berealty.lt

Someplace Else
www.someplaceelse.co.uk

## Estonia and Latvia

Ober-Haus Estate agents
www.ober-haus.com

www.homesgofast.com/Estonia

www.east-european-property-secrets.co.uk

# Lapland and Finland

Lapland log cabins:
www.sunshineestates.net/index.asp

www.davidstanleyredfern.com

www.abovethearctic.com

# Czech Republic

Executive Housing Specialists
www.ehs.cz

Alan Goss:
e-mail: handsonpost@aol.com
Tel: 07956 932669

www.worldpropertyshop.com

www.pragueproperty4less.com

www.euro-ventures.com

www.jekoo.com

www.ceres-group.com

www.EastPointConsulting.com

www.Czechpropertysearch.co.uk

# Poland

Filstan Investments (Cracow)
Tel: 0048 228261572

Churchill Properties Overseas:
Tel: 01983 550400
www.churchilloverseas.com

Also:
www.timesonline.co.uk/overseasproperty

www.polishpropertyinvestments.com

www.GlobalPropertyPlan.co.uk

www.propertyfinders.com/Poland

www.dreamhomesww.com

www.polandadventure.co.uk

# Romania

www.therightmoveabroad.com

www.emergingrealestate.com

www.landlordinromania.com

# Hungary

Duna House
www.dunahouse.co.uk

www.avatar-international.com

www.hungarinvest.com

www.propertyhungary.com

www.fpdsavills.com

www.engelvoekers.com

# Slovakia

The culture ministry website is on www.pamiatky.sk, where you can view properties for sale in Slovakia.
e-mail: uzkp@pamiatky.sk

www.sak.sk

www.slovakia-property.com

www.slovakia-investments.co.uk

www.worldpropertyshop.com

# Slovenia

www.slovenia-realestate.co.uk

www.slovenian-property.net

www.slovenianproperties.com
e-mail: enquiries@slovenianproperties.com

# Panama

www.escapes2.com

# Australia

www.realestate.com.au
Information on homes to buy or rent.

www.realestatecentre.com.au
Australian properties on the internet. Also access to other Australian
property sites.

www.specreloc.com.au
Information on relocating to Australia.

www.raywhite.com.au
Property experts in Australia.

www.ljhooker.com.au
Australian estate agents.

www.mcgrath.com.au
Australian real-estate company.

First National Bank
Tel: 00 61 29240 6165
www.firstnational.com.au
For essential information on financial aspects of relocating to
Australia.

www.therealaustralia.com

www.gumtree.com/property

www.knightfrank.com

www.clickcrawler.co.uk

www.easyexpat.com/sydney

# New Zealand

Bayleys Real Estate
www.bayleys.co.nz

www.NewZealandPropertyHomes.com

www.aranaproperties.co.nz

www.Gumtree.com

Arrowtown:
www.rwaarrowtown.co.nz

Queenstown:
www.southernlakes.co.nz
www.queenstownproperty.com

Auckland:
www.nzpropertysolutions.co.nz

General:
www.seek.co.nz

# Dubai

www.damacproperties.com
Tel: 020 7499 9001

FPDSavills
Tel: 020 7824 9030

Landmark Properties
Tel: 020 7083 0163
e-mail: lisa@landmark-dubai.com

Dubai Luxury Homes
www.dubailuxuryhomes.com

International Horizons
Tel: 01273 705630
www.internationalhorizons.co.uk

www.oryxrealestate.com

www.dubaiselect.co.uk

www.sherwoodproperty.com

www.propertyfrontiers.com

Financing a Dubai property:
www.halofinancial.com

## Egypt and the Red Sea

www.redsea.realestate.com
e-mail: elgounarealestate@orascom.net

Egyptian Experience
Tel: 01280 705630
www.egyptianexperience.com

## Thailand

www.katamanda.com

www.fpdsavills.co.uk

Siam Real Estate
www.siamrealestate.com

Phuket Property
www.phuketproperty.co.uk

Laguna Phuket
www.lagunaproperty.com

Royal Phuket Marina
www.royalphuketmarina.com

Bel Air Panwa
Tel: 000 66 7631 815158

www.investthai.com

International Horizons
Tel: 01273 705630
www.internationalhorizons.co.uk

New World Properties
Tel: 020 8819 6837
www.new-worldproperties.com

# India

Goa:
International Horizons
Tel: 01273 705630
www.internationalhorizons.co.uk

New World Properties
Tel: 020 8819 6837
www.new-worldproperties.com

Other parts of India:
www.CitiNRI.com/India/nri

www.MagicBricks.com

www.myhouseandgarden.com

www.gardenvisit.com

www.findIndiahome.com

www.hamptons.com

www.blueoceanestates.co.uk

www.india.assetz.co.uk

## China

www.soucring-cn.com

www.lihong.biz

## Rentals

www.holiday-rentals.com
Tel: 020 8743 5577

## Timeshare

Informational website: www.timeshare.org.uk/buy_web.html

The Holiday Property Bond
HPB House
Newmarket
Suffolk CB8 8EH
Tel: 01638 660066
www.hpb.co.uk

# Index

# Index of advertisers